Israel and the Nations

The Bible, the Rabbis, and Jewish-Gentile Relations

Emunot: Jewish Philosophy and Kabbalah

Series Editor:
Dov Schwartz (Bar-Ilan University, Ramat Gan)

Editorial Board:
Ada Rapoport Albert, University College, London (d. 2020)
Idit Dobbs-Weinstein, Vanderbilt University
Gad Freudenthal, CNRS, Paris
Gideon Freudenthal, Tel Aviv University, Ramat Aviv
Moshe Idel, Hebrew University, Jerusalem
Raphael Jospe, Bar-Ilan University, Ramat Gan
Ephraim Kanarfogel, Yeshiva University, New York
Menachem Kellner, Haifa University, Haifa
Daniel Lasker, Ben Gurion University, Beer Sheva

Israel and the Nations

The Bible, the Rabbis, and Jewish-Gentile Relations

Eugene Korn

Emunot: Jewish Philosophy and Kabbalah

BOSTON
2023

Library of Congress Cataloging-in-Publication Data

Names: Korn, Eugene, 1947- author.
Title: Israel and the nations: the Bible, the rabbis, and Jewish-gentile relations / Eugene Korn.
Description: Boston, MA: Academic Studies Press, [2023] | Series: Emunot: Jewish philosophy and Kabbalah | Includes bibliographical references and index.
Identifiers: LCCN 2022027888 (print) | LCCN 2022027889 (ebook) | ISBN 9798887190051 (hardback) | ISBN 9798887190068 (adobe pdf) | ISBN 9798887190075 (epub)
Subjects: LCSH: Gentiles in rabbinical literature. | Gentiles in the Bible. | Judaism--Relations--Christianity. | Christianity and other religions--Judaism. | Bible. Old Testament--Criticism, interpretation, etc. | Rabbinical literature--History and criticism.
Classification: LCC BM720.N6 K68 2022 (print) | LCC BM720.N6 (ebook) | DDC 220.8/3058--dc23/eng/20220709

LC record available at https://lccn.loc.gov/2022027888
LC ebook record available at https://lccn.loc.gov/2022027889

Copyright © 2023 Academic Studies Press
All rights reserved.

ISBN 9798887192550 (paperback), ISBN9798887190051 (hardback),
ISBN 9798887190068 (Adobe PDF),
ISBN 9798887190075 (ePub)

Book design by Kryon Publishing Services.
Cover design by Ivan Grave.

Published by Academic Studies Press.
1577 Beacon Street
Brookline, MA 02446, USA
press@academicstudiespress.com
www.academicstudiespress.com

וְנִבְרְכוּ בְךָ כֹּל מִשְׁפְּחֹת הָאֲדָמָה
"And all the families of the earth shall bless themselves by you"
Genesis 12:3

Contents

Introduction: Reassessing Jewish-Gentile Relations Today	1
Part One: Judaism, Jews, and Gentiles	7
1. The Covenant and Its Theology	9
2. Israel as Blessing: Theological Horizons	23
3. *Extra Synagogam Nulla Salus?* Judaism and the Religious Other	43
4. Revelation, Gentiles, and the World to Come	65
5. Idolatry Today	89
Part Two: Judaism, Jews, and Christianity	99
6. Rethinking Christianity: Rabbinic Positions and Possibilities	101
7. Esau Hates Jacob	132
8. The Man of Faith and Religious Dialogue	140
9. The People Israel, Christianity, and the Covenantal Responsibility to History	166
Bibliography	179
Index	190

Introduction
Reassessing Jewish-Gentile Relations Today

As the foundation of Jewish culture and identity, the Bible challenges the Jewish people in numerous ways to be "a blessing for all the families of the earth." This implies that the Jewish people should engage with gentiles in some way. Yet in both the Bible and the living historical reality of the Jewish people, Jewish experience with gentiles has been complex and fraught with difficulties. In biblical times most gentiles were idolators whom Jews were prohibited from befriending. Yet this is not the entire story: there were exceptions whom the Talmudic rabbis termed *benei Noaḥ* (those who follow the Noahide covenant) and resident strangers (*gerei toshav*) whom the Bible and rabbinic tradition directed Jews to respect and even protect.

In the post-Talmudic era also, most gentiles were assumed to be idolators. Throughout the Middle Ages, most rabbis considered their Christian neighbors in Ashkenaz (Germany, France, England, Poland, Russia) to be idolators. Moreover, Jewish-Christian enmity sharpened the sense of otherness that Jews felt toward their Christian hosts. Because Muslims were pure monotheists, most rabbis did not consider them idolators, and relations between Jews and Muslims were sometimes positive and other times difficult. With the advent of the modern era and secular tolerance, Jews found themselves in a new relationship with their gentile neighbors.

In addition, the last eighty years has transformed Jewish-gentile relations in an unprecedented way. Political Zionism and the establishment the Jewish State of Israel in the Middle East has given rise to increased adversarial relations with the Muslims—particularly Arab Muslims. And while Middle Eastern Christians remain largely supersessionist and hostile to the continued validity of Judaism, the Second Vatican Council in the 1960s caused a Copernican revolution in Christian theology about the Jewish people and Judaism among most Western Christians. The fruit of the revolution is continuing theological and empirical reconciliation between Christianity and the Jewish people. Lastly, because so much of modern life takes place in a shrinking global village, Jews today frequently meet non-Abrahamic believers and come to learn about Asian religions to a degree unprecedented in Jewish history.

What does Jewish thought and Jewish law (*Halakhah*) have to say about how Jews should understand, evaluate, and relate to Christians, Muslims, Asian believers, and secular gentiles in the past and today? And should Jewish-gentile relations change when Jews are a minority in the Diaspora and when Jews are the dominant majority in the State of Israel? What are the bounds of tolerance and Jewish religious pluralism? The essays in this book examine these issues.

The opening essay, "The Covenant and Its Theology," demonstrates that the central idea of covenant (*berit*) in Judaism requires theological principles to give Jewish religious thought coherence and urgency. The idea of the particularistic Jewish covenant immediately creates an insider/outsider problem: How should Jews inside the covenant relate to those people who stand outside the covenant? And does acknowledging the divinity of the particularist Jewish covenant imply that other purported religious covenants cannot not be valid?

At the very outset of God establishing a covenant with Abraham and his descendants stands the challenge to be a blessing to the world (Gen. 12:3). Blessing is also implicit in God's call for Israel to be a nation of priests (Ex. 19:15–16), since the function of priests is to be conduits of God's blessings to His[1] human children. But what is the meaning of this blessing, and how should the Jewish people fulfill this theological mission? Clearly, these biblical challenges entail Abraham's children exercising influence on humanity, but the Bible does not tell us how this blessing is to be achieved. Is Israel's role to actively engage gentiles, be passive models of excellence for non-Jews, or merely to engage in theurgic piety that results in divine overflow of goodness to gentiles? Chapter 2, "Israel as Blessing: Theological Horizons," analyzes these options found within rabbinic writings.

"*Extra Synagogam Nulla Salus*? Judaism and the Religious Other" argues from traditional rabbinic principles that authentic Jewish thought allows for limited religious pluralism, and requires Jewish moral and civil responsibilities

---

1 Throughout this book I use the masculine "Him," "His," and "He" in reference to God as a linguistic convention only, and do not want to imply any gender or gender preference to God. In the Jewish theological tradition, God transcends gender although in attempting to understand God it is helpful to ascribe to God traits traditionally associated with both masculinity (such as authority and punishment) and femininity (such as compassion and nurturing). This has significant pedagogical implications: *Imitatio Dei* would demand that human beings also strive to develop a combination of personality traits as religious and ethical ideals. According to Jewish mysticism, all these traits will merge into a perfect unity in the messianic era—in both God and His creatures.

to the gentile stranger (Hebrew: *ger toshav*). "Revelation, Gentiles, and the World to Come" extends the argument of the previous essay by analyzing the historic debate among Jewish thinkers regarding whether gentiles must acknowledge classic Mosaic revelation at Sinai to gain eternal life and be loved by God. "Idolatry Today" examines the two major biblical and rabbinic understandings of idolatry, asking whether idolatry has any application in today's world. It argues that a contemporary definition of idolatry that combines the two classical conceptions is necessary today as a basis for rejecting religious violence and intolerance.

In Europe and America Jewish exposure to and engagement with gentiles has predominantly meant interaction with Christians and their faith. The last four essays discuss philosophical, theological, and halakhic considerations of the particular relationship between Judaism and Christianity. "Rethinking Christianity: Rabbinic Positions and Possibilities" surveys traditional rabbinic evaluations of Christianity and Christians in light of the changes in Christian thinking about Judaism and the Jewish people, as well as contemporary social, political, and religious realities. Is it possible today to overcome the polemics and hostilities of the past to form sympathetic and constructive relationships for the future? The chapter points to a way for greater Jewish appreciation of Christianity as a faith and for Jews to see the Image of God in the face of a believing Christian—all within the parameters of Jewish law.

"Esau Hates Jacob" reviews an age-old but still influential rabbinic dictum. Using recent scholarship, the chapter analyzes whether hatred between Jews and Christians is built into the universe as an irreversible law of nature, as some traditional rabbinic hermeneutics imply. "The Man of Faith and Religious Dialogue" analyzes in detail the thought of Rabbi Joseph B. Soloveitchik regarding interfaith dialogue and its limits, which has become the dominant policy for Orthodox participation in interfaith events. The essay suggests that much of R. Soloveitchik's public policy on interfaith dialogue has been misunderstood and his concerns about supersessionist policy by the Catholic Church toward Jews are no longer a factor in today's Jewish-Catholic—and most Jewish-Christian—dialogue.

Lastly, "The People Israel, Christianity, and the Covenantal Responsibility to History," argues for a Jewish understanding of contemporary Christianity that allows traditional Jews to see Christians as participants in the covenant of Abraham, and partners with Jews in a mission to be a kingdom of priests to bring divine blessing to humanity and human history.

In sum, this book takes up texts, questions, and arguments essential to Jewish-gentile relations, Jewish law, and religious thought. It analyzes the issues standing at the heart of the critical discussion about Jewish teachings regarding gentiles and how Jews do and should behave toward others in contemporary life. It is my hope that this book will interest Christian scholars, clergy, and laity, as well as Jews interested in interfaith relations, and that the volume be a valuable resource for scholars, clergy, and laypersons in ongoing discussions about current Jewish experience and thought.

Unlike how traditional rabbis and theologians understood the primordial creation of the universe, no human thinking is done *ex nihilo*, out of a vacuum. Even scholars who achieve conceptual breakthroughs rely on intellectual antecedents and build on the work of those who come before them. In trying to explain the twists and turns of Jewish thinking about non-Jews and point to a constructive Jewish orientation of relating to humanity today, I have been blessed to be able to stand on the shoulders of previous giants, among them the Talmudic rabbis and medieval Tosafists, Maimonides, Rabbis Menaḥem Meiri, Yaaqov Emden, and Samson Raphael Hirsch, the historian Jacob Katz, and the contemporary theologians Joseph B. Soloveitchik, Abraham Heschel, and David Hartman. And much of this book would have been impossible without the Christian visionaries Popes John XXIII and John Paul II, A. Roy Eckardt, Alice L. Eckardt, and Krister Stendahl.

I am indebted to many scholars, rabbis, clergy, and friends with whom I have discussed these ideas over the years, who commented on my initial drafts of this material and improved it immeasurably. They include Professors Menachem Ben Sasson, David Berger, Phillip Cunningham, Shlomo Fisher, Yehuda Gellman, Alon Goshen-Gottstein, Robert Jenson, Menachem Kellner, Martin Lochshin, Gerald McDermott, Robert McKim, Don Seeman, and Noam Zion, as well as Rabbis Irving Greenberg, David Hartman, David Rosen, Shlomo Riskin, Jonathan Sacks, and Fathers Dennis McManus and John Pawlikowski and Sister Mary Boys.

Many of the chapters were published previously in different form. They have been updated and I have tried to weave them into a seamless coherent whole. I gratefully acknowledge the following for granting permission to republish the material, even when altered:

Meorot for "The Covenant and Its Theology";

Academic Studies Press for "Israel as Blessing: Theological Horizons," which appeared in *Judaism's Challenge: Election, Divine Love, and Human Enmity*, edited by Alon Goshen-Gottstein.

Brill Publications for "*Extra Synagogam Nulla Salus*? Judaism and the Religious Other," which originally appeared in *Religious Perspectives on Religious Diversity*, edited by Robert McKim.

Modern Judaism for "Revelation, Gentiles, and the World to Come," which originally appeared as "Gentiles, The World to Come, and Judaism: The Odyssey of a Rabbinic Text."

The Center for Jewish-Christian Understanding and Cooperation in Israel for "Religious Violence, Sacred Texts, and Theological Values," which originally appeared in *Plowshares into Swords? Reflections on Religion and Violence*, edited by Robert Jenson and Eugene Korn.

Littman Library of Jewish Civilization for "Modern Rethinking Christianity: Rabbinic Positions and Possibilities," which appeared in *Jewish Theology and World Religions*, edited by Alon Goshen-Gottstein and Eugene Korn.

Modern Judaism for "The Man of Faith and Religious Dialogue," which originally appeared as "The Man of Faith and Religious Dialogue: Revisiting 'Confrontation.'"

Eerdmans Publications for "The People Israel, Christianity and the Covenantal Responsibility to History," which originally appeared in *Covenant and Hope*, edited by Robert Jenson and Eugene Korn.

I would like to thank the staff of Academic Studies Press who helped bring this volume to fruition. In particular, Professor Dov Schwartz who enthusiastically supported this project from its inception. My gratitude also goes to Alessandra Anzani, who shepherded this volume to publication and to Kate Yanduganova for her keen editorial eye.

Eugene Korn, Jerusalem, 2022

Part One

JUDAISM, JEWS, AND GENTILES

1

The Covenant and Its Theology

Spiritual beings seek transcendent ends. Living humanly means to thirst for noble purpose that connects us to things beyond ourselves and to eternity. The search elevates our lives above mechanical behavior determined by material forces and transforms us into subjects who fashion our own destinies. In questing outwards for self-transcendence, we imitate the Divine, whose search for relationship moved Him to create the universe.[1]

To be a covenantal people is to participate in the unfolding of sacred history. That drama began at twilight of the sixth day, when God created Adam and Eve, endowing them with *Tselem Elokim*, and progressed through Noah, Abraham, and the revelation at Sinai. It continues until today and will ultimately end in the messianic era, when all persons recognize God's presence and His moral authority. As Isaiah, Micah, and Zechariah all taught, only when the entire world lives in blessing and peace will the Jewish people fulfill the sacred covenant that God made with Abraham and his descendants. The covenant beckons the Jewish nation to be a partner with the Divine, to complete creation as central actors in the redemption of humanity.

God's covenant with the Jewish people would be meaningless without this historical mandate. Unlike Christianity, whose purpose is individual salvation, the Jewish covenant is impossible without a historical dimension. Since

---

[1] Divine creation is philosophically superfluous. As least as early as Aristotle, thinkers understood that a perfect God has no need or motive to act at all. Yet Jewish tradition insists that God created the universe, not out of ontological necessity, but from the divine need for relationship. Maimonides defined this quality as *ḥesed* or *haflagah*—overflow into another. (*Guide of the Perplexed* III:53–54; hereafter *Guide*) There is only one thing Aristotle's self-sufficient God dwelling in splendid isolation could not do: relate to another. For Jewish theology this limitation renders God morally deficient. Although creation is metaphysically superfluous, it is essential to a Jewish spiritual and moral *weltanschauung*.

the God of TaNaKH made a pact with the Jewish people that endures throughout human history, this religious commitment can have a purpose only if His covenanted people has an enduring mission over the sweep of time. If personal transcendence is movement outward, then Jewish national redemption is movement inward, from the irrelevant margins of history to its center to be an impact-making people.[2] And if the State of Israel is the home of the Jewish people today, then it must play a central role in the unfolding of this universal sacred drama.

Berit Avraham and *Berit Sinai*

The Jewish theology of the covenant begins with the Torah's account of the founding of the Jewish people and its spiritual destiny. Genesis (12:1–3) relates that God created a unique relationship with Abraham, calling upon him to break from his father's home, culture and gods in pagan Mesopotamia and to travel to Canaan. It is there that Abraham is to become "the father of a great nation" whose destiny is blessing. Upon arrival, Abraham and his descendants receive eternal title to the Land, where Abraham immediately builds an altar "to call out the name of the Lord." This was the birth of the intimate covenant between God and Abraham, formalized soon thereafter in Gen. 15.

Similar to all contracts, each covenantal partner acquires benefits and assumes responsibilities: Abraham receives blessing, fame, and land. In return, rabbinic tradition understood that Abraham assumed the responsibility to be a witness to God's presence in heaven and on earth: "Before Abraham, God was called 'God of the heavens'; after Abraham, people called Him 'God of the heavens and the earth.'"[3] A bit later (Gen. 18:19), Abraham's responsibilities expand

---

2   This is the way R. Joseph Soloveitchik understood Israel's redemptive role in sacred history. See his "Redemption, Prayer and Talmud Torah," *Tradition* 17, no. 2 (1978): 55.

3   *Midrash, Sifre, Ha'azinu* 313. That is, Abraham taught people that God was present in human affairs. The rabbis derived the *midrash* from the text of Gen. 24:2–3, in which Abraham requires that his gentile servant, Eliezer, swear "by the Lord, the God of heaven and earth." After Christianity adopted this idea of religious purpose and popularized the term "witness," Jews have shied away from using it. However, neither God nor Isaiah hesitated to do so in reference to the Jewish people and its mission. Through Isaiah, God calls Israel "My witnesses" (Isa. 43:11–12). Moreover, the Hebrew term *Adat Yisrael* ("congregation of Israel"), so common in traditional texts and rabbinic parlance, is derived from the word *eidah*, meaning witness. R. Joseph Soloveitchik insisted that *Adat Yisrael* refers to the Jewish people in its spiritual capacity as bearing a message to the world, as opposed to *Maḥaneh Yisrael*, which refers to the Jewish people in its defensive capacities to defend itself

to "teaching the way of the Lord, to do righteousness and justice [*tsedaqah u-mishpat*]." As Genesis continues, the covenant is passed down to Isaac and Jacob, and the family covenant blossoms into a *national* covenant with the entire Jewish people at Sinai, where Jewish tradition teaches that God revealed to the Jewish people the written Torah and its 613 commandments. Rabbinic tradition understood the Sinai covenant to be a continuous extension of Abraham's covenant, theologically and spiritually identical although varying in detail.[4] In other words, in the mind of the rabbis Abraham is Israel and Israel is Abraham.

As the terms of the covenant, the Sinai *mitsvot* provide the content, meaning and commitment to Judaism; their conceptualization, Jewish intellectual endeavor. They shape Jewish spiritual life. They are, in the language of the Jewish liturgy, "our lives and the length of our days."

Like Abraham's covenant, *Berit Sinai* also establishes an intimate personal relationship between God and His people. As in all forms of intimacy, the relationship is particularistic and forms an exclusivist relationship between the covenantal partners. This is why Isaiah, Jeremiah and Hosea repeatedly use the metaphor of marriage to describe the covenant between God and the Jewish people. The sanctity of marriage lay precisely in the fact that husband and wife are devoted exclusively to each other. Because it is an exclusive relationship, the covenant's benefits accrue only to the Jewish people and the responsibilities of the covenantal commandments do not apply to the rest of humanity in the eyes of normative rabbinic thinkers. Unlike Christian theologians, the Talmud was

---

physically against outside enemies. See "Kol Dodi Dofeq," in *B'Sod ha-Yaḥid v'ha-Yaḥad*, ed. Pinhas Peli (Jerusalem: Orot, 1976), 381–383.

4   The verses in Exodus describing Jewish slavery in Egypt and Moses's deliverance of the Jewish people emphasize this continuity. "God remembered his covenant with Abraham" (2:24) and God is identified to the Jewish slaves as the God of Abraham (3:15). The exodus is but a fulfillment of the promise to Abraham (6:3–8). Thus, the religious dramas of Abraham and the theological events of the exodus and at Sinai are portrayed as being of one continuous cloth.

Though historically and textually difficult on a literal level, some Talmudic and medieval rabbinic opinions tried to emphasize this point by claiming that Abraham kept all of Mosaic (and even later rabbinic) commandments. This is the opinion of Mishnaic sage R. Nahorei, expressed in the last *mishna* in Babylonian Talmud (henceforth BT), tractate *Qiddushin*, and the late second-century and early third-century Talmudic sage, Rav, in BT *Yoma* 28b. (The same Talmudic text records the disagreeing opinion of R. Shimi bar Ḥiya.) Rav derives this conclusion from his exegesis of Gen. 26:5. It is also articulated by the popular medieval biblical commentator Shlomo ben Yitsḥaq (Rashi) in his commentary on that verse. As we shall see, this is a minority view, and one, I am convinced, that is made for pedagogical or polemical purposes only.

true to the biblical narrative and did not try to universalize God's covenant with Israel. Quite the contrary, the Talmud and *Halakhah* were suspicious of gentiles who studied Torah and followed the Sinai commandments, viewing them metaphorically as interloping third parties, adulterers who try to intrude on the intensely private betrothal between God and Israel, between the Lover and His beloved.[5]

On the surface, this dimension of Israel's covenant exposes a literary problem in the Torah, and in its depth it can lead to a more profound theological problem. As do all identity-forming relationships, the covenant erects boundaries, thereby creating an insider/outsider dichotomy. Nurtured in the covenant, Jews are under God's parental care; all else are "Other." If so, what are we to make of God's relationship with those outside my parochial covenant? The Bible seems to reinforce this challenge since, once Abraham appears in the biblical narrative, Hebrew Scriptures become almost an exclusive Jewish story. From Gen. 12 through Chronicles, the Bible is a history of the successes, failures, and journeys of the people of Israel. Gentiles never emerge from the background to play a primary role. With the arrival of Abraham, the cosmic drama of creation that pierced the farthest corners of the universe shifts with shocking discontinuity to a local family narrative.

On the theological level, this singular divine concern with his covenantal people radically narrows God's involvement with His vast creation. Throughout the Torah, the covenantal partners are so lovesick with each other that they leave the universe behind; those outside the covenant merit neither prolonged divine involvement nor Jewish attention. Abraham's travel from Haran to Canaan transformed not only Abraham, but also his Divine Partner. Sometime during the journey, the majestic all-caring Creator of Humanity voluntarily diminished Himself and became the demanding protective Father of the nation alone. But where is the Author of Creation, the God of resplendent holiness, Lord of Hosts, whose glory fills the entire universe, whose concern extends to all His children?

The covenant demands intense focus on performing and understanding the *mitsvot*, the commandments that connect the Jewish people to their God and Jews to their kin. As a result, Jews can easily interpret the covenant as

---

5   BT *Sanhedrin* 59a, Maimonides, *Mishneh Torah* (henceforth *MT*), Laws of Kings and Their Wars 8:10 and 10:9–10. Although Maimonides says in 10:10 that gentiles may perform commandments for their utilitarian value, he states in 10:9 that they should not do so *qua* commandment, that is, as a covenantal obligation, without conversion to Judaism and thus joining the Jewish people.

demanding that they remain a people "who dwells apart, not reckoned among the nations," residing in splendid isolation from the rest of the world, despite the fact that this fate was cast upon them by Bilaam, Israel's cruel enemy.[6] And certainly the long Jewish experience in exile conduces toward this withdrawal. Today, we Jews are a traumatized people, a nation suffering from battered wife syndrome.[7] The deep wounds of history inflicted upon us by Rome, the Church, the Tsars, the Nazis, the Communists, and contemporary Muslims who hate Israel are still raw, and they have led some Jewish thinkers to idealize our isolation from world affairs. It seems that whenever Jews engaged with the world, Jewish blood ran in the streets. So it is natural for the Jewish people to turn inward and elevate survival as its primary religious value.

Jews poignantly express our inward gaze in a central part of our liturgy:

> My God, guard my tongue from evil and my lips from deceitful speech. To those who curse me, let my soul be silent; may my soul be to all like the dust. Open my heart to Your Torah and let my soul pursue Your commandments. As for all who plan evil against me, swiftly thwart their counsel and frustrate their plans. Act for the sake of Your name; act for the sake of Your right hand; act for the sake of Your Torah. That Your beloved ones may be delivered, save with Your right hand and answer me. May the worlds of my mouth and the meditation of my heart find favor before You, Lord, my Rock and Redeemer. May He who makes peace in His high places, make peace for us and all Israel—and say: "Amen."[8]

This is the final prayer of the *Amidah*, the collection of nineteen statutory prayers that Jews recite three times daily as they stand before God. As the farewell in the direct communication with God, it represents the culmination of a Jew's personal petition. Note its major aspirations:

(1) personal piety,
(2) individual and national deliverance from hostile enemies,
(3) personal observance of the divine *mitsvot* (Torah),
(4) peace for all Israel.

---

6   Num. 23:9. The Torah is ambiguous as to whether this is a curse or a blessing.
7   I owe this vivid image to R. Shlomo Riskin.
8   *Koren Siddur*, American edition (Jerusalem: Koren Publishers, 2009), 134.

The prayer's religious vision is cautious and restricted. The penitent Jew sees the outside world not as a blessed manifestation of God's creation, but as wholly Other: an existential threat to him and the Jewish people ("Your beloved"). The fervent plea is for God to act as Deliverer of the Jewish people and Carrier of peace to Israel, not the Father of all humanity. The religious dream is personal piety disconnected from the world. Indeed, God's glorious creation as the arena of religious wonder and covenantal challenge has been left behind.

Covenant, Blessing, and Mission

Maimonides and all rabbinic rationalists insist that God's commandments (*mitsvot*) are rational.[9] A rational human act is a deed directed toward an adopted end, a purposive gesture. Similarly, for God's commandments to be rational each must have a purpose and be commanded with a constructive end in mind. The God of the Cosmos who created a world characterized by good cannot be arbitrary when He commands His children. To argue that the divine commandments have no purpose diminishes the Creator, lowering Him to a whimsical dictator who orders His children around simply to parade His authority over them.[10]

If this is true of individual *mitsvot*, so it must also be regarding of the system of commandments as a whole—the covenant at Sinai freely and voluntarily agreed upon by God and the Jewish people.[11] His covenant with us must be part of the divine rational economy, one with an overarching purpose that

---

9 *Guide* III:25–26; See also Saadyah Gaon, *Book of Beliefs and Opinions* III:1–3.
10 In *Guide* III:31, Maimonides implies this diminution of God by people who ascribe no rational purpose to divine commandments.
11 R. Joseph Soloveitchik, "The Lonely Man of Faith," *Tradition* 7, no. 2 (Summer 1965): pt. 6, particularly 29. (Originally appeared as *Ish ha-Emunah* [Jerusalem; Mossad ha-Rav Kook, 1968].) Rabbi Soloveitchik pointedly rejected the famous *midrash* ("*kafah aleihem har k'gigit*") found in BT *Shabbat* 88a, which claims that God coerced the Jewish people to accept the Torah at Sinai. R. Soloveitchik's insistence on the *voluntary* acceptance at Sinai was necessary halakhically (a coerced contract is invalid, and hence not binding according to *Halakhah*) as well as philosophically, since for R. Soloveitchik the acceptance and performance of *mitsvot* is essential to transforming ones' life from an object to a subject, as well as *Am Yisrael*'s living out its freely chosen collective destiny and its escape from slavery and the arbitrary winds of fate. R. Soloveitchik articulated this theology in 1956 in "Kol Dodi Dofeq," 368–380. For a fuller exploration of the tension between coercive and voluntary acceptance of the Torah, see "On Liberty and Halakhah" in Eugene Korn, *To Be a Holy People; Jewish Tradition and Ethical Values* (Jerusalem: Urim, 2021) chapter 5.

transcends the fulfillment of the particular *mitsvot* themselves. Commandments are the means to realizing a larger noble vision, a lofty divine end.

Here we confront the second consequence of the historical assaults on the Jewish people and its Torah: the sharp focus upon the technical analysis, definition and logical coherence of the covenantal terms, the *mitsvot*, to the neglect of the covenant's *telos* and theology. At their profoundest, Greek and Roman culture, Christianity, Enlightenment rationalism, and postmodernism all presented Jews with an ominous common threat: anti-nomianism. This threat led Jews to view the enterprise of *ta'amei ha-mitsvot* (finding reasons for the *mitsvot*) with a jaundiced eye and to eschew philosophic reflection on the purpose of God's covenant as essential to our religious life. One unfortunate result is that traditionalist Jewish thought is now exhausted by authority, by *yirat shamayim* [fear of heaven], and by the deontological experience of commanded-ness; theology, *ahavat ha-shem* [love of God], and spiritual ends have been eclipsed. Maimonides's *Mishneh Torah* fills the bookcases of traditional Jewish libraries, but there is hardly any room for his *Moreh Nevukhim*.[12]

However warranted, this reaction should be understood correctly as the Talmudic tradition understood it: as a defensive polemic forced upon us by our fate as victim, as a spiritual weakness rather than an ideal: "Since the day the Temple was destroyed, The Holy One, Blessed Be He, has nothing in His world except the four cubits of *Halakhah* alone" (BT *Berakhot* 8a). The Talmud claims that it was the disaster of the destruction of the Second Temple that forced God to contract Himself and limit our access to Him exclusively to *Halakhah*. It is no *a priori* ideal.

Yet while halakhic analysis and technical coherence have become our religious educational goals, transcendence remains a spiritual necessity. To paraphrase Immanuel Kant, "transcendence without analysis may be blind, but analysis without transcendence is impotent.[13]

Today *Am Yisrael* has returned home and reclaimed its national sovereignty. If so, has not God been "liberated"? Can we not find Him then also in the political, social and philosophical experiences of the Jewish people? In addition to the State of Israel as the guarantor of the survival of the Jewish people, should

---

12   MT is the paradigm of halakhic coherence whose analysis is suffused with citations of authority. By contrast, in *Guide* Maimonides never resorts to citing a biblical verse or a Talmudic passage to establish its authority, only as a secondary corroboration (*asmaḫta*) of a point he established previously by logical argument.
13   This is why *Halakhah per se* holds such little interest to Jews who have no commitment *apriori* to it. In our world that quests meaning, the dynamics of halakhic analysis are not by themselves spiritually compelling.

it not also be the instrument for enabling the Jewish people to recover its place in the family of nations and exercising its religious responsibility to influence humanity toward God's covenantal values?

This *telos* provides coherence to the Torah's puzzling conjunction of the cosmic account of creation with the remainder of the Bible as a particularistic narrative about the Jewish people. And it is this *telos* that gives the *berit* theological significance beyond Israel itself. As a covenantal people, the Jewish people fulfills a divine purpose in history, a unique mission as an *Am Segulah*—a treasured people. It is this message-bearing mission to others, this *charisma*, that endows the Jewish people with significance in universal history and redeems our covenantal life from narrow self-interest and spiritual narcissism.[14]

Not only rational Jewish theology, but the Torah itself testifies to this covenantal end and overriding religious purpose. In the very text that establishes God's particularist covenant with Abraham, God preserves divine concern for all His children when He issues the theological imperative for Abraham to interact with humanity: "You shall be a blessing. . . . Through you [Abraham], all the nations of the earth shall be blessed" (Gen. 12:2–3). Abraham and his descendants—the Jewish people—are challenged to play a role in human history. God demands that the Jewish people be neither a parochial nor a ghetto people relegated to an insignificant footnote in the larger drama of humanity. God's covenantal people is to be a central actor—*the* central actor—in the grand human story. This broad covenantal ideal is so important for Israel that the Torah reiterates it another four times, twice when God reaffirms the covenant with Abraham, when it is passed on to Isaac, and once more when it is bequeathed to Isaac's son, Jacob.[15] This is the divine paradox of sacred history: God shows an intimate and exclusive love to Abraham and his descendants, and this particular people is to bring God's blessing to all people everywhere.[16]

The Bible does not spell out the exact nature of the blessing that Abraham's children are to bestow upon the nations, but classical, medieval, kabbalistic, and modern Jewish thinkers have given it content, as we will see in the next chapter.

---

14 See R. Joseph Soloveitchik, *Worship of the Heart*, ed. Shalom Carmy (Jersey City, NJ: KTAV, 2003), 73–86, here 85. As R. Soloveitchik argues passionately elsewhere, the Jewish people dare not be like Peretz's unredeemed Bonstche Schweig, "who died without leaving a trace or a mark on others." "Redemption, Prayer and Talmud Torah," 61.
15 Gen. 18:18, 22:18, 26:4, 28:13–14.
16 The particularist/universalist paradox plays out on another level, that of geography: In the biblical vision, the Jewish Temple restricted to the particular locale of Jerusalem is the source of God's Word radiating outward to touch all the inhabitants of the earth, no matter where they reside: "My house shall be called a house of prayer for all nations" (Isa. 56:7).

The blessing blossoms forth out of two distinct theological obligations placed on Abraham and the Jewish people: spreading the knowledge of God[17] and teaching the world about divine moral values that are fundamental to human welfare.[18] The Jewish people achieve these goals and their resulting blessings by being active instructors and less directly as role models for the successful moral life when Jews shape their lives to be testimony about God and his moral law.[19] God charged Abraham to re-teach humanity what it lost in its spiritual descents from Adam and Noah and from Noah and Abraham.[20] God beseeched Abraham's covenantal children to become a partner with the Holy One to bring the nations of the world to their spiritual and moral fulfillment. This is the covenant's purpose in sacred history and the mission of the covenantal people. Though Jews tend to avoid "witness" and "mission" language because these terms were so widely appropriated by Christian theologians, nevertheless this language captures exactly the way rabbinic thinkers understood Abraham's behavior and his children's covenantal purpose: "Our task is to teach the Torah to mankind, to influence the non-Jewish world, to arouse in mankind a sense of

---

17 See commentaries of Isaac Abravanel and Menachem Ricanati on Gen. 12:2; *MT*, Laws of Idolatry 1:3; *Guide* III:29; and Yehudah Leib Alter, *Sefat Emet, Sukkot* 5664. This interpretation is supported by the numerous passages in Genesis where Abraham "calls the name of the Lord." (Gen. 12:8, 13:4, 21:33). Isaac does the same in 26:25. Gerald Blidstein claims that Maimonides "points to Israel's universalistic mission of the Jewish people as instructors of humankind in the worship of God," when he codifies in *MT*, Acts of Sacrifices 19:16, that Jews may teach gentiles how to offer sacrifices to God. See Blidstein, "Maimonides and Me'iri on Non-Judaic Religion," in *Scholars and Scholarship: The Interaction between Judaism and other Cultures*, ed. Leo Landman (New York: Yeshiva University Press, 1990), 31, n. 12.
18 This also has biblical support in Gen 18:19. See also *MT*, Laws of Kings and Their Wars 10:11, which states that the Noahide laws with their requirement of a legal order were given to humanity to help ensure that "the human society is not destroyed."
19 Deut. 4:6–7 explains how the model religious life will constitute a living "proof" to the nations of God's existence, wisdom, and morality: "Observe them [that is, divine commandments] faithfully, for that will be proof of your wisdom and discernment to other peoples, who on hearing all these laws will say, 'Surely that is a wise and discerning people.' For what great nation is there that has a god so close at hand as is the Lord our God whenever we call up on him? Or what great nation has laws and rules as perfect as all this Torah that I set before you on this day?" Also Zech. 8:23: "In those days it will happen that ten men of all the (different) languages of the nations, will take hold, they will hold the corner of the garment of a Jewish man, saying, 'Let us go with you, for we have heard that G-d is with you.'"
20 This is how Maimonides understands pre-Abrahamic history, although in Maimonides's account, Abraham discovered God rather than God commanding Abraham. See *MT*, Laws of Idolatry 1:1–3.

justice and fairness. In a word, we are to teach the world the seven *mitzvot* that are binding on every human being."[21]

The Torah also tells us the purpose of the covenant at Sinai and its commandments with the entire people of Israel: "If you will faithfully obey Me and keep My covenant, you shall be My treasured possession among all people. All the earth is Mine, but you shall be for Me a kingdom of priests and a holy nation" (Ex. 19:5–6).[22]

The Torah insists that priests are those who bestow God's blessings upon others of the community, and by doing so they receive God's blessings upon themselves[23]:

> Thus shall you bless the people of Israel: May the Lord bless you and keep you.
> May the Lord deal kindly and graciously with you.
> May the Lord bestow His favor upon you and grant you peace.
> Thus they shall link My name with the people of Israel and I will bless them.
> (Num. 6:22–27)

Yet if all Israel is to be a "kingdom of priests," it can only be the gentile nations who are the community that Israel is called upon to bless. Mirroring God's charge to Abraham to "be a blessing," Jewish theologians identified the Sinaitic priestly function as spreading blessing by teaching the world about God and divine ethical values.[24] This is why rabbis sometimes identified Abraham

---

21 Joseph B. Soloveitchik, *Abraham's Journey, Reflections on the Life of the Founding Patriarchs*, ed. David Shatz, Joel B. Wolowelsky, and Reuven Zeigler (Jersey City, NJ: KTAV, 2008), 182. R. Soloveitchik repeatedly insists upon this as Abraham's ethical and theological mission to the world. See also my review of this book: "Windows on the World," *Meorot* 8 (*Tishrei* 5771). Similar earlier rabbinic views of the mission of Abraham and the Jewish people are discussed later in this chapter.

22 See Alon Goshen-Gottstein, "A Kingdom of Priests and a Holy Nation," in *Judaism's Challenge: Election, Divine Love, and Human Enmity*, ed. Alon Goshen-Gottstein (Boston: Academic Studies Press, 2020), 13–49.

23 This is the formulation of R. Tsadoq ha-Kohen in his commentary on Deut. *Parshat Ki Tavo* 4.

24 See the commentaries of Rabbis Ovadiah Seforno and Samson Raphael Hirsch on Ex. 19:6. Maimonides's son, Abraham ben ha-Rambam, also insists that this is his father's understanding of the Jewish mission, quoting him in his commentary on Ex. 19:6, s.v. "kingdom of priests."

as a *kohen* despite his life predating the formal institution of priesthood.[25] His theological mission announced in Gen. 12:3 foreshadowed the challenge God uttered at Sinai for *benei Yisrael* to be a *Mamlekhet Kohanim*. This challenge is the meaning of election at Sinai, the reason for Israel's covenantal destiny. Rabbi Naftali Tsvi Yehudah Berliner (Netsiv) went so far as to claim that in establishing the covenant at Sinai, God completed His plan for all of creation that began in Genesis.[26] As the *Am Segulah*, the treasured nation, Israel is the culmination of creation, not because Jews are the center of the universe, but because Sinai charged the new nation to be humanity's teachers, to instruct all people of God's authorship of creation and His moral rules for continuing the human social order. Israel was created for the world, not the world for Israel.

The prophet Isaiah poetically expresses this same covenantal calling to Israel, when he proclaims in God's name:

> I have called you in righteousness, and will hold your hand and keep you. And I will establish you as a covenant of the people, for a Light of the Nations. . . . Behold, darkness shall cover the earth, and a thick darkness the nations. But God will shine upon you. Nations shall then go by your Light and kings by your illumination. (Isa. 42:6; 60:2–3)

The disparity between Gen. 1–11 and the rest of the Torah is now closed by God's paradox of sacred history: a particular people, a tiny people, is tasked with the mission of bringing God's blessing to all of humanity and the light of divine morality to every corner of creation.

At times Jewish tradition focuses on knowing God as the goal of the covenant; other times it stresses the blessings of peace and ethical perfection. Genesis through Deuteronomy repeatedly calls on the Jewish people to "know God," and in his *Guide of the Perplexed* Maimonides understood this intellectual virtue to be the ultimate purpose of God's covenant and its commandments. Indeed, neither the Five Books of Moses nor the *Guide* refer at all to the era of messianic moral bliss that Isaiah, Micah, and Zechariah dream of so beautifully and insist upon so passionately.

---

25 *Midrash Aggadah* (Buber ed.) on Gen. 12:3. This appellation is applied to Abraham because he is seen as functioning as a priest/teacher to the pagan community around him.
26 *Ha-Emeq Davar*, introduction to book of Exodus.

Yet the two visions are one, and both purposes merge into unity. This is clear in Maimonides's culmination of *MT*:

> At that time, there will be neither hunger, nor war; neither will there be jealousy, nor strife. Blessings will be abundant and comfort within the reach of all. The single preoccupation of the entire world will be to know the Lord. Therefore there will be wise persons who know mysterious and profound things and will attain an understanding of the Creator to the utmost capacity of the human mind....[27]

Here it is our knowledge of God that leads naturally to messianic tranquility.[28] For Isaiah, too, peace and knowledge of God are inevitable natural partners, as he announces in the same verse with which Rambam [Maimonides] concludes his great halakhic code: "There will be neither hurt nor destruction in My holy mountain for the earth will be filled with the knowledge of God, as the waters cover the seabed" (Isa. 11:9). So too in the Torah, the knowledge of God and the fulfillment of His covenant yield human blessing, security and tranquility.[29]

---

27 *MT*, Laws of Kings and Their Wars 12:5 (according to the Yemenite manuscript). Most printed texts include the word "Israel" to qualify those who will attain ultimate knowledge of the divine. This qualification is inconsistent with the earlier, more accurate manuscripts. See *MT*, Shabse Frankel ed. (New York: Congregation Benei Yosef, 1998). It is also inconsistent with the earlier emphasis on the universal nature of messianic blessing ("The single preoccupation of the entire world . . ."). See Menachem Kellner, "*Farteicht un Farbessert*: Comments on Tendentious Corrections to Maimonidean Texts" [Hebrew], in *Be-Darkei Shalom: Iyyunim be-Hagut Yehudit Mugashim li-Shalom Rosenberg* [In the paths of peace: Topics in Jewish thought in honor of Shalom Rosenberg], ed. B. Ish-Shalom (Jerusalem: Beit Morasha of Jerusalem Press, 2006), 255–263. For English translation, see "*Farteicht un Farbessert* (On Correcting Maimonides)," *Meorot* 6, no. 2 (*Marheshvan* 5768), https://library.yctorah.org/files/2016/07/Kellner-on-Rambam-FINAL.pdf.

28 This is also the case in the conclusion of *Guide* (III:54), where Rambam explains that the achievement of the intellectual virtues has as its natural consequence the abundance of *ḥesed, tsedaqah*, and *mishpat*. See also *MT*, Laws of Servants 9:8, where Rambam stresses that the correct living of *mitsvot* nurtures empathy, responsibility and compassion for all people, without any distinction between Jew and gentile, master and servant.

29 In the Torah also, knowledge of God and fulfillment of His covenant yield blessing, harmony, and human security. See Lev. 26:3–13; Deut. 28:1–12.

Abraham

We do well to reconsider Abraham and God's covenant with him—and by implication the entire book of Genesis. Jews who are nurtured by the rich biblical story of Abraham through Moses as told by rabbinic tradition and *midrash* know that Abraham was the first Jew. Yet, in what ways was Abraham a Jew? We can ask the question in legal terms: "Was Abraham obligated by the 613 *mitsvot* given at Sinai or did he observe only the seven commandments of Noah?" Posing the question this way, we understand that most rabbinic authorities did not see Abraham as a Jew who is similar to post-Sinai Jews because they believed that he was not obligated by or observe the Sinaitic commandments.[30]

Yet Abraham was no mere Noahide. According to most biblical authorities, *Abraham was a theological Noahide:* He observed the fundamental Noahide laws and other individual *mitsvot*, such as circumcision. Abraham's uniqueness—and the reason we claim him as our father—lay in his recognition of the One Creator of Heaven and Earth, in his understanding of the theological foundation for the Noahide moral laws,[31] and in his public witness to these beliefs. This is the significance of Abraham repeatedly "calling the Name of the Lord." This gesture was testimony to all his neighbors of God's existence and it constituted a public prayer announcing God's continuing involvement with His children.[32] God's covenant with Abraham, then, was the seed for the covenant at Sinai but was far from identical with it.

---

30 See commentaries on Gen. 26:5 by Rabbis David Qimḥi (Radaq), Ovadiah Seforno, Moses ben Naḥman (Naḥmanides), Abraham Ibn Ezra, Samuel ben Meir (Rashbam), Ḥizqiya bar Manoaḥ (Ḥizquni). See also *MT*, Laws of Kings and Their Wars 9:1. For a contemporary expression of this position by a traditionalist rabbinic authority, see Soloveitchik, *Abraham's Journey*, 58. These interpretations comport well with the biblical text, which indicates that the patriarchs violated some of the Sinai commandments, and they eliminate the need for historical anachronism. (How could Abraham observe Passover in commemoration of the exodus from Egypt, which was yet to occur?). They have no reason to ascribe prophetic powers to Abraham to enable him to know later biblical or post-biblical Jewish history. As such, they are more rational than the minority view of the Talmudic sages R. Nahorei (BT *Qiddushin* 82a) and Rav (BT *Yoma* 28b), and the medieval commentator Rabbi Shlomo ben Yitsḥaq (Rashi).
31 None of the Noahide commandments require a positive theological commitment.
32 According to the Talmudic authorities (*Ḥazal*), Abraham established the practice of *shaḥarit*, morning prayer. See BT *Sanhedrin* 26b; and *MT*, Laws of Kings and Their Wars 9:1. This is also the way in which medieval rabbinic biblical commentators understood "calling the name of the Lord." For Rashi, it was an act of prayer and for Naḥmanides it was public proclamation of God's existence. See their respective commentaries on Gen. 12:8.

Abraham was the pre-halakhic man, and he remains our paradigm of the faithful Jew. *Mitsvot and Halakhah* are built upon *berit Sinai* and *Torat Moshe*, but Jewish theology is rooted in Abraham and his covenantal life—and just as Judaism would be unthinkable without our patriarchs and matriarchs, the full understanding of God's commandments cannot be detached from Abraham's covenantal life and its theology.

This intrinsic connection between the covenant's theology and religious life dedicated to *mitsvot* is why the Torah does not begin with the first divine imperative found in Ex. 12 to fashion Jewish time around the new moon of Nisan, but with the noble experiences of our ancestors throughout Genesis. It is why the Torah cannot end with the last *mitsvah* of *hakhel* found in Deut. 12, but continues through the covenantal experiences of the Jewish people and the messianic visions of the prophets.

Without the life and historical mission of Abraham the covenant would be devoid of theological purpose. And without the account of the historical trials of God's treasured people that will culminate in the messianic dream, the covenant at Sinai would lack historical significance and spiritual direction. Only when we combine the *mitsvot* with their underlying theology does Jewish covenantal life and its spiritual destiny blossom into full splendor:

> Come, let us go up to the mountain of the Lord and the God of Jacob, that He teach us His ways, and we will walk in His paths.... Let the peoples beat their swords into plowshares and their spears into pruning hooks. Nations shall not lift up sword against nation, nor shall they learn war anymore. Let every man sit under his vine and under his fig tree; and no one shall make him afraid....Let all the people walk, each in the name of his God; and we shall walk in the name of our Lord our God forever and ever. (Micah 4:2–5)

This is the religious dream of Abraham, of Moses, and all the prophets of Israel. It is the ultimate role that the Torah asks the Jewish people to play in human history. Indeed, it is the dream of the Creator of Heaven of Earth Himself, the God of Israel, and of all His children who are faithful to the covenant.

2

Israel as Blessing: Theological Horizons

Israel and the Biblical Blessing

As we have seen, blessing appears in the Torah's account of the birth of the Jewish people as well as its destiny in human history:

> Be a blessing... I will make of you a great nation, and I will bless you; I will make your name great, and you shall be a blessing. I will bless those who bless you and curse him that curses you; and all the families of the earth shall bless themselves by you. (Gen. 12:2–3)

The nexus between Abraham and blessing is not limited to this one textual reference or to Abraham alone. Blessing as part of God's promise appears twice more to Abraham, in Gen. 18:18–19 ("Since Abraham is to become a great and populous nation and all the nations of the earth are to bless themselves by him. For I have singled him out that he may instruct his children and his posterity to keep the way of the Lord by doing what is just and right, in order that the Lord may bring about for Abraham what He has promised him") and in 22:17–18 ("I will bestow My blessing upon you and make your descendants as numerous as the stars in the heaven and the sand on the seashore.... All the nations of the earth shall bless themselves by your descendants because you have obeyed My command"); to Abraham's son Isaac in Gen. 26:4 ("I will make your heirs as numerous as the stars of heaven, and assign to your heirs all these lands, so that all the nations of the earth shall bless themselves by your heirs"); and also to Isaac's son Jacob in Gen 28:14 ("All the families of the earth shall bless themselves by you and your descendants").

Curiously, however, the theological idea (*theologoumenon*) of Israel as a blessing does not appear again in the remainder of the Pentateuch. Moreover, in the rest of TaNaKH the blessing's reference to the Jewish people after Jacob appears *explicitly* only in the later prophets.[1] Nevertheless, the blessing's application to the post-patriarchal Jewish people is mentioned explicitly in Gen. 18 ("his children and *his household after him*"), in Gen. 22 ("All the nations of the earth shall bless themselves *by your descendants*"), in Gen. 26 ("all the nations of the earth shall bless themselves *by your heirs*"), as well as in Gen. 28 ("All the families of the earth shall bless themselves *by you and your descendants*"). Importantly, Gen. 28 is directed at Jacob, and thus this blessing must also refer to Jacob's progeny down through the generations.

Blessing is also implicit in God's charge to the entire Jewish people at Sinai to become a "kingdom of priests" (Ex. 19:6) and the prophetic call for Jews to function in history as a "light unto the nations" (Isa. 42:6 and 49:1–6). A primary function of the priest—particularly in the post-Temple life of Israel—is to be a conduit of God's blessing to the community, in which case the call to become "a nation of priests" implies bestowing blessing on the world community. "Light to the nations" also carries the undeniable connotation of providing goodness and understanding to the gentile world. If so, this analysis assumes that the bestowal and predictions of blessing are not limited to the patriarchs, but apply to the Jewish people over the sweep of their history, just as rabbinic tradition assumed that God's covenant with Abraham applies to Abraham's Jewish descendants in perpetuity. Blessing, therefore, constitutes an intrinsic part of the Bible's understanding of Israel's destiny and theological calling. And as Abraham's progeny are called upon to extend blessing to "all the families of the earth," it should play a central role in defining the Bible's covenantal conception of the Jewish people's relations with the gentile world.

Yet blessing has not played a prominent role in past rabbinic biblical and Talmudic interpretation. This may be due more to the trauma experienced by the Jewish people in throughout in diasporic history rather than to the idea that blessing was limited to the patriarchs. Jewish interaction with gentile powers

---

1   Zech. 8:13, Ezek. 34:26, Jer. 4:1–2, and Isa. 19:24–25, all of which will be discussed later in the essay. One theological option is to confine the bestowal and imperative of blessing exclusively to the patriarchs, which would cancel blessing as central to the life, election, and theological mission of Israel after Jacob. As indicated above, this narrow interpretation runs afoul of some of the other Pentateuchal texts and the above prophetic references.

have often been tragic, thereby causing rabbinic commentaries to pass over the Bible's theological calling for the Jewish people to enter world history by influencing the gentile nations.

Another possible explanation for why these texts have not enjoyed wide circulation is that it is only in modernity that Jewish readers are deeply interested in developing the theological concept of Israel as blessing. Reading texts is not only about what the texts say but also about the interaction between what they say and what the reader seeks to find or is able to recognize. Thus, different texts and themes may naturally be emphasized in different periods. Some generations may have been less interested, or less able, to hear the notion that Israel is to be a blessing unto others. This points to a challenge of contemporary interpretations in our present times. To develop a theology of Israel that offers possibilities for how Israel should relate theologically to other peoples and religions, modern thinkers may be in a better position than previous generations were to hear messages in Jewish sacred texts and later rabbinic writings.

To preserve the coherence and integrity of the above biblical texts regarding blessing must be understood as a constituent element of Israel's mission and election. Identifying the centrality of the biblical concept of blessing and how its uses have been limited to specific contexts presents us with the challenge of developing the principles and application of the concept.

The Bible provides few details regarding the nature of this blessing and the dynamics of its transmission. However, rabbinic tradition provides an array of sources regarding these subjects, which have significant implications for Israel's role in sacred history and its ideal relationship to gentiles. Studying these sources allows us to reveal important conceptions of Israel's covenantal mission, to engage in constructive thinking and to explore some of the covenantal challenges before Jews today.

This chapter surveys the rabbinic interpretations of Israel's blessing, outlining their implications for different theological approaches to Jewish self-understanding, and to Israel's relationship to humanity. The different theologies, attitudes, and practices that emerge from this variety are expressed in contemporary Jewish self-definition, behavior, and attitudes toward other religions. Rather than prescribe a specific interpretation or view of Israel's mission, my goal now is be a catalyst for independent thinking that can contribute to future constructive Jewish theology.

The texts under consideration come from a broad range of sources representing different periods and schools of Jewish thought. The eclectic use of sources is designed to achieve several purposes. It makes us aware of the broad range of options available for Jewish theology, and it allows us to revisit the fundamental dynamics of Jewish thought and the inherent tensions in performing the task of constructing a contemporary Jewish theology. Finally, it allows us to recover voices sometimes overlooked in Jewish religious discourse, and thereby broaden the theological possibilities at our disposal.

Prophetic Conceptions of Israel as Blessing

A number of prophetic texts mention the idea of blessing as essential to Jewish identity. Despite the existence of these texts, it is striking how little attention they have received in the history of interpretation and commentary, and how much most students of the Torah are unaware of them or their significance. Certainly, no Jewish theology has been built around the centrality of blessing in Israel's covenant.

Israel as blessing appears in the prophets Zechariah, Ezekiel, and Jeremiah, as well as Isaiah:

> And just as you were a curse among the nations, O House of Judah and House of Israel, so, when I vindicate you, you shall become a blessing. Have no fear; take courage! (Zech. 8:13)

> I will make these and the environs of My hill a blessing, I will send down the rain in its season, rains that bring blessing. (Ezek. 34:26)

Rabbi David Qimhi (Radaq), a primary rabbinic commentator on the prophets, relates the promises of blessing that appear in Zechariah and Ezekiel to the specific blessings to Abraham as recorded in Gen. 12:2–3.[2] This reinforces the idea that Abraham's blessing also applies to all of Israel in its relation to the nations. However, the prophets extend the meaning of being a blessing in relation to Abraham into a continuation of the promise for salvation. This might be understood as indicating that *the purpose* of salvation for Israel to function as blessing to the nations, or alternatively that the blessing will occur not in normal history but only in the *eschaton*, that is, only at the end of history (*aharit ha-yamim*, the messianic era) when salvation is fully realized—and not before.

---

2   See Radaq's commentary on those verses.

And if the messianic era represents a rupture or discontinuity with pre-messianic history, then Israel need not strive to be a blessing to the nations prior to that time.

The mandate or prediction to function as a blessing in Zechariah is couched between the promise of salvation and the encouragement to be fearless. This detracts from the force of the categorical message of blessing appearing in Genesis. Is this due merely to the literary context of the prophets, or is it more central to their visions and theologies? In either possibility the de-emphasis may have contributed to the blessing prophecy failing to achieve great popularity in rabbinic tradition.

Radaq again sees Ezekiel's reference to blessing as an extension of Gen. 12. However, he appears to emphasize the divine bestowal of rain as the result of (or constituting) blessing with the actions of Israel functioning as the conduit for the blessing. This can easily elude the reader, so that the prophecy of Israel as blessing will be relegated to the background.

Israel as blessing also appears in Jer. 4:1–2:

> If you return, O Israel—declares the Lord—if you return to Me, if you remove your abominations from My presence and do not waver, and swear, "As the Lord lives," in sincerity, justice, and righteousness—nations shall bless themselves by you [lit. "him"] and praise themselves by you.

R. Shlomo Yitshaqi (Rashi) interprets the meaning of this verse similar to his interpretation of Gen. 12:2–3: "If you [Israel] do so [return to the Lord], then nations will bless themselves by Israel. Every non-Jew will say to his son, 'You shall be like So-and-So the Jew.'" Thus, Israel seems to stand almost as an introverted religious model to be seen and emulated by the gentiles of the world.

Radaq comments on this verse in Jeremiah:

> Nations will bless themselves by him and will glory in him. There will yet come a time also when the other nations will bless themselves in Him and will take pride in Him and not in idols. It is also possible that the words "in him" refer to Israel—that is, if Israel will do all of this, then the nations will bless themselves by you, as it is written, "All the nations of the earth shall bless themselves by your heirs" (Lev 26:4).

Similar to Rashi, this latter interpretation again seems to imply that Israel's active return to God will occasion the blessing to the nations, with Israel's direct relationship with the gentile nations being secondary.

Rashi's strong reading of Jer. 4:1–2 suggests that *all* nations will be blessed through Israel. (Radaq also recognizes this reading.) Similar to his reading of Gen. 12:2–3, Rashi highlights how Abraham serves as a model for others. In Gen. 12:2–3, as in his interpretation of Jeremiah, Rashi understands the verse to indicate that gentiles will say to their sons, "be like Abraham," even though there is nothing in the biblical text to indicate that this blessing/role modeling should be in the framework of father-son relations. It may that Rashi implies here that Israel's relationship to the nations should be regarded as parallel to that of a parent to a child: role model and teacher by example. In his second interpretation Radaq appears to agree with Rashi, but his first interpretation suggests that God is the one who is being blessed, not Israel. That the verse can be read in more than one way may have contributed to the limited influence that this verse has had over the generations in expressing the notion of Israel as a blessing to the nations.

Finally, Isaiah announces blessing in 19:24–25:

> In that day, Israel shall be a third partner with Egypt and Assyria as a blessing on earth; for the Lord of Hosts will bless them, saying, "Blessed be My people Egypt, My handiwork Assyria, and My very own Israel.

These verses in Isaiah are unique in the Bible in that they appear to extend the covenantal blessing of Israel to Egypt and Assyria, thus implying that those nations have achieved (or will achieve) theological parity with Israel. They imply that, at some future time, Israel will share its status with Assyria and Egypt, the two reigning empires of Isaiah's time. Terms of status and endearment hitherto exclusive to God's relation with Israel are now shared with other peoples. They may suggest that Israel's status and election are but instrumental, and that Israel will influence Egypt and Assyria, who will in turn bestow blessing on other gentile nations. Thus, ultimately, God's design is for others to enjoy the same elected status and relationship that Israel enjoys. Since this diminishes Israel's unique character and religious calling, these verses also have not been stressed in rabbinic tradition and Jewish thought. Yet they may give fertile ground for understanding Israel's instrumental role in shaping Christianity and Islam and these later religions in turn influencing humanity.

Radaq comments on these verses:

> In that day, Israel shall be a third partner. They will share a third in the faith of God, and they will be a blessing in the midst of the land. For they will enjoy an advantage of blessings over the other nations for as long as they maintain their faith in God.

Here Radaq introduces the notion of faith in God as the foundation for the new status of Assyria and Egypt. Faith—presumably knowledge of the One God of heaven and earth—is the basis for shifting relations between Israel and the nations. One possible understanding of this idea is that Israel's goal is to spread the knowledge of God in the world. When Israel is successful, others will share in Israel's special status and enjoy its particular blessings.

According to Radaq, blessing is what the nations receive from God as a consequence of their true faith. This interpretation does not seem to have the rich understanding of "blessing" that characterized the interpretations of Gen. 12. While Radaq emphasizes the three nations enjoying the advantage of blessings, one can also imagine that blessing conveys the idea of spreading the faith in God to others and seeing Israel's special status as instrumental to the task of teaching humanity about God. This has obvious ramifications for Jewish understandings of other religions, and raises the questions for Jewish theology of identifying which conditions are necessary for others to recognize God, whether the other faiths must mirror the Jewish concept and worship of God, and whether other nations can be considered as sharing Israel's blessings and Abraham's covenant. It also leaves open the question of how faith itself leads naturally to blessing understood biblically as peace, security, and human flourishing.

Blessing as Active Universal Engagement: Teaching Theology and Morality

How aware are Jewish thinkers, both throughout the generations and today, of the idea of being a blessing to the nations? This question is related to the diverse understandings of what it means to be a blessing. Traditional interpretations of the biblical blessing oscillate between active understandings that promote Jewish engagement with gentiles and their culture, and more passive ones that restrict blessing to introspective Jewish modeling that naturally engenders gentile emulation. Thus, we can imagine different degrees of activity, awareness, and intentionality of the biblical blessing. Each of the understandings represents a paradigm for contemporary relations between Jews and gentiles, and for ideal Jewish interaction with humanity.

This is not a strictly theological or "metaphysical" question since different educational and social initiatives follow from the adoption of particular interpretations. Should Jews be "out there" doing good and striving to influence gentiles? Should they seek to share the knowledge of God as a way of being a blessing? If so, should they seek to convert gentiles, either minimally to the Noahide commandments or maximally to the Mosaic covenant? Should Jews keep gentile humanity as part of their spiritual intention, even as they face God and practice their particular Mosaic covenant within the Jewish people? Alternatively, perhaps Jews need do nothing other than function as a model worthy of others' praise, emulation, and blessing. Ought Jews focus inward exclusively with role modeling taking place without Jewish concern for the presence of others, or do they also have to consider some degree of intentionality toward others?

This presents a twofold spiritual challenge. First, what does blessing imply regarding ideal Jewish action and to what extent should Jews direct their actions toward others to extend blessing to them? Second, how closely should the rest of the world be present in Jewish thoughts and intentions, even as we serve God in the context of our particularist covenant?

One major understanding of the biblical blessing and charge sees blessing in active terms. God has challenged Abraham, and consequently Israel, to share their theological understanding with the nations. Thus, teaching is a form of creating universal blessing. According to this view, Abraham is the prototype of a teacher who shares Judaism's message with others. By emphasizing teaching, we begin to move from blessing peoples to recognition of their religions. This is most evident in Maimonides's statements about the theological and historical function of Abraham:

> He [Abraham] began to call in a loud voice to all people and inform them that there is one God in the entire world and it is proper to serve Him. He would go out and call to the people, gathering them in city after city and country after country, until he came to the land of Canaan, proclaiming (God's existence the entire time), as (Gen. 21:33) states: "And He called there in the name of the Lord, the eternal God." When the people would gather around him and ask him about his statements, he would explain (them) to each one of them according to their understanding, until they turned to the path of truth. Ultimately,

thousands and myriads gathered around him. These are the souls of Abraham's house. He planted in their hearts this great fundamental principle, composed texts about it, and taught it to Isaac, his son. Isaac also taught others and turned (their hearts to God). He also taught Jacob and appointed him as a teacher. (*MT*, Laws of Idolatry 1:4)

"You shall love God," that is, make Him beloved among the creatures as your father Avraham did, as it is written, "The souls that he made in Ḥaran" (Gen. 12:5). Avraham, as a result of his deep understanding of G-d, acquired love for God, as the verse testifies, "Avraham, who loved Me" (Isa. 41:8). This powerful love therefore caused him to call out to all mankind to believe in God. So too, you shall love Him to the extent that you draw others to Him. (*MT*, Book of Commandments, positive commandment 3)

In Maimonides's understanding Abraham is a Socratic instructor who dispenses blessings to the world by teaching the pagans around him about the true nature of God and correct faith. Aside from Abraham's correct metaphysical understanding that God is unique and non-physical, Maimonides believed that Abraham was aware only of the moral Noahide commandments, the commandment of circumcision, and possibly the commandment to pray.[3] It is likely, therefore, that Maimonides believed that Abraham taught those around him about the moral commandments as a necessary means to understanding theological truth. If so, according to Maimonides, the mission of Israel includes teaching humanity about the accurate nature of God and divine moral law.[4] In fact, Maimonides acknowledged that these truths were spread to the nations of the earth partially by both Christians and Muslims, whose religions were derived from Judaism.[5] Thus this idea of blessing has implications for how Jews should understand Christians and Muslims theologically in the context of sacred history.

In his commentary on Gen. 12:2, the medieval exegete Don Isaac Abravanel (fifteenth-century Spain) also understands blessings this way:

---

3   *MT*, Laws of Kings and Their Wars 9:1.
4   As we saw, in chapter 1, Maimonides's son, Avraham ben ha-Rambam, testifies to his father's interpretation. See his commentary on Ex. 19:6, s.v. "kingdom of priests."
5   See *MT*, Laws of Kings and Their Wars 11:4 (uncensored edition).

> The purpose of the process referenced here and the phrase "You shall be a blessing" that God commanded him [Abraham] is that when he travels he should be a blessing among the nations in teaching and informing them about the true faith in a way that will complete the world through him and his teaching so that divine providence will extend to those who accept his teaching and study His faith. Regarding this it says, "I will bless those who bless you."

According to Abravanel, Abraham's success is measured by the fact that so many consider themselves to be his heirs, even though they are not genealogically related to him. This bold statement appears to be made without reservation, and likely constitutes an acknowledgement that Christianity and Islam—the religions to which Abravanel was exposed—were also carriers of a true teaching sourced in Abraham.

There is another more behavioral interpretation of "being a blessing." Some sources highlight the cognitive knowledge of God, while others, highlight the path of righteous and justice—*tsedaqah* and *mishpat*—as emphasized in the reference to blessing in Gen. 18:18–19.

Whether God's charge to Abraham to function as a blessing to the world connotes teaching the world about the reality and metaphysical character of God or basic moral norms of righteous and justice, under this conception of blessing Israel has an active mission toward gentiles. Its mission consists in sharing this teaching and following in the footsteps of Abraham, who is the first one to both share his theological awareness with others as well as acting as a defender of justice and righteousness (Gen. 18) and thus functioning as a model of ethical relations toward others. Hence Israel actively brings blessing to the nations in two ways. Teaching faith in God itself is an act of blessing, while the moral consequences of that theological sharing are also a blessing to humanity as they lead to individual and social flourishing.

A third instance of interpreting the election of Israel as blessing to the world is offered by R. Naftali Berliner (Netsiv), who sees the book of Exodus as the theological extension of the book of Genesis, and the Sinaitic revelation as the culmination of God's creation of the universe that proceeds from Gen. 1 through the covenantal blessing bestowed upon Abraham in Gen. 12 through Exo. 20[6]:

---

6   *Ha-Emeq Davar*, introduction to book of Exodus.

It thus emerges that the giving of the Torah is the completion of creation, and this is identical with the Exodus from Egypt, as then Israel were fit to accept the Torah and to complete the Creation, and to come through it to the *telos* of their formation, in relation to the People of God. This is analogous to the function of human reason and forthright qualities in the Torah of Humanity, regarding which even though the land and what fills it did not reach this completion until after a long time after the creation of Heaven and Earth, and even nowadays there are many human beings that have not reached this height, nonetheless the matter is comprehended even by the nations of the world that only this is the telos of the advantage/raised status of the human being. Similarly we have reason to believe that even though Torah and her principles were not given until after the Exodus from Egypt, and even now there are many of Israel who have not achieved a Torah mindset, nonetheless, the Torah is the sole reason for the advantage/raised status of Israel, who were formed to be a covenantal people for a light unto the nations. Thus the book of Exodus is the second book of the first book [Genesis], as if they are one subject separated into two books of the book of creation.... The general completion of the world is that there will be a nation who will be God's people. This was not achieved until Israel left Egypt and arrived at its goal that it be fit to be a light unto the nations and to establish the knowledge of God in the world.

Rather than understanding revelation at Sinai in parochial or national terms, Netsiv proceeds in the opposite direction, insisting like Isaiah (49:6) that Sinai revelation has universal value. The purpose of Sinaitic election is for the Jewish people to serve as "a light unto the nations" by teaching the world the true knowledge of God. According to Netsiv, Israel's religious identity cannot be understood without Israel's connection to the gentile nations because Israel's election is the center of a universal strategy for disseminating divine truth to humanity.

It should be noted that understanding Israel's blessing as active teaching (or universal mission) is an instrumentalist conception of election, and this, in turn, leads to a theological and national paradox: when Israel's uniqueness consists in its mission to bless and teach others, the very success of that blessing entails the loss of Israel's uniqueness. By succeeding in its mission Israel would no longer enjoy the benefits of its unique relationship with God. Isaiah's prophecy in 19:24–25 approaches this idea, and Maimonides and his rationalist theological followers developed this understanding of Jewish religious identity most fully and downplayed the meaning of Jewish election.⁷

Blessing as Passive Modeling

We saw how Rashi and Radaq often understood Genesis's blessing to Abraham as providing a model whose influence naturally spreads to the nations ("They [the gentiles] will say to their sons, 'be like Abraham'") without entailing any necessary Jewish intentionality toward gentiles This is a significant difference between the first concept of blessing as active engagement with gentiles and this more passive modeling interpretation of blessing. Even in this model of blessing, however, it is clear that Jews need to be aware of the presence of gentiles and the impact of Jewish behavior on others, albeit that such awareness need not be the primary element in Jews leading their religious lives. Moreover, this model may function as an important stimulus for Jews to evaluate themselves in their spiritual and behavioral lives. It may demand that they continuously ask themselves, "Am I an admirable model? Are my actions worthy of emulation by others?"

The interpretation of blessing by Ovadiah ben Jacob Seforno in sixteenth-century Italy represents an integration of these disparate conceptions. For Seforno, the ideal Jewish religious intention is toward God, yet ultimately being a blessing to God results in human flourishing because God finds joy in correct human belief and progress. Focusing on God's joy is thus coupled with action in relation toward others. Relating to Gen. 12:2, Seforno offers a synthesis of religious intention toward God and concrete action in relation to gentiles:

> The blessing of God is that He should rejoice in His creation, as our sages have said, "(God said to me,) 'Ishmael, My son, bless Me.' I replied, 'May it be Your will that Your mercy may prevail over Your other attributes'" (BT *Berakhot* 7a). Therefore He [God] says, "become a blessing to Me by (your) deep understanding (whereby) you will acquire perfection, and teach knowledge (of God) to the people."⁸

---

7   Maimonides does not mention Jewish election at all in *Guide*. The end of his *MT* describes the fullness of the messianic era—when Israel's mission and blessing has been fully realized—in thoroughly universalistic terms. See also *MT*, Laws of Kings and Their Wars 12:5 (according to Yemenite ms.) quoted earlier.
8   Ovadiah Seforno, commentary on Bible, Gen. 12:2 (Pelcovitz ed., 64).

Seforno here couches his understanding of blessing in terms that relate to God directly: Being a blessing means being a blessing to God, so the correct understanding of Gen. 12 is that God challenged Abraham and his descendants to be a blessing for Him. God finds joy in His creation—specifically when His human creatures achieve spiritual perfection. Abraham is commanded to reach spiritual perfection, through attaining the perfected understanding of God who acts toward His human creatures with the moral attribute of mercy. He takes this interpretation a step further by asserting that perfected knowledge is the basis for teaching others and hence Abraham is to share his knowledge with others. In the end it is this activity of teaching that makes Abraham a blessing to God.

Seforno cites the Talmudic passage in which a righteous person (R. Ishmael) gains the upper hand over divine justice, implying that blessing increases divine joy because it allows for the continued existence of God's children who will withstand divine justice with the aid of divine compassion. Thus, anything that advances the project of maintenance, evolution, and perfection of creation can be considered a divine blessing. Unique to Seforno's reading is that Abraham—and by extension all Israel—are simultaneously a blessing to themselves, to God, and to the world.

Yet who are the others that Abraham is bidden to teach and perfect spiritually? While it is possible that in Seforno's mind Abraham is to teach his offspring exclusively (as suggested by Gen. 18:19), it is more likely that, because the Jewish people had not yet been formed and according to rabbinic tradition Abraham converted the "strangers" around him, the others who Abraham was commanded to teach are those "souls" he acquired outside his biological family.

Blessing as Non-Relational Theurgic Agency

While philosophical and rational schools of interpretation emphasized blessing as active teaching or influencing (either theologically or morally) and the medieval biblical exegetes emphasized passive modeling, still others stressed more solitary dimensions of blessing, and avoided the possibility of Israel's losing its unique status through the sharing of blessing. One specific mode of this interpretation, which is popular among kabbalistic thinkers, is that blessing is directed toward, and connecting with, the supernal world. This is achieved through ritual and religious intent that draws the divine flux into the physical, human plane. Blessing refers to the drawing of a celestial reality to the human realm—almost exclusively to the life and experience of the Jewish people. The covenantal blessing emerges constitutes and important concept in this spiritual transfer. Abraham's specific blessing is understood in the context of the broader kabbalistic understanding of blessing, and thus biblical and classical sources are reread in light of the particularities of the kabbalistic understanding of how the celestial realm above relates to the human realm below.

Drawing forth blessing from above seems largely divorced from any direct Jewish interaction with other nations, and thus it eliminates the need for Jews to be concerned with gentiles while they lead their religious and spiritual life. Blessing is the natural effect of living in accordance with the divine commandments, a radically more introverted way of generating blessing than either active engagement or passive modeling.

This is concept is expressed by the kabbalist R. Joseph ben Abraham Gikatilla of thirteenth-century Spain:

> This is the secret of the blessing that God, blessed be He, granted to Abraham. For the abundance of bounty and emanations that are drawn from the Supernal Eden, which is called *keter* [crown], and subsequently flow through the conduit of *tiferet,* which is called *nahar* [river], are all gathered into the tenth pool which is the secret of *malkhut* [kingship], and this is the pool that the stories of the wells of Abraham and Isaac refer to. God entrusted Abraham with this pool through which all the nations shall be blessed. This is the meaning of what He said, "I will make of you a great nation, and I will bless you; I will make your name great, and you shall be a blessing" (Gen. 12:2). What is the meaning of "be a blessing"? That the *shekhinah* [the immanent presence of God] that is the pool shall dwell in you.... Even though God gave Abraham the pool He did not give him nor Isaac the gate, because their progeny contained dross, that is, Ishmael and Esau; but He did give the gate to Jacob whose progeny did not contain any dross. The meaning of God's words to Abraham, "and all nations of the earth shall be blessed in you" is clear and well understood, for seventy families attach themselves to Abraham and Isaac. This is the meaning of the word *berakhah* [blessing], which comes from the word *ve-arkhavah ha-variakh* [to graft unto], that is, that the seventy nations are grafted unto and spiritually connected to Abraham and Isaac.[9]

---

9 Joseph ben Abraham Gikatilla, *Gates of Righteousness*, First Gate.

The author here plays on the Hebrew words *berakhah* (blessing) and *beraikhah* (pool). The tenth sphere of *malkhut* (divine kingship) is the pool, into which all higher blessings gather and which is also associated with the notion of blessing. The divine grant of blessing to Abraham means that God provided him with access to *malkhut*. As *malkhut* is responsible for the drawing forth of all blessings to the physical world, it is also the source of sustenance and bounty for gentiles. God granted this to Abraham so that the nations may also receive blessings. Hence blessing for the nations is inherently linked to this *sefira*, and it is only through the access entrusted to Abraham that blessing is available to others. Blessing is a form of spiritual graft, of extending spiritual power from God to Israel to the nations. Only Abraham's blessing keeps gentiles connected to the divine.

Note that blessings to the nations stem from the metaphysical endowment God bestowed upon Israel rather than from any knowledge that Israel possesses or actions that Israel manifests. This concept does, however, stress the importance of Israel maintaining a high spiritual state to remain connected to "pool" of divine kingship of *malkhut* and hence blessing.

R. Menachem Mendel Schneerson, the Rebbe of Lubavitch who lived in twentieth-century America, followed a related line of thinking:

> This is the meaning of the verse, "Praise the Lord, all you nations; extol Him, all you peoples, for great is His steadfast love toward us" (Psalms 117:1–2). . . . How is the demonstration of God's love to us [Israel] a reason why other nations should praise Him? The explanation is well known: the intensification of God's love toward us causes a purification, refinement, and elevation among the Gentiles and nations, to the extent that they visibly recognize its effects and as a result, they extol and praise God. This process is accomplished through the offering of the seventy oxen and similarly through the service of "Instead of bulls we will pay (the offering of) our lips" (Hos. 14:3), that is, prayer.[10]

This teaching provides a further proof for Israel's continuing obligation to serve as a blessing for the nations. Gentile nations rejoice because whatever God's grace is shown to Israel also extends to the nations. Israel, then, becomes

---

10   Menachem Mendel Schneerson, *Torat Menahem*, pt. 1, 131.

a—perhaps the exclusive—spiritual conduit of blessing for the nations. Because the blessing is fully observable to the nations, it induces them to offer praise to God. However, this interpretation again omits any explicit reference of Jewish mindfulness toward gentiles when experiencing God's love. Israel "earns" God's blessing through ritual (the sacrifice of seventy oxen on the festival of *Sukkot*) or through prayer—both of which are actions directed toward God alone.

This raises an important spiritual and theological question: to what degree should the energetic transfer of blessing to gentiles be conscious and intentional in Jewish religious life? One possible interpretation of this teaching is that throughout the religious life of the Jewish people, Israel and the nations engage in a conscious exchange of blessing, an extension of divine love that reaches out to all humanity, in turn leading to the praise of God. And this extension of divine love should be a spiritual aspiration for Jews not only annually during the festival of *Sukkot*, which intimates the era of full blessing for all nations, but also every day as Jews engage in daily prayer.

A third expression of blessing as theurgic agency is provided by R. Elimelekh of Lizhensk, the influential ḥasidic master in eighteenth-century Poland:

> This is the meaning of the verse, "See ... I set before you blessing and a curse" (Deut. 11:26): The word "see" hints at and refers to the righteous ones [*tsaddiqim*] who are on the level of (serving God with) love, which is also identified with sight. "I set before you a blessing and a curse," refers to the curse that is placed upon the nations, and the blessing consists of compassion for Israel. All this is delivered in your hands [in your power]; by virtue of your righteousness, you will be able to accomplish the foregoing.[11]

Unlike the two earlier sources that highlight blessing between Israel and the nations, R. Elimelekh portrays Jewish-gentile relations in diametrically opposite terms, corresponding to good and evil and other similar dichotomies. This counterpoint of Israel and gentiles is not uncommon in kabbalistic and ḥasidic writings, in which blessing to Israel carries a theological concomitant of curse for gentiles. The righteous (Jewish) *tsaddiqim* are on the level of love and they extend that love, expressed through compassion, upon Israel. In contrast,

---

11 Elimelekh of Lizhensk, *Noam Elimelekh*, Re'eh.

they stimulate the opposite of blessing—"curse"—upon the nations. The duality of blessing and curses is paralleled by the duality of Israel and the nations. The curse to gentiles is the dialectical concomitant of Israel's blessing, rather than a conduit to universal blessing, as Gen. 12:2–3 indicates. It also ensures Israel's enduring uniqueness and superiority.

It may well be that historical circumstances led to this polarized worldview. Whatever its genesis, it is now firmly entrenched in a number of rabbinic writings and presents contemporary Jews with the challenge of understanding, evaluating and potentially adopting this worldview.

With its active and missionary emphasis, the philosophical tradition allowed for natural sharing between Abraham and the world, between Israel and humanity. By contrast, kabbalistic tradition largely focuses on ritual and interior spiritual life as the arenas of religious activity, with its correlative de-emphasis of Jewish-gentile relations. The first interpretations present the flow of blessings from Israel to the nations, a desirable sharing in divine bounty. The latter present a discontinuity and a limit, positing the nations as polar opposites of Israel. The extreme version of this theology is Elimelekh's teaching in which divine intent of blessing for the nations is replaced by a curse upon them. The spiritual depth of that theology is matched by oppositional, even hateful, statements concerning gentiles, projecting Jewish-gentile relations as theologically undesirable and to be strenuously avoided.

How should we evaluate this strand of interpretation? Do we accept it as a permanent truth of Jewish theology and spiritual life, merely as a temporary insight resulting from difficult historical circumstances, or as a denial of the biblical aspiration for Jews to spread the divine blessing to all God's children, and hence to be rejected?

In the context of a Jewish approach to gentiles and their faiths, interpretations of the concept of Israel as blessing run the gamut of Jewish-gentile relations. They range from proactive and ultimately harmonious relations posed by the interpretation of blessing as active engagement, to indifference and the potential self-critiquing function posed by the passive model interpretation, to obliviousness and perhaps the theologically necessary adversarial relationship posed by the theurgic interpretation of blessing.

The three modes of interpreting blessing (active engagement, passive modeling, and non-relational theurgic agency) demonstrate that there are multiple and sometimes contradictory ways of relating to the gentile "other." Which theological strand ought Jews to choose today to shape their attitudes and behavior? One fundamental challenge for theological Jews today is to consciously accept one understanding of blessing—with both its spiritual and behavioral implications—over the others. Developing a contemporary theology of Jewish-gentile relations religions forces us to examine difficult elements within Jewish tradition and to make critical choices from the tradition that yield the most fruitful results for our given social, cultural and spiritual circumstances. In the process we come to understand that the tradition is neither monolithic nor consistent, and that some aspects of tradition need to be reinterpreted constructively. The choice of favoring one theological motif over another is an important way of purifying tradition from within.

Blessing, History, and the State of Israel

It is fruitful to examine the concept of Israel as blessing as it relates to the changing historical and political conditions of the Jewish people. The passive, even quietist, understanding of blessing, that is, theurgic agency, may be interpreted as Israel standing outside the realm of history and political life. In such a view, Israel is a source of blessing to the world because of its spiritual life and religious observance. However, by the same logic, the flaws in Israel's worship, stemming from exile and the destruction of the Temple, might be considered an impediment to fulfilling the divine biblical mandate to the Jewish people and to sharing its blessing with the nations. In the more extrovert understanding (active engagement), the harsh historical reality of exile proved to be a hindrance to Israel's fulfilling its mission of blessing realized as its vocation to teach the human family. When diaspora Jews experience oppression and exclusion, these historical conditions undermine the theological value and activism prescribed by this interpretation of blessing, and the more passive or introverted understandings of blessing flow more naturally and appropriately.

Conversely, during times of Jewish flourishing, optimistic Jewish thinkers taught that exile held the greater opportunity for Israel's active fulfillment of blessing because it affords the Jewish people positive interaction with gentiles and their cultures. This was particularly true in Jewish homiletical, rabbinic and philosophic writings following the Emancipation and the European Enlightenment,[12] as it is true in America today, where the theme of *tiqqun olam* has become commonplace among centrist and liberal American Jews. It is no accident that following in the post-Emancipation era the question of the Jewish

---

[12] The early twentieth-century Jewish German philosopher, Hermann Cohen, is another example.

people's role for the nations surfaces as a more conscious spiritual direction. When Jews live in relative harmony among gentiles, the question positive Jewish relations toward gentiles become sharper and more desirable.

The existence of the State of Israel creating the condition of Jewish sovereignty is particularly relevant to interpreting the covenantal blessing. The urgency of this theological task flows from the recognition that today Jews are living in a new moment in history. Its novelty derives not merely from modern developments in interreligious relations and global interdependency, with their recognition that "no religion is an island," but also from the reality that with sovereignty and independence amidst the family of nations, the State of Israel has become the primary representative of the Jewish people to the world community. These transformed political conditions require us to reassess Israel's relationship to gentile nations, which takes on new importance when "Israel" is not only a people, but also a country that is well known on the world scene. Hence it seems clear that the current existential and political conditions of the Jewish people mandate new religious thinking, or at least new implications of prior theological options. Moreover, these ideas have dramatic political, cultural and historical consequences today.

The reality of Israel generates a theological paradox. On the one hand, Israel's prolonged continuous fight for survival in a region where the majority of its neighbors refuse to acknowledge its *de jure* legitimacy and its *de facto* existence constitutes a threat and naturally fosters an inward Jewish turn focusing on self-concern. In this condition the theological option stressing internal religious values without primary consciousness of their effect on the world, that is, passive modeling, has great currency. Further still, a significant percentage of Israelis are fervently Orthodox Jews (*ḥaredim*) whose religious lives are close to the model of non-relational theurgic agency. Their theological orientation is to live outside of history and politics, convinced that only isolated spiritual immersion and individual Torah study will bring blessing and security to the Jewish people. If the gentile nations achieve blessing, it will only be in the *eschaton* and directly initiated by God rather than in empirical history as we know it. And, as one would expect, kabbalistic theology, with its portrayal of Jews and gentiles as polar opposites, is popular in both groups.

On the other hand, sovereignty and independence provide the Jewish people with unprecedented voice in the family of nations and influence in world events. It has led to the recognition of Jewish dignity and equality in Israel's relations with others. One need only contrast the acceptance of full dignity and influence of Jewish people today with the Jewish condition in medieval Christian Europe or during the *Shoah* in the twentieth century to see that Israel represents an unparalleled historic opportunity for the Jewish people to exercise influence on, and foster progress for, the nations of the world. Whether it be through its technological, scientific and security achievements, its democratic and humanistic values unique in the Middle East, its demanding military ethics or its academic prowess, Israel today plays a significant role in world culture and events. Never before has the Jewish people had such an opportunity to teach and influence others on a global scale, and with it the opportunity to spread blessing by contributing to the progress and flourishing of human life.

Contemporary sovereignty has given Jews today the power to flourish as well as the access to teaching other nations to bring dignity and blessing to their lives. Yet, as the rabbinic sources divide on the meaning of Israel as blessing and how that blessing is best achieved, so also do contemporary Jews divide on how their lives can realize this biblical mission and on the means to achieve this blessing.

Do Jews and the State of Israel have a universal mission to teach the world? If so, is that teaching exclusively theological or does it also include the keys for moral, political, and technical progress? Should Jews ignore the gentile nations and attend only to their own spiritual and physical security, leaving it up to God alone to spread blessing? Lastly, should Jewish religious life devoted to connecting to divine blessing be above all history and politics, focusing instead on exclusively spiritual and theurgic matters?

In sum, what should the religious, moral, and political aspirations of the State of Israel and the Jewish people be? Many options exist, both religious and secular, but for Jews who measure their individual lives and the life of their people in spiritual terms, the answers to this question cannot be divorced from the theological reflection that the Bible charges the children of Abraham be a blessing, and "that through them all the families of the earth be blessed." And for them, Jewish destiny and Jewish mission will be driven by what theological interpretation they give to the central covenantal notion of Israel as blessing.

3

Extra Synagogam Nulla Salus? Judaism and the Religious Other

> Why was Adam created alone? To tell of the glory of The Holy One, for when a person mints many coins from the same die, all the coins are identical. But while the King of Kings, The Holy One, mints all persons from the same die, no person is identical to another. (*Mishna Sanhedrin* 4:5)

Introduction

The above rabbinic statement acknowledges that human diversity is an undeniable empirical fact. Further still, it insists that our diversity is not merely a *de facto* reality, but a theological *desideratum* that testifies to the uniqueness and glory of the Divine. And the diversity the Mishna extols is not limited to differences in physical appearance, but includes all dimensions of human personhood.

Yet does this affirmation of diversity also extend to *theological* pluralism, that is, the acknowledgement of a plurality of valid religions? Is the multiplicity of religious belief a value to be permanently celebrated or a lamentable condition to be naturally overcome at some point in the future? Or is religious uniformity among the goals reserved for the *eschaton*, the messianic era, when human life will be mysteriously and supernaturally transformed? These are the more crucial and complex questions.

Similar to the Christian and Muslim thinkers who shaped their respective religious traditions, Jewish prophets, rabbis, philosophers, poets, and pietists also prized theological agreement and endowed it with a powerful thrust throughout Jewish thought. In the words of the prophet Zechariah, "The Lord shall be King over all the earth; and in that day shall the Lord be One, and His name one" (Zech. 14:9). In practice, Jewish religious life, too, affirms: *lex orandi, lex credendi* ("The law of praying [is] the law of believing"). The *Aleinu* prayer that religious Jews recite thrice each day proclaims: "We place our hope in you, Lord our God, that we may soon see your glory when . . . all humanity will call on Your name . . . and all the world's inhabitants will realize that to You every knee must bow and every tongue must swear loyalty."

In the face of these potent visions of religious uniformity, it is not self-evident that the idea of religious diversity functions as a serious Jewish *desideratum*. Can traditional Jews see the Image of God in the face of the religious Other?[1] In our contemporary world where Western people interact daily with others of different faiths, these questions are critically important for our theological, moral, and social lives.

I want to approach the broad question of how Judaism regards religious diversity and the religious Other by considering the following more specific questions:

1. Does Judaism manifest a fundamental position of tolerance, pluralism or indifference toward other faiths and their worshippers?
2. Is the endorsement of tolerance and religious pluralism an ideal or merely a pragmatic concession?
3. What are the limits of legitimate religious diversity?
4. Is religious uniformity a value we should actively pursue in history or an ideal reserved only for the end of history?
5. If religious uniformity is an ideal, what are legitimate methods for achieving that consensus?

Preliminary Clarifications

Before analyzing these questions, I would like to make a number of preliminary observations about the nature of Jewish theological, legal, and philosophic traditions. When referring to Judaism or Jewish tradition, I have in mind the

---

1 For an incisive approach to Jewish religious diversity, see Jerome Gellman, "Jewish Chosenness and Religious Diversity: A Contemporary Approach," in *Religious Perspectives on Religious Diversity*, ed. Robert McKim (Boston: Brill, 2016), 21–36.

sacred Jewish Scriptures and their rabbinic commentaries, the Talmud, and the corpus of post-Talmudic rabbinic commentary on the legal, moral, and theological Talmudic passages, medieval and modern Jewish philosophical writings as well as the living experience of the Jewish people throughout history. This is a vast field consisting of many voices, and rarely is there unanimity on any given issue. The Jewish intellectual religious tradition is a culture of dialectics and disagreement where dissent is present on issues both large and small. Even axiomatic principles and foundational texts often give rise to diverse and conflicting interpretations.

Consider the following example that, as we shall see, has extensive implications for our analysis: Is Mosaic revelation (the Torah) directed exclusively at Jews or is it ideally a divine code for all humanity?

One popular rabbinic source announces:

> The Torah was given in a free place [the desert of Sinai], for had the Torah been given in the land of Israel, the Israelites could have said to the nations of the world, "You have no share in it." But now that it was given in the wilderness publicly and openly, in a place that is free for all, everyone wishing to accept it could come and accept it.[2]

This rabbinic statement posits that the Torah was given in the desert to demonstrate that it is not exclusively applicable to Jews. On the contrary, the giving of the Torah in no-man's land was a clear signal that the Torah was intended for all peoples. Implicitly, then, "Torah is available to all those who come into the world. It remains in place, available for anyone to take it. Torah is the litmus test for all humanity, not just Jews."[3]

Conversely, the Talmudic authority Rabbi Yoḥanan declared that "a non-Jew who studies the Torah deserves death, for it is written, 'Moses commanded us with the Torah, (it is) the inheritance of the congregation of Jacob' (Deut. 33:4)—it is our inheritance, not theirs." Similarly, R. Simeon ben Lakish taught that "a non-Jew who keeps a day of rest deserves death."[4]

---

2   *Mekhilta de-Rabbi Ishmael, Ba-Ḥodesh.*
3   Marc Hirshman, "Rabbinic Universalism in the Second and Third Centuries," *Harvard Theological Review* 93 (2000): 101–115. For other rabbinic statements implying this, see *Sifrei*, Num. 119.
4   BT *Sanhedrin* 58b–59a. It is undetermined whether "deserves death" is to be taken literally, or is only hyperbole, meant to signify harsh condemnation. Such rhetorical hyperbole is

These are two absolutely incompatible rabbinic positions. Which is correct? Is God's revelation to the Jewish people universal or limited only to that people? The answer is "both," depending on time, context and inquiry. Jewish tradition and theology are in their essence dialectical and pluralistic, with few absolutely categorical truths: "These and these are the words of the living God,"[5] in rabbinic parlance. One should hesitate, therefore, to infer conclusions simplistically from isolated scriptural verses or individual rabbinic pronouncements. Understanding Jewish teachings demands working diligently to ferret out normatively accepted positions from minority or non-normative claims.

Closely related to the above methodological point is the fact that neither Jewish theology, nor law, nor philosophy are apodictic deductive disciplines that yield logically necessary conclusions. The conclusions and rulings in the rabbinic corpus are influenced by historical experience, time, and place. In other words, Jewish theology places a premium on the lived experience of the Jewish people rather than on dogma or theoretical first principles. As our human experiences and conceptions of God evolve, so does Jewish theology.

One highly relevant example for our study is how Jewish law understood and evaluated Christianity over time. In the first and second centuries, Jewish Christians were considered *minim*—intolerable heretics. After Christianity broke from Judaism and became primarily a gentile religion, rabbis considered Christian belief in the trinity and incarnation to be unacceptable violations of the belief in the One Creator of the universe because it violated pure monotheism and divine incorporeality. But during the late Middle Ages rabbis living in Christian Europe staked out a position that Jewish law required only Jews to believe in pure monotheism, and validated belief in the trinity for Christians because the triune Christian conception included the true Creator of heaven and earth. This position became normative Jewish teaching for European Jews from the late Middle Ages into modernity, primarily because of the social, economic, and political changes in relations between Jews and Christians.[6]

---

common in rabbinic statements. Whether literal or only hyperbole, it was, of course, never practiced.

5   BT *Eruvin* 13b. Another bold rabbinic expression of Jewish pluralism and its problematics is: "This person prohibits and this person permits. How, then, can I learn Torah? . . . All the words have been given by a single shepherd, one God created them, one Provider gave them, the Lord of all deeds, Blessed be He, has spoken them. So make yourself a heart of many rooms and bring into it the words of the House of Shammai and the words of the House of Hillel" (*Tosefta Sotah* 7:12).

6   See Jacob Katz, *Exclusiveness and Tolerance* (Springfield, NJ: Berman House, 1961), ch. 10. The details of this historical evolution are developed in chapter 7 of this book.

In other words, the normative Jewish theological and legal position shifted. In fact, very few positions in Judaism are absolute dogma that are immune to reconsideration and change.[7] The debate about what constitutes core unchangeable belief in Judaism is robust, yet few maintain that recognition of other religions, tolerance, and legitimate religious pluralism are included in this small subset.[8] On the contrary, attitudes to gentiles and their faiths are among the subjects in Jewish tradition most influenced by the fluctuating Jewish experience with gentiles throughout history.

Unlike the Christian tradition, formal law (*Halakhah*) plays the dominant role in rabbinic thought, with philosophy and theology playing secondary roles. While law does not exhaust rabbinic tradition (as the Augustinian and other harsh patristic polemical portraits of Judaism incorrectly asserted), theological principles and concepts are frequently derived from case law or legal categories, rather than the reverse. Hence, halakhic analysis and historical context are often indispensable keys into Jewish theological, philosophic, and ethical ideas.

The Jewish Covenant

Judaism is a covenantal faith. At its foundation, Judaism is the expression of the biblical covenant between God and the Jewish people. The sacred pact was initiated with Abraham (Gen. 12–15) and was in turn later bequeathed to Isaac, Jacob, and their progeny. The family covenant later blossomed into a national covenant when the Israelite nation experienced the exodus from Egyptian slavery and accepted Mosaic revelation at Sinai (Ex. 19–20). Since that revelation, the starting point of rabbinic theology has been that each Jew is bound by the 613 divine commandments of the Mosaic covenant, whose details are defined by Jewish law. Indeed, responsibility to this covenant and the sense of "commandedness" is the traditional definition of Jewish identity. The most prominent sign of male Jewish identity is circumcision, whose original Hebrew name is *berit*—covenant.

---

7   Minority opinions in Jewish law were preserved and studied because under different circumstances or eras, they might become normative opinions to be followed (*Mishna Eduyot* 1).
8   For an extensive treatment of the debate on the content of Jewish dogma, see Marc Shapiro, *The Limits of Orthodox Theology* (Portland, OR: Littman Library of Jewish Civilization, 2004); and Menachem Kellner, *Must a Jew Believe Anything?* (Portland, OR: Littman Library of Jewish Civilization, 2006).

As we have seen, some rabbinic speculation pointed in the direction of this covenant (Torah) having relevance for all humanity, but in practice Jewish tradition limited the obligations of the Abrahamic/Mosaic covenant to the Jewish people. At best, the Torah of Moses might apply to all humanity only in the distant messianic era, after history as we know it has ended. But prior to the *eschaton*, the Jewish covenant remains particularistic: the Torah addresses the Jewish people uniquely, and the nation of Israel is singularly elected by God. The biblical prophets and the Talmudic rabbis poetically conceptualized the covenant as an intimate partnership between God and the Jewish people. The private and exclusive nature of this relationship is why Isaiah, Zechariah, Jeremiah, and Hosea repeatedly use the metaphor of marriage when referring to the covenantal relationship between God and the Jewish people.

Judaism has taken much unkind and unfair criticism—primarily from Christian polemicists, Enlightenment rationalists, and twentieth-century universalists—for its particularist conception of the biblical covenant. It is, to use Soren Kierkegaard's phrase, "a scandal of particularity." Those critics were seduced by "Plato's ghost," who insisted that truth was universal, so that what is true for one person must be true for all persons at all times.[9] Judaism resisted the urge to universalize the biblical covenant, and it is precisely the particularistic nature of the Sinai covenant that provides Jewish theology and law with the logical opening for acknowledging valid non-Jewish religions and conceptions, that is, theological pluralism. Because it is particular to Jews, the covenant creates space for other modes of human-divine contact, and for different theological conditions that bestow dignity and legitimacy upon the gentile Other.

Universalism exhibits an ambivalent logic. Universal theological schemes possess the virtue of providing all people with the possibility of a relationship of love, grace, salvation before God. However, universal doctrines are also imperialistic and rapacious. By their very nature they deny valid alternative schema, thus easily leading to delegitimization of those not subscribing not submitting to the universal vision. They seek to eliminate differences by imposing one faith, one regime, or one empire on all humanity. They are the logical converses of pluralism and often the natural opponents of tolerance. Isaiah Berlin noted this well:

> Few things have done more harm than the belief on the part
> of individuals and groups (or tribes or states or nations or

---

9   I owe this formulation of Plato to Jonathan Sacks, *Dignity of Difference* (London: Continuum, 2002), 49.

churches) that he or she or they are in sole *possession* of the truth. ... It is a terrible and dangerous arrogance to believe that you alone are right, have a magical eye which sees *the* truth, and that others cannot be right if they disagree. This makes one certain that there is one goal and only one for one's nation or church or the whole of humanity, and that it is worth any amount of suffering (particularly on the part of other people) if only that goal is attained—even "through an ocean of blood to the Kingdom of Love" as said Robespierre. Hitler, Lenin, Stalin, and I daresay leaders in the religious wars of Christian vs. Muslim or Catholics vs. Protestants sincerely believed this: the belief that there is one and only one true answer to the central questions which have agonized mankind and that one has it oneself—or one's Leader has it. This belief was responsible for the oceans of blood. No Kingdom of Love ever sprang from it, nor could it.[10]

From Paul onward, Christian theology universalized the biblical covenant, expanding the original biblical view from the descendants of Abraham to all humanity. Concomitants of this universalizing logic were the insistence on one universal redemptive covenant and Christian belief as the exclusive way to theological truth. Thus *"extra ecclesiam nulla salus"*: those standing outside Christian belief were locked out of eternal salvation. Perhaps more critically for our study, those *extra ecclesiam* were deemed inferior and barely tolerated in this world as well.[11] Jews experienced this in their flesh as the only non-Christians in medieval Europe: Christians considered Judaism blasphemous

---

10 Isaiah Berlin, *Liberty* (New York: Oxford University Press, 2002), 345.
11 The early Church father, Irenaeus (died 202 AD), explained the original import of the principle: "(The Church) is the entrance to life; all others are thieves and robbers. On this account we are bound to avoid them. ... We hear it declared of the unbelieving and the blinded of this world that they shall not inherit the world of life which is to come. ... Resist them in defense of the only true and life-giving faith, which the Church has received from the Apostles and imparted to her sons" (*Against Heresies*, Book 3). After the Second Vatican Council and its document, *Lumen Gentium*, the Catholic Church accepted a more expansive interpretation that allowed salvation to some outside the Church. Today the official Catechism reads, "This affirmation is not aimed at those who, through no fault of their own, do not know Christ and his Church: Those who, through no fault of their own, do not know the Gospel of Christ or his Church, but who nevertheless seek God with a sincere heart, and, moved by grace, try in their actions to do his will as they know it through the dictates of their conscience—those too may achieve eternal salvation." *Catechism of the Catholic Church*, 847, https://www.vatican.va/archive/ENG0015/__P29.HTM. See also Daniel Madigan and Diego Sarrio Cucarella, "Thinking outside the Box: Developments

and illegitimate, and saw Jews as unbelievers to be treated as social and spiritual outcasts. Jewish stubbornness and "blindness" to universal Christian truth were grounds for imposing humiliation, discrimination, conversion and physical persecution upon them. Some of this hostility was defended on the grounds that it expressed love and concern, for without conversion to Christianity, Jews were "lost." In other words, the claim of universality by the Church led directly to a denial of legitimate religious pluralism in principle and only minimal toleration in fact.

The Noahide Covenant

In addition to the Mosaic covenant, a universal covenant known in rabbinic language as the Noahide covenant is a core element of Jewish theology. The necessity of this covenant is theologically and ethically necessary, and follows logically from the biblical axiom (Gen. 1:26) that God created each human being in the Image of God (Hebrew: *Tselem Elokim*, Latin: *Imago Dei*), and hence that all humans are endowed with intrinsic dignity and spiritual capacities. If so, the Creator of all humanity could not possibly restrict divine involvement to one people. Rather, God must in some way relate to all His children with love and responsibility. The God of the first eleven chapters of the Bible, the Creator of the cosmos, cannot be a parochial, tribal God.

The Bible (Gen. 9) relates that after the great flood God established a covenant with Noah and his descendants, that is, all humanity. According to Jewish teachings, this covenant contains exactly seven commandments: the six prohibitions against murder, theft, sexual wildness, idolatry, eating a limb of a live animal (the prototype of cruelty and disdain for life), and blasphemy, as well as the one positive injunction to establish courts of law that would justly enforce those six prohibitions and ensure that people do not live in a pre-civilized brutal and chaotic Hobbesian jungle.[12] The rabbis understood blasphemy in this context to mean intolerance directed toward any true religion teaching about the universal Creator. Thus, the Noahide covenant is the vehicle that enables non-Jews to

---

in Catholic Understandings of Salvation," in *Religious Perspectives on Religious Diversity*, ed. Robert McKim (Boston: Brill, 2016), 63–119.

12 *Tosefta Avodah Zarah* 8:4; and *MT*, Laws of the Kings and Their Wars 9:1. For full explication of the Noahide Commandments, see David Novak, *The Image of the Non-Jew in Judaism* (Portland, OR: Littman Library of Jewish Civilization, 2011), chs. 1–8.

stand responsible before God, and it is the theological principle that grants them social, moral, and theological legitimacy in Jewish thought.

It is important to note that technically the Noahide covenant does not require a gentile Noahide to believe in God.[13] The obligations associated with this covenant are primarily, if not exclusively, moral. At most, Noahides might be required to believe in a generic creator who implanted a moral order in the world and who ensures punishment to people who violate that order.[14] That is, Noahides might be required to believe in a transcendent authority, that "God is," but not in any more specific theology or particular way to worship God.

The rabbis thus subscribe to a double covenant theory. Jews have a covenant of 613 commandments (Hebrew: *mitsvot*), while all gentiles are members of the covenant of the seven Noahide commandments. Importantly, each covenant is theologically valid for its respective adherents, and Noahides are not expected to convert to the Jewish covenant or Judaism. All gentiles who live faithfully by these basic laws of civilization are considered to be worthy gentiles, *benei Noaḥ* (children of Noah) in rabbinic parlance.[15] Their covenant is independent and authentic, and observing the Noahide covenant is a valid way of life in the eyes of both God and the rabbis.[16]

In sum, we may say that Jewish theology divides humanity into three categories: Jews, righteous Noahides whose beliefs dictate that they obey the moral Noahide commandments, and pagans whose beliefs do not respect the basic civil Noahide obligations and who were therefore deemed illicit.

Idolatry as the Limit of Tolerance

Judaism's double covenant theology creates a wide opportunity for acknowledging the legitimacy of religious diversity, the validity of non-Jewish religious

---

13 Maimonides may have thought that theological knowledge was necessary, but the content of that knowledge is in question. See chapter 4, as well as Steven Schwarzschild, "Do Noahides Have to Believe in Revelation?," *Jewish Quarterly Review* 58 (1962).
14 The rabbis who formulated the concept of the universal Noahide covenant believed that one could not lead a coherent moral life without believing in a divine authority who punished the guilty and rewarded the innocent. As for other pre-moderns, a secular ethic was unthinkable for them.
15 *MT*, Laws of Kings and Their Wars 8:10.
16 Noahides are accorded positive status in this worldview. According to some rabbinic opinions, gentiles who faithfully keep the Noahide commandments are even regarded by God as more beloved than Jews who violate the fundamentals of their covenant of 613 commandments.

forms, and respect for gentiles, all without Jews sacrificing the primacy of their unique status in God's economy or their particularistic Jewish theological convictions.

Yet a thorny problem lurks behind this simple picture. The complexity turns on defining the criteria for violating Noahide commandments, and more specifically what constitutes the Noahide prohibition against idolatry. Jewish Scriptures, the Talmud, and Jewish law all insist upon intolerance toward idolatry and its worshippers—sometimes to the point of annihilation.[17] The definition of idolatry and the delineation of who falls within the idolatrous domain is thus the key to determining Judaism's acceptance of the religious other and the limits of legitimate religious pluralism.

Throughout the Bible idolatry represents what is morally and spiritually intolerable, and so numerous religious texts require its destruction. So harshly did the Bible assess idolatry that it commanded the Israelites to "let no (idolatrous) soul remain alive" (Deut. 20:16) upon entry to the Land of Canaan.[18] In later rabbinic legal, ethical and theological discourse too, idolatry represented the line where tolerance ends and where intolerance is warranted.[19] The covenant of Noah allowed for theological pluralism and practical tolerance, yet only within limits.

The Hebrew term most frequently employed for idolatry in rabbinic and Jewish legal literature is *avodah zarah*, literally, "foreign worship." Technically, *avodah zarah* means all worship deemed illicit by Jewish law, both in its idolatrous and non-idolatrous manifestations.[20] While often identified with the

---

17 Since the demand to exterminate the Canaanite and Amalekite nations appears repeatedly and insistently in the books of Deuteronomy, Joshua, and Samuel, and because King Saul lost his kingship due to his failure to execute this this commandment literally, the harsh requirement of annihilation was understood literally by Jewish legal tradition. Rabbinic tradition largely avoided the practical problems of this legal demand not by interpreting it figuratively, but by rendering the commandment inoperative. See the following footnote.
18 This refers to the seven idolatrous Canaanite nations inhabiting the land. The biblical accounts of the actual conquests found in the book of Joshua reiterate that his army did not leave any idolatrous Canaanite alive when possible. There is extensive discussion in Jewish literature of the moral problematics of this command. See Katell Berthelot, Menachem Hirshman, and Josef David, eds., *The Gift of the Land and the Fate of the Canaanites in Jewish Thought* (New York: Oxford University Press, 2014); as well as Avi Sagi, "The Punishment of Amalek in Jewish Tradition: Coping with the Moral Problem," *Harvard Theological Review* 87, no. 3 (1994): 323–346; and Eugene Korn, "Moralization in Jewish Law: Divine Commands, Rabbinic Reasoning and Waging a Just War," in my *To Be a Holy People: Jewish Tradition and Ethical Values* (Jerusalem: Urim Publications, 2021), 103–124.
19 See the trenchant analysis of idolatry and its function in Moshe Halbertal and Avishai Margolit, *Idolatry* (Boston, MA: Harvard University Press, 1994).
20 For further elaboration, see chapter 7.

pagan idolatry that the Bible so loudly condemns, it is in fact a wider category that also includes non-pagan yet still illegitimate worship.

Rabbinic thinkers understand the category of *avodah zarah* and who falls under the rubric of an intolerable idolator differently. Fundamentally, two competing conceptions are dominant in Jewish thought, and both are inferred from biblical texts. Jewish Scriptures sometimes describe idolators as people who worship celestial bodies, stars, and trees[21] (that is, any finite physical object) because they mistakenly understand them to be divine, while other times the Bible portrays idolators as people or cultures with abominable immoral practices.[22] The first more cognitive conception was emphasized by rabbis with philosophic bents, most prominently the twelfth-century polymath Maimonides, who lived in Spain and Egypt. As the greatest Jewish legal authority in Jewish history, Maimonides exerted a prodigious influence over the Jewish canon. And as rationalist philosopher steeped in the metaphysics of Aristotle, he understood idolatry as any conceptual error that identifies God with something that is in fact not divine,[23] specifically anything that is physical, plural, has emotions, or is subject to change.

Because of this conception, Maimonides considered not only ancient sun worship, star worship, and polytheism to constitute idolatry, but also judged Christianity to be idolatrous since its theology asserts that God has become incarnate and is trinitarian. He considered Christians who held these beliefs to be idolators and subject to all the same strictures of alienation and intolerance as were the biblical Canaanites and other ancient pagans. Maimonides was consistent in applying his criteria for idolatry: he also considered Jews who harbor personalistic conceptions of God, that is, who imagine an emotional, angry, loving, or regretful God, to be worse offenders than gentiles who believed that God was physical.[24] By contrast, Islam's conception of Allah is free of any corporeal dimension and insists on absolute monotheism (similar to Judaism in that respect). Hence Maimonides considered Muslims to be observant Noahides and Islamic theology regarding God to be legitimate. As we shall see in chapter 7, Maimonides's biography influenced his legal views.

The other conception of idolatry emphasizes the biblical identification of idolators as primitive immoral pagans with abominable ethical, religious, and

---

21 For example, Deut. 4, 12, 16.
22 See, for example, Lev. 18; Deut. 12.
23 This is why Maimonides placed the laws regarding idolatry in his great legal code, *MT*, in the Book of Knowledge (*Sefer Madda*).
24 *Guide* I:36.

sexual practices. Rabbi Menaḥem Meiri in thirteenth- and fourteenth-century Christian Provence championed this definition, conceptualizing idolatry in moral terms: idolatry is cultic worship whose primary character is the absence of moral demands upon its worshipers. It is any religion that does not impose on its adherents the fundamental ethical restraints against murder, theft, sexual wildness, lawlessness, that is, the foundation of orderly civilized society.[25] Thus, according to this definition, even polytheists and corporealists who subscribe to fundamental moral values can belong to the domain of valid believers. The Torah, it seems, requires pure monotheism only of Jews, but not of gentiles.[26] Thus, Jewish limits of tolerance, diversity, and theological pluralism will vary significantly depending on how "foreign worship" is understood.

Both the Bible and Jewish law affirmed the residency and civil rights of gentiles in an ideal Jewish polity governed by Jewish religious law. The Bible denotes such a person as a *ger* (alien) and repeatedly warns Jews not to oppress or take advantage of this stranger in their midst.[27] Under Jewish law, Jews have rigorous religious obligations to support and sustain this gentile stranger economically, and ensure that he not dwell "close to the border (due to danger of an enemy attack) or in an unseemly place; rather, he should reside in a goodly dwelling in the midst of the Land of Israel, in a place where his business or artisanship can prosper."[28] This is the rabbinic expansion of Jewish civil obligations toward the religious Other that is derived the biblical commandment, "He [the gentile] shall dwell in your midst, in whatever place he will choose, in any one of your cities, wherever it is beneficial to him; you must not taunt him" (Deut. 23:16).

It is important to note that the insistence on legitimate religious diversity in Jewish society and the religious obligations devolving upon Jews to protect the safety, dignity and economic health of the religious Other in their midst obtain in the *ideal* Jewish polity, where Jews are sovereign. This indicates that acceptance and protection of the gentile is not a practical concession to *realpolitik*, but an obligatory value that religious Jews must implement when they possess political power and social dominance. While the status of the *ger toshav* is technically applicable only in the Jewish homeland under Jewish sovereignty,

---

25 See Menaḥem Meiri's commentary on the Talmud, *Beit ha-Beḥirah*, Sanhedrin 57a and Avodah Zarah 20a.
26 For more detail on this idea, see chapter 7.
27 Ex. 22:21, 23:9; Lev. 19:33; Deut. 24:17, 27:19. While the Bible speaks only of *ger*, rabbinic tradition refers to *ger toshav* (resident alien).
28 BT *Gerim* 3:3, 4.

the concept is rich in general implications for the values of pluralism, tolerance, and obligations toward the religious Other in Judaism. The Bible, the Talmud, and Jewish law could have constructed the ideal as a monolithically Jewish polity in which there was no religious diversity and no need to extend recognition or protection of gentiles. Pointedly, they did not.

Who qualifies as a *ger toshav* with rights of residency and protection in this ideal Jewish polity? The Talmud decided that it is any non-Jew who forswears idolatry and accepts the ethical requirements of the Noahide commandments.[29] Given that this status is a civil and social one, it is reasonable to assume that the renunciation of idolatry required of the resident stranger is achieved by his commitment to obey the fundamental moral responsibilities required for membership in a stable and just society—that is, Meiri's conception of idolatry. Testing the stranger for the purity of his metaphysical understanding of God (that is, Maimonides's understanding of idolatry) makes no sense in this context. It is more logical for the residency requirement to provide warrant that the would-be resident be a law-abiding civilized member of Jewish society than that he be a sophisticated theologian.

Similarly, it would seem that in our pluralistic modern and postmodern societies where people of different Abrahamic and Asian religions interact regularly, where theological ideas play a less significant role than in the past, where democracy is a dominant ethos, where atheists exhibit social and moral responsibility no less than believers, and where the concept of universal human rights is an intrinsic part of our Western worldview, the moral conception of idolatry as behavior bereft of civil and ethical restraints stakes out the proper conception of Jewish tolerance of the Other and its limits.[30] This conception grants legitimacy to anyone committed to ethical principles, social responsibility, compassion for others and improving the world that God created for his creatures to flourish. In practice, most Jews— religious and secular, lay and rabbinic—adhere to this policy, whether or not they are conscious of its theory. In a word, it has become Judaism's normative approach today.

---

29 Ibid. See also *MT*, Laws of Kings and Their Wars 8:10.
30 While Meiri thought that idolatry was found only in the far-flung corners of the earth, today that is not so. A Muslim or Jewish terrorist should not be tolerated because of his behavior, even though his theology may be monotheistic. See also Alon Goshen-Gottstein, "Concluding Reflections," in *World Religions and Jewish Theology*, ed. Alon Goshen-Gottstein and Eugene Korn (Oxford: Littman Library of Jewish Civilization, 2012).

The Afterlife and the Messianic Era

Thus far I have analyzed Jewish law and theology's approach to religious diversity in the empirical world as we know it. What of the afterlife, that is, eternal salvation? Who is entitled to such exalted status? The reward of eternal life is a fundamental principle of Judaism, but unlike Christian theology, Jewish religious thought devotes little time to soteriology, eschatology, and the nature of life after death. Its focus is life on earth and the responsibilities of Jews while alive in this world. Also Jews do not talk of "eternal salvation," rather of "a share in the world to come." This is not an exclusively distant metaphysical concern. In all theological traditions, as in Judaism, earning eternal afterlife is an indicator of what is understood to be a meritorious life in this world, both for ourselves and others.

There are a few significant Jewish texts that speculate about the afterlife. The Talmudic and medieval rabbis paid some gentiles the ultimate theological compliment by teaching that "righteous gentiles have a share in the world to come."[31] Again, it was the twelfth-century rabbi-philosopher Maimonides who set the normative Jewish position on this question. He ruled in accordance with the Talmudic opinion that righteous gentiles do participate in the world to come, and rejected the rival opinion that such salvation was confined to Jews.[32] Even after accepting this broad principle, two critical questions remain: (1) what earthly life qualifies a person to gain "a share in the world to come"; and (2) what, if any, religious belief is required to merit this eternal life. If theological belief *is* necessary and that required belief is the acceptance of all Mosaic revelation at Sinai, then *de facto* the only gentiles with a share in the world to come would be those few who subscribe to strictly traditional Jewish theology. Thus, potential universal salvation could easily be denuded of its breadth—in other words, "*extra synagogam nulla salus*"[33]—only Orthodox Jews have a share in eternal life.

Only a few Jewish particularists took this extreme position based on an idiosyncratic reading of a key Maimonidean text on the question,[34] yet

---

31 BT *Sanhedrin* 105a; and *MT*, Laws of Repentance 3:5, Laws of Testimony 2:10, and Laws of Kings and Their Wars 8:11. For an extended discussion of salvation for righteous gentiles, see chapter 4 and Schwarzschild, "Do Noahides Have to Believe in Revelation?"
32 *MT*, Laws of Kings and Their Wars 8:11.
33 This would be the Jewish analogue to the Christian principle "*extra ecclesiam nulla salus*"—outside the Church there is no salvation.
34 See chapter 4.

nothing suggests that this particular view became normative in Jewish thought. Significantly, even Jewish rationalists like Maimonides himself and moderns like Moses Mendelssohn subscribed to the more universal thesis, believing that while Jewish tradition gives Jews some advantage over others due to their possession of divine revelation, true knowledge of God is a rational capability open to any dedicated human being.[35]

Most rabbinic thinkers were not as metaphysically oriented as was Maimonides, and hewed close to the explicit requirements of the Noahide covenant. They insisted that gentiles merited eternal life when they scrupulously commit themselves to the moral life of social responsibility and restraint required by the seven practical Noahide commandments.[36]

In other words, the majority rationalist Jewish position regarding salvation is close to the ethical interpretation of idolatry and the Noahide covenant. It is important to understand, however, that whether we accept Maimonides's metaphysically oriented requirement of eternal salvation or Meiri's more ethical conception, the "world to come" is a religiously diverse community. The difference lies primarily in the density of its population: the rationalist's world to come is a sparsely populated realm of metaphysically sophisticated Jewish and gentile souls (that is, intelligences), while the ethicist's is a more populous diverse community of beings who had lived a morally committed responsible life.

What of the messianic era, not the eternal metaphysical realm of the afterlife, but the culmination of sacred history when the divine covenant is fulfilled?[37] This conception is actually more significant for our study, since Jewish thinkers have understood the messianic era to represent the ideal state of human affairs of our social and religious orders in empirical history. The messianic ideal

---

35 MT, Laws of Jubilee 13:13; *Guide* I:1-2 and III:51. For full explanation of this point in Maimonides, see Menachem Kellner, "We Are Not Alone," in *Radical Responsibility: Celebrating the Thought of Chief Rabbi Lord Jonathan Sacks*, ed. Michael J. Harris, Daniel Rynhold, and Tamra Wright (London: School of Jewish Studies; New York: The Michael Scharf Publication Trust of Yeshiva University Press, 2012), 139–154; Menachem Kellner, *Maimonides' Confrontation With Mysticism* (London: Littman Library of Jewish Civilization, 2006), 229–264; and Menachem Kellner, *Gam Hem Qeruyim Adam: Ha-Nohkri be-Einei ha-Rambam* [They also are called Adam: The gentile in the eyes of Maimonides] (Tel Aviv: Bar-Ilan University Press, 2016). For Mendelssohn, see Alexander Altmann, *Moses Mendelssohn: A Biographical Study* (Tuscaloosa: University of Alabama Press, 1973), 217–218.
36 See, for instance, Rabbi Abraham Kook, *Letters* [Hebrew] (Jerusalem: Mosad Harav Kook, 1923), vol. 1, 100.
37 While some early rabbinic opinions identified the messianic era with the afterlife, Maimonides sharply distinguished between the two. Owing to his prodigious influence, most post-Maimonidean rabbinic opinions accepted his distinction.

also highlights the relationship between the theological mission of the Jewish people and the rest of humanity.

As we saw, the central paradox of the Bible is that the universal God of creation enters a covenant with a particular people (the Jews) that is ideally situated in a limited particular geography (Canaan/Israel). The tension between the universal God and the particularist covenant is resolved by the covenant's universal mission. The Torah teaches that the purpose of God's election of the Jewish people is for it to serve all humanity, since at the first moment of covenant God tells Abraham, "You shall be a blessing. . . . Through you (and your progeny) all the nations of the earth shall be blessed" (Gen. 12:2–3). The Jewish covenantal mission is delineated further when God demands that Abraham "instruct his children and his posterity to keep the way of the Lord by doing what is right and just" (Gen. 18:19). Later the Bible indicates that Jewish covenantal mission connects to humanity when it demands that the Jewish people be "a kingdom of priests" (Ex. 19:6), that is, the entire Jewish people is charged with the priestly function of bestowing divine blessing upon the other nations of the world. And later still, this universal mission is repeated in different formulation by the Jewish prophets: "I will make you a light of the nations, that My salvation may reach the ends of the earth" (Isa. 49:6). It is this universal dimension of the Jewish covenant that rescues the coherence of the biblical narrative, bridging the disparity between the cosmic concern in the Bible's first eleven chapters and the intensely particularistic focus on the Jewish people dominant throughout the remainder of the Hebrew Bible.[38]

As we have seen Jewish tradition fleshed out these covenantal goals of blessing and instruction to refer to bearing witness to and informing all humanity of the one transcendent Creator as well as to demonstrating commitment to the divine ethic of righteousness and justice—what is sometimes referred to as ethical monotheism."[39] The patriarch Abraham is understood to have been a model and teacher, and the rabbinic stories contend that he converted others through rational persuasion and living the life of compassionate ethical witness. Significantly, however, Abraham's faith was not the particular faith of Judaism,

---

38   For further elaboration on the paradoxical particularistic/universalistic character of the biblical covenant see Jon D. Levenson, "The Universal Horizon of Biblical Particularism," in *Ethnicity and the Bible*, ed. Mark R. Brett (Boston: Brill, 2002), 143–169.

39   For an expansion of this idea, see Shlomo Riskin, "Covenant and Conversion: The United Mission to Redeem the World," in *Covenant and Hope*, ed. Robert W. Jenson and Eugene B. Korn (Grand Rapids, MI: Eerdmans, 2012), 99–128.

but a more generic faith in the single Creator of the universe and His moral law.[40] Since Abraham lived generations before the Mosaic revelation that provides the foundation for Judaism as we know it today, as we saw in chapter 1, technically Abraham was a theological Noahide, not a Jew commanded by the particularistic law given to Moses at Sinai.

Abraham is the prototype of covenantal responsibility in Jewish tradition. His model together with the independent validity of the Noahide covenant are the primary reasons that for nearly all of Jewish history, Jews eschewed attempts to convert others to Judaism. There simply was no theological need to do so. Even today, there is a distinct aversion to proselytizing gentiles. However, Jews do have the religious obligation to influence gentiles toward the universal Noahide moral code without any hint of making them Jews.[41] In this way, the rabbinic theology of religious diversity entails a sensitive dialectic between the Noahide and Mosaic covenants. From the Noahide covenant emanates the responsibility to maintain concern for the welfare of all human beings and to teach ethical commitment whenever possible, and from the particularistic Mosaic covenant emerges the aversion to forcing upon others unique Jewish religious requirements and commitments.

Jewish prophets provide a stunning picture of what human society will look like when the Jewish covenantal mission is achieved. Isaiah, Micah, Amos, Zechariah, and Jeremiah portray the messianic era as a human society committed to ethical monotheism, one shorn of violence and suffused with harmony, peace, and human flourishing. This ideal is at once both unified and diverse: all peoples have come to accept the moral authority of the God and fundamental moral values, yet the diverse nations of humanity retain their separate religious identities and worship the one Creator of the universe in their own ways. Micah's vision explicitly states this pluralism as part of this messianic ideal:

> It shall be in the end of days that the mountain of the Lord shall be established on top of all mountains and shall be exalted above the hills. And (many) peoples shall stream onto it. Many nations shall come, and say, "Come let us go up to the mountain of the Lord and to the house of the God of Jacob; and He will teach us His ways and walk in His paths. For the Torah shall go forth

---

40 MT, Laws of Idolatry 1:1–3, Laws of Kings and Their Wars 9:1, Book of Commandments, positive commandment 3.
41 MT, Laws of Kings and Their Wars 8:10; and Riskin, "Covenant and Conversion."

from Zion, and the word of the Lord from Jerusalem." They shall beat their swords into plowshares and their spears into pruning hooks. Nation shall not lift up sword against nation, nor shall they learn war anymore. But every man shall sit under his vine and his fig tree; and none shall make him afraid. . . . *"For let all people walk, each in the name of his God* [emphasis by EBK] and we will walk in the name of the Lord our God for ever and ever." (4:1–5)[42]

Maimonides too sees this idyllic messianic picture as the culmination of Jewish covenantal life.[43] Whether Maimonides believed that all people will subscribe to the same theological truths and religion at that time is subject to scholarly debate,[44] yet even those who claim that Maimonides envisaged religious unity in the messianic era understand that for him this ultimate universal religion would be a theologically pure worship unlike any specific religious form of worship today. This unity will be achieved by teaching fundamental theological truth, not by forcing particularist forms of religion or ethnic religious policies upon others. If there is conversion, it is neither to any single church, synagogue, mosque, or ashram, nor to one particular liturgy, but to commitment that allows for non-idolatrous differences in worship and practice.[45]

The Open Future

The biblical principle that all persons are created in the Image of God, the rabbinic doctrine of the Noahide covenant with all humanity, and the

---

42 The parallel passage in Isa. 2:1–4 does not include "For let all people walk, each in the name of his God and we will walk in the name of the Lord our God for ever and ever." I also note that a number of Jewish commentators interpret the final verse of this passage differently. See commentaries of Rabbis Shlomo Yitshaqi (Rashi) and David Qimḥi (Radaq) on Micah 4:5, who interpret the verse not as *de jure* pluralism but as *de facto* toleration of all who accept ethical monotheism.

43 See *MT*, Laws of Kings and Their Wars 12:5.

44 See the debate between Menachem Kellner and Chaim Rapoport on this question in *Meorot* 13 (2008), http://www.yctorah.org/content/view/436/10.

45 Maimonides maintained that pure monotheism without hint of ethnic or Mosaic ritual was the ideal form of religion and that Mosaic ritual was a result of contingent (and therefore probably temporary) historical circumstances (*MT*, Laws of Idolatry 1:3). In addition, he believed that contemplation constituted a higher form of worship than verbal prayer. Hence we can assume for him this silent meditation would be the common form of worship in the ideal messianic era.

particularistic Mosaic covenant together provide the legal and theological framework for the normative Jewish attitudes regarding religious diversity. These Jewish theological elements naturally give rise to an approach of tolerance toward the non-idolatrous religious others. We may go further still: the category of *ger toshav*, the alien resident in a Jewish polity whom Jews are obligated to sustain and protect, establishes the basis for more than mere toleration. It is the theological and legal foundation for Jewish engagement with and responsibility for the gentile Other.

Of course there are perils to unbounded particularism also. A particularistic covenant can lead—and sometimes has led—to arrogance and narrow chauvinism. If Jews are uniquely loved and elected by God, as the particularistic Mosaic covenant asserts, Jews can come to regard gentiles as theologically and ontologically inferior, as mere background noise to the central biblical drama played out in religious history between God and the Jewish people. Such particularism leads not to the unmitigating pressure on the Other that so often characterizes theological universalism, but to its opposite—indifference and hostility.

The key to constructive religious pluralism is a sensitive dialectic that navigates carefully between the poles of particularistic and universalistic theological claims. This dialectic accepts my universal concern for all people and particularism's virtue of not absolutizing my own faith, which allows me to accept the differences of others. This dialectic balances the two opposing religious sensibilities, with each pole exercising a constraint on the other.

Only today can Jews truly test this dialectic. When Jews were a weak minority scattered throughout Europe, Northern Africa, and the Middle East for nearly two thousand years, they rarely practiced active intolerance toward the majority gentile populations in whose midst they lived, be they Christians or Muslims. Yet as Yehudah Halevi already noticed in the tenth century, perhaps it was only because they lacked the means to do so.[46] Were exilic Jews pluralists out of religious principle and Jewish teachings, or were they tolerant only due to the exigencies of historical conditions over which they had little control?

Tolerance as a virtue and pluralism as a principal can be demonstrated only with the ability to exercise control and intolerance. The sovereign and majority status of approximately half of all Jews in the world today in the State of Israel is now testing the Jewish commitment to tolerance and acceptable religious diversity on moral, political, and social levels. As a pluralistic democracy, Israel

---

46   Yehudah Halevi, *The Kuzari* I:113–115.

is legally committed to the rights of non-Jewish minorities. Yet neither pluralism nor tolerance is an absolute value, and the proper limits of those values are being vigorously debated today among Israeli politicians and religious authorities alike. At stake is whether the sovereign Jewish majority in Israel can express its national integrity without falling prey to a narrow chauvinism that overlooks the dignity, equal rights, and religious integrity of non-Jews and their beliefs.

The new Israeli conditions of independence, majority status, and national sovereignty create the possibility for both liberal pluralism and particularism to express themselves. Yet, under this freedom, narrow particularism sometimes runs unchecked among some insulated and hypernationalistic Israelis. Counter to national Israeli values and policies, at times these extremists have denied the legitimacy of religious pluralism, advocated restricting the freedom of Israeli gentiles and limiting their residency rights, and even physically assaulted those in their midst—all on allegedly theological grounds.[47] Tragically, God's particularist covenant with the Jewish people that grants it election and title to the Land of Israel has led these particularists to deny the universal human equality endowed by the Image of God, the rights of resident aliens and the legitimacy of religious diversity that the Noahide covenant entails.

As we have seen, absolute universalism can easily lead to a harmful doctrine of forced imperial inclusion, while the opposite ideology of extreme particularism can also evolve into a troublesome doctrine of religious exclusion. The latter one-sided parochialism leaves the God of all creation and the universal mission of the Jewish people in the deep background. Its proponents are led to absolutize the Jewish covenant for everyone on the Land and support a policy of religious imperialism and intolerance. The most extreme Jewish particularists have seized on elements of Jewish mysticism (*qabbalah*) and begun to advocate ethnic superiority, maintaining that Jews are ontologically superior to gentiles—in contradiction to the biblical and Jewish rationalist theological tradition.[48] They come morally close to the very antisemitic universalist enemies

---

47 In 2009 Rabbis Yitshaq Shapira and Yosef Elitsur, two religious extremists, published *Torat ha-Melekh* [The teaching of the king] (Lev ha-Shomron: Yeshivat Od Yosef Hai, 2009), which justifies killing innocent gentiles in war. In 2010, a number of Israeli nationalist rabbis wrote a public letter prohibiting selling Israeli land to gentiles. In 2015 Jewish nationalists set fire to the Church of Loaves and Fishes in the Galilee, claiming it to be a house of idolatry. And frequent incidents continue today of Jewish religious extremists defacing church properties in the ancient part of Jerusalem and assaulting Armenian priests living there.

48 One example is the mystic Rabbi Yitshaq Ginsburg, who has a significant following including Yitshaq Shapira and Yosef Elitsur (see previous note). His racial theory of Jewish ontological superiority is directly opposed to the rationalist strain of Jewish thought and ethics, again

who victimized Jews in the medieval and modern diaspora. Thus *les extremes se touchent*. Importantly, the prominent contemporary Jewish theologian, Irving Greenberg, has defined contemporary idolatry as all absolute monistic theological doctrines—whether universalist or particularist—that deny religious pluralism. They are idolatrous both because they mistake the finite for the infinite Divine and because they inevitably lead to conflict, destruction, and death.[49]

This phenomenon points to another truth about religion. No religion is intrinsically tolerant; nor is any religion violent and intolerant in its essence. Each religion's sacred texts and theologies at times counsel peace and tolerance, and at other times display intolerance and hostility. Which is essential and which marginal? What are the limits of its tolerance?

While mostly tolerant and accepting of diversity today, Christianity in the Middle Ages was intolerant of religious diversity. Islam was largely tolerant and comfortable with religious pluralism in some countries during the tenth–twelfth centuries, but today its Middle East varieties commonly exhibit intolerance and violent extremism. While Jews were largely pacifistic and tolerant in exile and continue to be so today, the phenomenon of Jewish intolerance has begun to rise in Israel. Religious intolerance and violence has stained, and continues to stain, religious Muslim, Christian, Jewish, Hindu, and even normally pacifist Buddhist communities. Thus, while at a particular time some religions tend more than others toward intolerance, extremism and violence, there is no "essential nature" of any faith—only the actions, thoughts, and testimonies that a living community of believers manifests at a given time in history. It is not sacred texts or theology that define a religion's essence or its character; rather it is *how the believing community interprets, prioritizes, and lives the meanings of those sacred texts and theologies that defines that community's religion.*

In light of this truth it is clear that there is no single permanent Jewish theological position on religious diversity and tolerance of the Other. At times Jewish particularism emphasizing gentile otherness and an expansive

---

most clearly exemplified by Maimonides. For a full explication of Maimonides's universal understanding of humanity, see Menachem Kellner, *We Are Not Alone* (Boston: Academic Studies Press, 2021). For more on Ginsburg, see Don Seeman. "God's Honor, Violence, and the State," in *Plowshares into Swords? Reflections on Religion and Violence—Essays from the Institute for Theological Inquiry*, ed. Robert W. Jenson and Eugene Korn (Jerusalem: Center for Jewish-Christian Understanding and Cooperation in Israel, 2014). Much of the impetus for the assertion of Jewish ontological distinctiveness and superiority comes from the medieval foundational text of Jewish mysticism, the *Zohar*, and its subsequent commentators in the kabbalistic tradition.

49 Chapter 5 examines Greenberg's modern thesis of idolatry in detail.

definition of idolatry that frowns on legitimate religious diversity may gain ascendency. At other times a more open universalistic position may prevail that is built around the ideas of all people created in the Image of God, the Noahide covenant, and Jewish obligations toward the *ger toshav*. In the best of times a dialectic balance operates, one that sustains Jewish identity and helps shape a constructive theological respect for diversity and acceptance of the Other. Like God Himself, whom the Bible names "I will be Who I will be" (Ex. 3:14), the future of Jewish theology is not determined. The responsibility for its future is in our human hands.

The nature of emerging Jewish doctrines toward religious diversity will depend greatly on the quality of Jewish relations with gentile religions, persons and nations. When Jews feel oppressed and victimized, the former particularistic motif will naturally gain prominence. When Jews experience more security, tolerance and acceptance, they will feel sufficiently secure to open themselves to principled theological diversity and mutual religious appreciation. At those times, Jewish thinkers and rabbis may begin to tackle the challenges that contemporary pluralistic life poses for Jewish theology and ethics.

Will Jews use their theological tradition to refashion the legal category of *ger toshav* to all peace-loving gentiles both inside and outside of a sovereign Jewish polity, emphasize the intrinsic dignity and equality of each person derived from his Divine Image, reformulate Jewish theological categories to better understand Asian theologies and their believers, and develop a positive appreciation of ethical secularism?

Out of the ideals of tolerance, *de jure* pluralism, and appreciation of human difference a bold comprehensive Jewish theology of religious diversity awaits us. This theology will encompass Jews, Christians, Muslims, Asian believers, and ethical secularists; it will be borne of freedom, principle, and independence. While new in application, this understanding will reflect the ancient dream of the Jewish patriarchs, biblical prophets, and traditional rabbis alike. It is the covenantal dream of peace attained, moral values implemented, and harmony lived among all God's human children.

4

Revelation, Gentiles, and the World to Come

Preface

"Explain this Rambam to me," implored the yeshiva student. "Is Rambam saying that a person must believe in the revelation of Torah at Sinai through Moses for him to be one of the *ḥasidei umot ha-olam* [righteous gentiles] who qualifies for *olam ha-ba* [the world to come]?"

"That's what Rambam is saying," responded the American born, college-educated *Gemara rebbe*.

"But look," persisted the vexed student, "let's assume there is a coolie in China, a perfectly exemplary person. He lives by moral principles, and influences others to do so. Human life is precious to him. He doesn't steal, break the law, worship idols, and he is sexually modest. He is kind to animals and would never eat flesh from a living animal. He even believes in one non-corporeal God. But having never been educated, this coolie knows nothing about occidental or Semitic cultures, nothing of Jews, Jewish history, *Moshe Rabbenu*, Torah or Mount Sinai. He never had the opportunity to learn about these things. Is it possible that such a person never has a chance to enter *olam ha-ba*, and that he can never acquire moral or religious wisdom?"

"That's correct," snapped back the Talmudic authority. "Our history is crucial for all humanity. If one doesn't know Jewish history, and believe in the divinity of our Torah, then he is doomed."

The *rebbe* couldn't understand the urgency of the question. The student couldn't accept the insensitivity of the answer. It was no accident that within a year the student had left the yeshiva to study philosophy. His favorite work was entitled "Justice as Fairness."

For many years thereafter, the Talmud student tried to forget about Maimonides's disturbing text—and its "authoritative" interpretation. To him it seemed intellectually primitive and morally intolerable. Yet, Maimonides pursued him relentlessly. The passage cropped up in mysterious but regular fashion, no matter what he studied or wherever he went. Every new encounter with the text stirred up passionate feelings of disbelief and embarrassment, denial and alienation.

Some fifteen years after the interchange with the *rebbe*, the student found himself studying Torah in Jerusalem with a professor of philosophy. "Of course, you know that the printed version of this text is corrupt," commented the Israeli professor. "The printer used a manuscript with an incorrect letter. Maimonides never wrote the text the way you are reading it."

Heartened, the student began to consider the passage anew and discovered he was not alone: The text had engendered passionate and scholarly debate among Jewish thinkers for hundreds of years.

I

The text under consideration is one of the most discussed passages in Maimonides's august legal code, *Mishneh Torah*. It appears in Laws of Kings (*Hilkhot Melakhim*) 8:10–11. All printed editions of the text read as follows:

> 8:10. Moses our teacher bequeathed the Torah and the commandments only to Israel, as it is said, "(It is an) inheritance of the congregation of Jacob," as well as one who wants to convert from the nations, as it is said, "(There shall be one law) for you and for the convert" (Num. 15:15). However, one who does not wish (to convert) is not forced to accept Torah and commandments. Thus commanded Moses our teacher on the authority from God to compel all human beings to accept the commandments that were commanded to Noah, and he who does not accept (them) may be killed. One who accepts them is called everywhere a resident alien [*ger toshav*] and he must accept them before three rabbis. . . .

> 8:11. Everyone who accepts the seven commandments (of Noah) and is careful to do them is of the righteous of the nations of the world [*ḥasidei umot ha-olam*] and has a share in the world to come. This is so if he accepts and observes them because God commanded them in the Torah, and He informed us through Moses our teacher that Noah had previously been commanded (to observe) them. However, if he does them because of his own rational conclusions, he is not a resident alien, nor one of the righteous of the nations of the world, nor one of their wise men [*ve-lo me-ḥakhmehem*].

The context of Maimonides's injunctions in Laws of Kings is his description of an ideal polity under Jewish sovereignty. While detailing the norms for how this Jewish society should be organized and governed, the questions arise whether this society would include non-Jews, and if so what their status and obligations would be. Hence, the frame of reference is clearly political and the primary focus of laws 8:10 and 8:11 is the category of the gentile resident alien (*ger toshav*). This text raises serious problems in three categories: logical, philosophical, and moral.

1. Multiple logical problems are apparent. Even novice students of Maimonides recognize that the writing style of *MT* is precise and complete. Maimonides's keen analytic mind expressed itself with linguistic elegance and logical coherence. He invariably defined his terminology, carefully established categories, rarely introduced extraneous ideas, and inevitably wove various logical strands into a coherent unity. Yet in this text, Maimonides seems to be guilty of violating all of these standards.

Maimonides mentions five categories of gentiles in 8:10–11. There are:

(1) pagans—those who reject the seven Noahide commandments;
(2) Noahides (*b'nei Noaḥ*);
(3) resident aliens (*gerei toshav*);
(4) righteous gentiles (*ḥasidei umot ha-olam*); and
(5) wise gentiles (*ḥakhmehem*).

In 8:10 Maimonides proceeds to define a *ben Noaḥ* as one who accepts the seven Noahide laws, and a *ger toshav* as one who proclaims his commitment to those laws before a rabbinic judicial court (*beit din*). In 8:11 Maimonides defines the category of righteous gentiles as those who are careful to observe the Noahide laws and have accepted them because they believe that "God commanded them in the Torah and made them known through Moses our teacher." Maimonides does this even though these three categories are well known and found elsewhere in his writings and in the Talmud.

However, at the end of 8:11 Maimonides introduces an entirely new category—wise gentiles. He then proceeds to exclude from this category someone who accepts the seven Noahide laws out of exclusively rational considerations. Yet how does one qualify as a wise gentile? How does he differ, if at all, from a righteous gentile? Quite inexplicably, Maimonides never defines a wise gentile, nor does he tell us who is included in this category, nor does he indicate how a wise gentile is different from a righteous gentile. In fact, since such sages remain indistinguishable from righteous gentiles, it is not apparent why Maimonides mentions this category at all.[1] This class of gentiles is not necessary to his main subject, namely, gentiles who reside in the Jewish polity. As an independent category, the class of wise gentiles lacks definition, and as a category coextensive with righteous gentiles it is superfluous. Such sloppy categorization would be highly unusual in Maimonides's writing.

Another lesser-known logical problem lurks in the background. Throughout 8:10–11 Maimonides speaks of the acceptance of Noahide laws employing the same Hebrew verb, *leqabel* ("to accept"), uniformly for all of the above categories. In 8:10, he implies that the Noahide's acceptance and that of the resident alien are similar, the sole difference being the procedural requirement that the resident alien proclaim his allegiance before a rabbinic court of three. It appears that the content of the resident alien's acceptance is identical to that of a Noahide. In 8:11 Maimonides posits that essential to the resident alien's acceptance is belief in divine revelation. Because of the substantive identity of acceptance between the resident alien and the Noahide, it may be that even a Noahide must also accept revelation.[2] We will analyze the implications of this interpretation later, but consider now that under this reading the righteous gentile does not differ at all from the Noahide, since both have identical substantive requirements and neither requires formal acceptance by a court. Here again we are led to category confusion and logical imprecision so unlike Maimonides.

---

1   See A. Kirschenbaum and N. Lamm, "Freedom and Constraint in the Jewish Judicial Process," *Cardozo Law Review* 1, no. 1 (1979): 1–18, who make a similar observation relative to the superfluousness of the category of *ḥakhmei umot ha-olam* in this text.
2   Evidently, this is the way that R. Velvel Soloveitchik read the text. More on this interpretation and its socio-political consequences later.

2. Philosophical problems arise from the requirement at the end of 8:11 that resident aliens, righteous gentiles, and wise gentiles must accept the Noahide laws on the basis of divine revelation. Further still, Maimonides insists that to qualify for any of these categories one must accept not merely any heteronymous imposed revelation, but specifically the Jewish tradition's version of Mosaic revelation at Sinai. ("God commanded them in the Torah and informed us through Moses our teacher.") As Maimonides denies the appellation "wise men" to those who lack acceptance of revelation at Sinai, it follows that that wisdom can be found only among those who accept Sinaitic revelation and in those disciplines that posit the Sinaitic revelation as axiomatic or accept it as a demonstrated fact. In effect, wisdom and truth can emerge only from a community of believers and their intellectual enterprises. This renders philosophy, Aristotelian metaphysics and physics, the sciences of medicine, logic, and mathematics—all disciplines to which Maimonides was passionately devoted—cognitively and spiritually sterile. In principle, they are incapable of yielding truth and devoid of intellectual value.

Moreover, excluding from "the world to come" one who rationally accepts the moral and theological restrictions of the Noahide commandments implies that they and their philosophies lack spiritual integrity and religious truth—even in "this world." Since for Maimonides the afterlife is a non-physical world of eternal spiritual truth, it is logical to assume that one who attains a measure of religious truth through his earthly deliberations would somehow assume identification with that everlasting verity and participate in its immortality, that is, have a share in Maimonides's world to come. Exclusion from the afterlife is thus a sign of spiritual and religious bankruptcy on earth.

Indeed, many Jews once believed and some still believe today that truth and spiritual integrity can emerge only from a community of believing Jews and a framework that first acknowledges divine revelation at Sinai. Those ignorant of Jewish history with its traditional theological presuppositions have little chance of acquiring wisdom or religious truth. Such a parochial outlook informed Yehudah Halevi's *Weltanschauung* and appears to be the inevitable conclusion of his major work, *The Kuzari*.[3] It is also the guiding principle of

---

3   See Yehudah Halevi, *The Kuzari* 1:25–43 and 95. For Halevi, Jews were categorically different from other people. Only they possessed the mystical divine power (*inyan elohi*) that was bestowed upon them during their unique history. Thus, as "the pick of humanity," they had exclusive access to ultimate religious truth that no non-Jew could share. Even the faithful converts to Judaism lacked this capacity as they did not experience the exodus from Egypt nor receive revelation at Sinai.

separatist ultra-Orthodox Jews, who see no value in either social contact with non-believers (gentile or Jewish), or in intellectual contact with their philosophic, literary, or cultural "wisdom."

Maimonides, however, was no such Jew. Can one study either his religious or philosophic writings without quickly discerning the hand of Aristotle in the background? Is it possible to plumb the depths of the Laws of the Fundamentals of the Torah (*Hilkhot Yesodei ha-Torah*) without recognizing the contribution of Aristotle's metaphysics? Can one fully understand the Laws of Human Dispositions (*Hilkhot De'ot*) or his *Eight Chapters* on ethics with their typologies of ḥakham, tsadiq, and ḥasid, their idealization of the mean (*derekh benonit*), or their appropriation of acting beyond the letter of the law (*lifnim m'shurat ha-din*) without discovering the influence of Aristotle's *Nicomachean Ethics* and other Greek ethical writings?[4] Is it possible to comprehend Maimonides's reasoning regarding the incorporeality of God and his concept of *olam ha-ba* as expounded in Laws of Repentance (*Hilkhot Teshuvah*) and in his introduction to BT *Sanhedrin*'s chapter Ḥeleq separate from Aristotle's metaphysical arguments?

True to the advice he gave others, Maimonides "accepted truth from whoever pronounced it"[5]—even those who had no concept of an immanent divinity, let alone a God who could meet the Jewish people at Sinai and bestow the gift of Torah revelation upon it. For Maimonides, truth was determined by validly constructed arguments, and wisdom was a function of the rational content of propositions. These are universal logical properties, not limited to a parochial source or tradition. Because of his rationalist conception of truth, Maimonides was able to interpret all biblical references to the physical properties of God as anthropomorphic metaphors,[6] and consider denying the fundamental biblical teaching of creation should there exist a valid argument in favor of the universe's eternity.[7] Similarly, because he had uncompromising conviction in the ability of all people to utilize their rational faculties in order to discover spiritual and moral truth, he could maintain that prophecy was a natural category

---

4   For an analysis of how Maimonides understood these character typologies, see Norman Lamm, "The Sage and the Saint in the Thought of Maimonides" [Hebrew], in *Samuel Belkin Memorial Volume*, ed. Norman Lamm, Moshe Sokolow, Gershon Churgin, Moshe Carmilly, Hayim Leaf (New York: Yeshiva University Press, 1981), 11–28.
5   Maimonides, *Shemonah Peraqim* [Eight Chapters], introduction.
6   *Guide* I:1–60.
7   *Guide* II:25.

of mankind[8] and that the gentile "Aristotle omitted nothing that is within the scope of true ethics from his writings."[9]

Yet, incomprehensibly, according to our text Maimonides considered his teacher Aristotle neither a wise man who possessed a measure of earthly wisdom, nor a righteous gentile who earned any right to bask in the glory of eternal truth.

3. This text poses another problem, a moral one rooted in an essential characteristic of justice. If a necessary condition for salvation is the belief that revelation at Sinai provides the basis for Noahide commandments, then due to sheer accidents of time and place of birth, most of humanity is denied the possibility to achieve salvation. This arbitrary denial of opportunity constitutes an injustice regarding perhaps the greatest reward available to human beings.

The moral problem is highlighted when we compare the position Jews and that of non-Jews with regard to salvation. As the *Mishna* and *Hilkhot Teshuvah*[10] indicate, "All Jews have a share in the world to come." Only with the commission of grievous sins are a small minority of Jews excepted from salvation. The reverse proportion appears to be true gentiles: immortality for non-Jews would be the exception, open to a small minority. Thus we arrive at an arbitrary inequality, the hallmark of distributive injustice.

It is precisely this principled injustice that haunted the young Talmudist and many modern thinkers. Moses Mendelssohn expressed this same concern almost 200 years earlier in 1773 in a poignant letter to R. Jacob Emden. Mendelssohn took his cue from R. Yosef Karo, who stated that Maimonides developed the qualifying condition at the end of 8:11 from his own reasoning, even though it is a correct opinion.[11] In asking R. Emden whether there was any Talmudic authority for Maimonides's claim, Mendelssohn poured out his soul in the following impassioned argument:

> These words are to me harder than flint. Are then all the inhabitants of the earth from the rising of the sun unto the going down thereof except us doomed to descend unto the pit and become an object of abhorrence to all flesh if they do not believe in the Torah that was given as an inheritance only to the congregation of Jacob?... What then is expected of the nations unto whom

---

8   *Guide* II:32.
9   Yosef ibn Shem Tov, *Kavod Ha-Elokim* (Ferrara, 1555), 30a.
10 BT *Sanhedrin* 10:1; and *MT*, Laws of Repentance 5:3.
11 Yosef Karo, Commentary on *MT* (*Kesef Mishna*), ad loc.

the light of the Torah does not shine and who received no tradition except from their untrustworthy ancestors? Does God act tyrannically with men by destroying them and blotting out their name without their committing any iniquity? Shall such a view be termed a correct opinion?[12]

Mendelssohn was scandalized by the injustice of the restrictive requirement and understood that the moral critique naturally leads to a theological problem regarding the benevolence of the Creator. Could any God, who is "merciful to all His creations," doom to oblivion the ninety-nine percent of humanity who do not know of revelation at Sinai? Indeed, even Christians and Moslems who accept Mosaic prophecy—at least with respect to moral commandments—would probably not qualify for salvation. How many Christians or Moslems honestly refrain from eating the limbs of live animals (the seventh Noahide commandment) because it is prohibited in the Torah? Possibly only the relatively few members of the fledgling "Sons of Noah" sect in the southern United States could honestly be said to have this motivation.

In effect, Maimonides's qualification evolves into Judaism's analogue of the traditional Catholic principle *"extra ecclesiam nulla salus"* ("outside the Church there is no salvation"). Good works alone avail men little when it comes to salvation. Only when combined with correct belief does moral behavior take on significant religious value. Thus, the world to come has been transformed into an Orthodox neighborhood, rather than being a spiritual destination for all created in the image of God.

Could this be a correct opinion? So disturbing was this qualification to Mendelssohn that he considered its denial and the universal opportunity for salvation to be one of the central arguments for the superiority of Judaism over Christianity. For Mendelssohn, Judaism was unlike Christianity because it taught that all men who professed the fundamental doctrines of God, providence and afterlife and observed basic moral laws qualified for salvation. Since R. Yaakov Emden was unable to supply Mendelssohn with an authoritative Talmudic source for this limiting condition,[13] Mendelssohn felt free to consider

---

12   Moses Mendelssohn, *Gesammelte Schriften Jubilaeumsausgabe*, vol. 19, letter 154, 178–179, quoted in Alexander Altman, *Moses Mendelssohn: A Biographical Study* (Montgomery: University of Alabama Press, 1973), 217–218.

13   Emden advanced several arguments for the correctness of Maimonides's claim. These arguments, however, did not constitute discovery of any authoritative Talmudic source. See Schwarzschild, "Do Noahites Have to Believe in Revelation?," 38. The source of Maimonides's stipulation is still under dispute. A passage in *Mishnat R. Eliezer (Midrash*

Maimonides's original idea to be in error, and proceeded to disregard Emden's opinion by maintaining that:

> according to the concepts of true Judaism, all the inhabitants of the earth are destined to felicity; and the means of obtaining it are as widespread as mankind itself, as charitably dispensed as the means of warding off hunger and other natural needs.[14]

Ignoring the weighty legal opinion of Maimonides is always a risky strategy. To claim that normative Judaism disagrees with him on this question, however, is particularly difficult. Jacob Katz has shown[15] that it is none other than Maimonides himself who coined the phrase, "Righteous gentiles have a portion in the world to come," transforming a cryptic reference to *tsaddiqim* found in the Talmud (BT *Sanhedrin* 105a) into an authoritative and popular principle of Judaism. As a result, a cogent argument against Maimonides's interpretation of this concept in favor of a dissenting formulation by "true Judaism" would require tracing this concept throughout rabbinic writings, and demonstrating that it evolved beyond the author's original meaning into a more universal interpretation that eventually became normative. Absent this, intellectual honesty demands that we not disregard Maimonides on this principle.

Most philosophers and rabbis who discussed this issue acknowledged the need to accept Maimonides's opinion and confronted his text. Ironically, it was Baruch Spinoza in the latter half of the seventeenth century who accepted the text faithfully and accorded Maimonides the authority to represent Judaism and "the opinions of the Jews." In a famous passage in the *Tractatus*, he cites Maimonides as the basis for a merciless attack upon Judaism. Our text demonstrates that Jewish beliefs "are mere figments, grounded neither on reason, nor to be found in scriptures." Maimonides's opinion—and, by extension, all of Judaism—is "harmful, useless and absurd."[16]

Aqur), ed. H. G. E. Enelow (New York: Block, 1933), 121, appears to the only rabbinic text that mentions a similar requirement. However, the authenticity of this text has been questioned by scholars. See Schwarzschild, "Do Noahites Have to Believe in Revelation," 34–35; and Jacob Dienstag, "Natural Law in Maimonidean Thought and Scholarship," *Jewish Law Annual* 6 (1987): 72–74.

14 Moses Mendelssohn, *Jerusalem*, trans. Allan Arkush (Hanover: Brandeis University Press, 1983), 66.

15 Jacob Katz, "The Vicissitudes of Three Apologetic Statements" [Hebrew], *Zion* 23–24 (1958–1959): 174–193.

16 Benedict Spinoza, *Theological-Political Tractatus*, trans. R. H. M. Elwes (New York: Dover Publications, 1951), vol. 1, 80, 1–15.

Hermann Cohen, in his polemic against Spinoza's critique of Judaism, also refused to consider Maimonides in error. Cohen believed that monotheistic biblical Judaism represented the point in history at which the concept of humanity began. The Bible was first in recognizing messianic humanity, the concept of every human being possessing inherent dignity and value, independent of race, religion, or nation.[17] Cohen attempted to universalize the text by claiming that the restrictive requirement of belief in Mosaic revelation applied to the resident alien only, as a political prerequisite for citizenship rights in Jewish society. Thus, he cites the end of 8:11 only in part: "However he who does them out of rational considerations is not a resident alien," and consciously omits the remaining exclusions, "nor of the righteous gentiles, nor of their wise men."

Cohen's interpretation contravenes the explicit wording of Maimonides's complete formulation of 8:11. Cohen was able to adopt this interpretation only by tampering with the text and assuming an illicit emendation. Under his interpretation, the end of 8:11 should read, "However he who does them out of his own rational conclusions is not a resident alien, *but is one of the righteous gentiles* and is one of their wise men" (emphasis added). As we will discuss, textual variants do exist, but none matching Cohen's version or supporting his interpretation. In the end because Cohen could not preserve the integrity of Maimonides's text, he failed to show that the Maimonides's position was consistent with universal justice or theological benevolence.[18]

"Could such a view be termed a correct opinion?" The world was to wait a century and a half after Mendelssohn posed this question until a mystic personality, sensitive to the demands of justice and faithful to rabbinic tradition, attempted another answer.

II

As noted earlier, the above text appears to be a corrupt version of Maimonides's own manuscript. Evidence indicates that at the end of 8:11, Maimonides wrote,

---

17 Hermann Cohen, *Religion of Reason out of the Sources of Judaism*, trans. Simon Kaplan (New York: Oxford University Press, 1972), 121–122.
18 Ibid., 332. See also Schwarzschild, "Do Noahides Have to Believe in Revelation?," 39–41 for a further analysis of the failings of Cohen's critique of Spinoza. Michael Nahorai makes an important contribution to the reading of Maimonides's text in "Righteous Gentiles Have a Share in the World to Come" [Hebrew], *Tarbits* 61, nos. 3–4 (1992): 465–487. Like Cohen, Nahorai considers the subject of the law to be restricted to the resident alien. However, Nahorai adduces significantly more textual and philosophic for this claim than Cohen does.

"However, if he does them because of his own rational conclusions, he is not a resident alien, nor of the righteous of the nations of the world, but of their wise men [*ela me-ḥakhmehem*]," rather than "nor of their wise men [*ve-lo me-ḥakhmehem*]." Somehow the letter *aleph* of *ela* was mistaken for a *vav* and read as *ve-lo*. The substitution of *ela me-ḥakhmehem* for *ve-lo me-hakhmehem* succeeds in including rational moralists in the category of wise gentiles. How does *ela* affect our textual difficulties? Does it resolve any of the logical, philosophical and moral problems cited above?

Before attempting to answer these questions, it should be noted that the *ela* version is not universally accepted. Much of the vigorous contemporary debate revolves around the question of whether Maimonides—and Judaism—subscribe to any natural law theory, with natural law supporters advocating the *ela* reading, while halakhic positivists and natural law opponents preferring *ve-lo*.[19] Moreover, just as in Mendelssohn's time during the struggle for Jewish emancipation when apologetics was a dominant motif in the discussion of this issue,[20] today a good bit of the vigorous debate amongst contemporary writers seems heavily influenced by both apologetical and polemical considerations. This is not surprising, for at stake is more than a theoretic demographic profile of the world to come. The real issue before us in modern times is the nature of ideal Jewish/gentile relationships. This subject raises compelling and ideologically

---

19 Many of the essays in *Jewish Law Annual* 6 (1987) and 7 (1988) are devoted to the question of whether Jewish law is consistent with any theory of natural law. Of particular interest within these volumes to our question regarding Maimonides's law are the following articles in issue 6: Emmanuel Rackman, "Secular Jurisprudence and Halakhah"; Dienstag, "Natural Law in Maimonidean Thought and Scholarship"; Oliver Leaman, "Maimonides and Natural Law"; and in issue 7: J. David Bleich, "Judaism and Natural Law," and David Novak, "Natural Law, Halakhah, and the Covenant." Other important contributions to this discussion include Schwarzschild, "Do Noahides Have to Believe in Revelation?"; Marvin Fox, "Maimonides and Aquinas on Natural Law," *Dine Israel* 3 (1972): V–XXXVI; Jose Faur, *Studies in Mishneh Torah: Book of Knowledge* [Hebrew] (Jerusalem: Mosad ha-Rav Kook, 1978), 61–65, 161–176; David Novak, *Image of the Non-Jew in Judaism: An Historical and Constructive Study of Noahite Laws* (Portland, OR: Littman Library of Jewish Civilization, 2011), ch. 10; and Kirschenbaum and Lamm, "Freedom and Constraint in the Jewish Judicial Process." Bleich, Fox, and Faur are the most vocal opponents of a natural law interpretation of Jewish law and each argues for the correctness of *ve-lo me-ḥakhmehem*. Lamm and Kirshenbaum, Rackman, Schwarzschild, and Novak all advance natural law interpretations and each maintains that *ela me-ḥakhmehem* is the correct version of the text. It should be stressed that while *ve-lo* precludes a Maimonidean natural law theory, *ela* does not necessarily imply one. That is, *ela* is a necessary condition for a natural law claim, but not a sufficient condition.
20 Katz, "The Vicissitudes of Three Apologetic Statements," 176–177, and Schwarzschild, "Do Noahides Have to Believe in Revelation?," 35.

charged questions in our day: how does tradition assess the worth of gentiles who do not share Judaism's faith assumptions? Is there any spiritual gain by entering their social and intellectual universe? Ought Jews to coexist with gentiles in an atmosphere of social pluralism and religious tolerance? Can they do so and continue to believe in the uniqueness and divinity of Mosaic revelation? As is often the case, our discussion of eschatology here serves as a mask for political, sociological and intellectual judgments about life in this world.

Nevertheless, many argue on scholarly grounds that *ela* is the correct text. The inclusive reading is found in numerous early manuscripts, in the authoritative manuscripts housed in the Bodleian library at Oxford and the British Museum, as well as in the Yemenite manuscripts, generally considered to be most faithful to Maimonides's original text.[21] It is also quite easy to understand how the configuration of an *aleph* in *ela* could become defaced or worn away and read as a *vav* in *ve-lo*. The reverse process, that of a *vav* being naturally transformed into an *aleph*, is much less probable. As Isadore Twersky claims, "practically all texts support the '*ela*' reading."[22] Thus bibliographic evidence is weighted heavily toward reading *ela*, even though most printed editions of our text contain *ve-lo*.

Let us now consider the logical, philosophical, and moral evidence for the inclusive reading of the text, and determine what impact it has upon our three problems.

1. If Maimonides indeed wrote *ela* ("but of their wise men"), the logical difficulties cited are resolved. The category of wise gentiles is now well defined and independent: it is those persons who accept Noahide laws from rational considerations. Moreover, "wise man" is a term of approbation and positive value, so it is impossible that Maimonides considered such persons as pagans to be disqualified as Noahides. Since the acceptance of Noahide law by the wise gentile does not require acceptance of revelation, *a fortiori* the lesser category of plain Noahides would not require belief in Mosaic revelation as part of the acceptance of Noahide laws either.

Thus in 8:10–11 Maimonides delineates five clearly independent categories of gentiles:

---

21 For an excellent account of the textual variants of this passage contained in various manuscripts see Dienstag, "Natural Law in Maimonidean Thought and Scholarship," Appendix, 75–77.

22 Isadore Twersky, *Introduction to the Code of Maimonides* (New Haven: Yale University Press, 1980), 455.

(1) the pagan—one who rejects the seven Noahide commandments;
(2) the Noahide—one who lives by the Noahide laws for whatever reason or motive. Such a person might do so unreflectively, simply because such behavior is the prevailing ethos of his society or peer group;
(3) the resident alien—the Noahide living under Jewish sovereignty who lives by the Noahide laws, accepts them as obligations from Mosaic revelation, and swears this allegiance before a rabbinic court;
(4) the righteous gentile—the Noahide who lives by the Noahide laws, accepting them as revealed Mosaic commandments;
(5) the wise gentile—the Noahide who lives according to the Noahide laws because he has concluded rationally that they are correct principles of behavior.

In effect, Maimonides's use of *ela* succeeds in defining the class of wise gentiles in classic philosophic style, *per genus et differentia*. Such sages are in the generic category of Noahides, but differ from plain Noahides because of their commitment to Noahide laws as principles, and from the more exalted Noahides (righteous gentiles and resident aliens) because their commitment is rooted in autonomous reason and not from any theological awareness.

It now also becomes apparent why Maimonides introduced the category of wise gentiles: He is creating an exhaustive list of all gentile categories. Maimonides is using this opportunity in *Hilkhot Melakhim* to give a comprehensive listing of different ways Jewish law classifies and evaluates gentiles.

2. If Maimonides wrote that persons living by autonomously accepted morality could be considered wise men, this statement would constitute an explicit claim that wisdom—in all its senses—can be found among all rational persons, even those with no substantive religious commitments. It should be noted that the theological dimensions of the seven Noahide commandments require only that a person refrain from idolatry and exercise a limited sense of tolerance, that is, refrain from undermining the correct belief in God. As we saw earlier, Noahide law does not require that one have any positive belief in God.[23] Perhaps the most that should be claimed regarding the Maimonidean concept of wisdom is that it requires an acknowledgement of a sole power higher than man that has necessary, not merely contingent, existence.

---

23 It is sometimes mistakenly assumed that because Noahide law prohibits idolatry and blasphemy, it also requires affirmation of some theology. Both of these religiously oriented Noahide laws are prohibitions, however, and do not imply any positive belief. See *MT*, Laws of Kings and Their Wars 9.

Maimonides implies this in his opening statements of *MT*: "The foundation of foundations and the pillar of wisdom is to know that there exists a first being who brought every existing thing into being. All existing things, whether celestial, terrestrial, or belonging to an intermediate class, exist only through His true existence."[24] Here Maimonides described a primary being, above both humanity and nature. This power is closely identified with Aristotle's wholly transcendent unmoved mover, who never comes into contact with human beings. Clearly what this passage does *not* demand as a prerequisite for wisdom is a personal, immanent God who created the universe, who entered human affairs and bestowed commandments upon the Jewish people in a revelatory meeting at Sinai. It is the God of the philosophers, not the God of human history. This is why Maimonides quoted only the beginning of Ex. 20:2, "I am the Lord, your God," and consistently omitted the latter part of the verse, "who brought you out of the land of Egypt, out of the house of bondage," when discussing the positive commandment to know God.[25] Nowhere in the initial four chapters of the *MT*, where Maimonides discussed this higher metaphysical power, did he mention creation, revelation, or even the Jewish people. Writers err who use this beginning passage as proof that wisdom requires traditional Jewish belief in revelation, and hence Maimonides must have written "*ve-lo me-ḥakhmehem*." Either they simply neglected to read full text of chapter 1 of *MT* or they have been blinded by their ideological fervor. For Maimonides, wisdom might require belief in the God of the philosophers, but not the historically experienced God of Jewish history.

It follows that Maimonidean wisdom is an open category, not necessarily tied to Jewish theology or confined to Jews. Hence, it is quite logical that Maimonides studied non-Jewish writings, accepted their claims when he thought their arguments were valid, and integrated their wisdom into his own philosophic and religious works. Aristotle certainly qualified as a wise man, as could other philosophers, thinkers, and scientists who accepted basic Noahide moral norms. In principle, any intellectual enterprise—such as philosophy, science, medicine, or literature—could discover truth and possess wisdom as long as that discipline does not ultimately deny the Noahide prohibitions against homicide, theft, sexual license, anarchy, blasphemy, cruelty, and idolatry.

The result is that the philosophical difficulties cited earlier are also solved by the *ela* reading. In 8:10–11, Maimonides should not be understood to have

---

24 *MT*, Laws of the Foundations of the Torah 1:1. Translation from Isadore Twersky, *A Maimonides Reader*, (New York: Behrman House 1972) 43.
25 Ibid. 1:6; *MT*, Book of Commandments, positive commandment 1; and *Guide* II:33.

defined *a priori* the theological requirements for intellectual and spiritual truth. Rather, he may have offered a halakhic standard for tolerance: Jewish tolerance extends up to the edge of paganism, the culture that rejects any of the restraints of Noahide law.[26]

3. However, the moral problem that so vexed Mendelssohn proves to be more intractable. Mendelssohn had the standard printed edition with its *ve-lo* text,[27] but had he possessed the *ela* version, he would have found little comfort. As Steven Schwarzschild notes:

> The emendation of the text does not relieve us of the difficulties that arise from Maimonides' statement, however. It still remains true that he excludes what we might call the philosophical rather than the religious Noahides from the class of the righteous of the gentile nations of the world and thus from the world to come.... All the questions raised with respect to this dictum, therefore, retain their validity.[28]

Ela me-ḥakhmehem accords only wisdom to those outside the tradition, but not immortality. This point is borne out by the experience of Hermann Cohen, who was faced with the same problem even though he knew of both the *ve-lo* and the *ela* versions of the text. To support his theory he was forced to emend the *ela* version by moving the location of *ela* so that it applied both to wise men and to righteous gentiles. Without this illicit change, Spinoza's critique and the moral/theological problem stand with either version of the text.

---

26 See Michael Rosenak, "The Religious Person and Religious Pluralism," in *The Meaning and Limits of Pluralism Today*, ed. Allan Brockway and Jean Halpérin (Geneva: World Council of Churches, 1987), 13–20. The author subscribes to a natural law interpretation of the Noahide laws and argues that they form a minimum universal ethical code for humanity. As such, the halakhic requirement to accept Noahide law is identical with the moral requirement to accept the laws of civilized existence rather than to live in an immoral pagan order. Under this conception, Judaism's acceptance of all Noahides is identified with tolerance for all people willing to live morally. See also chapters 3 and 5 of this book.
27 See Dienstag, "Natural Law in Maimonidean Thought and Scholarship," 26.
28 Ibid., 33.

III

We can briefly sum up the various responses to Maimonides's controversial claim that the status of resident alien and righteous gentile (and possibly wise gentile) requires belief in Mosaic revelation:

- In the sixteenth century, Yosef Karo accepted Maimonides's opinion as correct, but could not find a source for it within Jewish tradition.
- In the seventeenth century Spinoza accepted Maimonides's opinion as authoritative, but found it so obviously incorrect that it provided the basis for his argument undermining the validity of Judaism.
- In the eighteenth century, Mendelssohn could not accept the opinion as correct, considered it to be idiosyncratic, and rejected it as an element of true Judaism.
- In the early twentieth century, Cohen realized that he could not reject Maimonides as authoritative Judaism, and therefore exploited the fact that some texts were corrupt. He proceeded to change the text, so that it he could interpret Maimonides to say that belief in Mosaic revelation was required only of gentiles wishing to live under Jewish sovereignty (resident aliens), but not required for righteous or wise gentiles.

Ostensibly, both versions of the text—*ve-lo me-ḥakhmehem*—and *ela me-ḥakhmehem* leave us with equally untenable options with respect to our moral problem: either reject Maimonides's opinion (Mendelssohn), change the wording of the text without any bibliographical warrant (Cohen), or accept the authority of Maimonides's text and suffer the undesirable moral and theological consequences (Spinoza).

In the twentieth century, there was one Jewish personality who made a bold interpretive move, attempting to be faithful to Maimonides, the text, and the considerations of justice. For Rav Abraham Ha-Kohen Kook, the *ela* text was the key to cutting the Gordian knot. By granting that Maimonides ascribed wisdom even to those who accepted Noahide commandments from reason alone, Kook was able to reinterpret the comparative merit of wise gentiles:

> Behold the correct version is "but [*ela*] of their wise men." My opinion is that Maimonides intends (to convey) that the status "possessing a share in the world to come" is a low level, even though it is also a great good. Since even Jewish sinners and

ignoramuses merit this status, it is a low status amongst spiritual values. Maimonides reasons that ideas improve man much more than does righteous behavior. Therefore he reasons that the level of "possessing a share in the world to come" is a status specifically for righteous gentiles, who were not superior in their ideas but accepted faith in wholehearted purity and acted in an honest way because they accepted that their commandments were so given by God. However, someone who through his rational conclusion merited accepting the seven Noahide commandments—he is truly wise of heart and full of understanding. He is considered "of their wise men." Since the status of wisdom is very great, and there is no need to state that they "possess a share in the world to come." Rather he [the rational person] is on a level of holiness that requires interpretation in an expression greater than the language of "possessing a share in the world to come."[29]

Kook inverts the rankings of the wise and righteous gentiles. For him a wise gentile is spiritually superior to the righteous gentile since the sage recognizes moral truths in an autonomous manner, from the innermost spirit of his being, rather than passively accepting them through tradition as heteronymous imposed commandments. Thus the wise man has both rational and moral virtues, while the righteous gentile has only the latter. Kook maintains, moreover, that both of those virtues are open to all people. Just as every person has the free will to determine his behavior and refrain from killing, stealing, and raping, so too does every person have the natural capacity to recognize that these actions are morally wrong.

Kook's interpretation grows out of his conviction that the act of acquiring moral wisdom is more than a sterile cognitive moment within secular experience. It is, rather, a transcendent achievement filled with religious significance, one that elevates the gentile sage to a high level of spirituality and endows him with holiness. Although he never explicitly says so, Kook's interpretation has the strong implication that the wise gentile also merits salvation. Being on a higher spiritual level, he certainly earns at least the level of spiritual reward that the righteous gentile does. Thus salvation is a possibility available to all humanity. Approximately 250 years after the *Tractatus*,

---

29   Kook, *Letters*, vol. 1, 100.

Rav Kook's has finally rebutted Spinoza's argument. Indeed, according to Kook, Maimonides's view "should be termed a correct opinion."

In this interpretation we see a classic expression of Kook's worldview, where all forms of knowledge are suffused with holiness and God's presence. Kook's religious universe was radically open: every aspect of the world, history, and truth necessarily reflected a divine light waiting to be perceived—and Kook saw God's light in every far-flung corner of the universe. He saw Hegel's dialectics of history expressing a working out of God's presence in human affairs, and even the theory of evolution was a corollary to divine creation. His unshakable faith led him to conclude that the activity of atheistic Zionists, although resulting from a total rejection of God and His law, paradoxically realized God's will. The story of atheistic Zionism was an example of how history proceeds dialectically towards an inexorably spiritual result: a thesis (religion) clashes with an antithesis (political Zionism) and together they produce a holy synthesis (the return of the Jewish people to the land of Israel). Perhaps in a similarly paradoxical way, the moral convictions of the rational and autonomous wise man attest to God's worldly presence more effectively than unreflective and habitual behavior based on acceptance of revelation.

Given Kook's religious sensibility, it is not surprising that he maintained the possibility of salvation for all men. But Kook makes a stronger claim, namely, that this is also the conviction of Maimonides ("Maimonides intends . . ."). Clearly, he read the text contrary to the majority of interpreters on this point. What evidence exists that Maimonides also shared this universal religious sensibility? Perhaps Kook is illicitly recreating Maimonides in his own image?

Despite its novelty, there is logical warrant both within our text and from the larger corpus of Maimonides's writings for Kook's interpretation. The dictum "Righteous gentiles have a share in the world to come" has traditionally been interpreted as "*Only* righteous gentiles have a share in the world to come." That is, a gentile merits salvation if and only if he is classified as a righteous gentile. Yet, this is not the precise connotation. Logically the wording allows for other categories of gentiles to merit the world to come also, as Kook reads the phrase. Even the text at hand implies this interpretation since in *MT*, Laws of Kings and Their Wars 8:11 Maimonides requires of a resident alien everything that he does of a righteous gentile, namely acceptance of Noahide laws from belief in Mosaic revelation. Thus, it is logical that if a righteous gentile qualifies for salvation, so must a resident alien.[30] So, at least one type of person other than righteous gentiles also has a share in the world to come. If "righteous gentiles" is not the exclusive category of persons meriting salvation, then wise gentiles can also qualify since they are on a higher spiritual level.

This interpretation supplies additional coherence to the text, as it succeeds in explaining why Maimonides deemed it relevant to mention wise gentiles at all in the end of 8:11. At this point in the text he took pains to list all categories of people who have a share in the world to come for the sake of completeness in order to prevent the incorrect inference that it is *only* righteous gentiles and resident aliens who merit salvation.

It is instructive to note that in no other passage where Maimonides mentions immortality does he stipulate the requirement belief in divine revelation at Sinai.[31] This is true whether Maimonides mentions righteous gentiles or not in these passages. Consider one of the most important of these texts:

> Anyone in the world whose spirit moves him and who understands by his own knowledge to stand apart before the Lord to minister to Him and to serve Him, to know the Lord and to walk straight as God made him. . . . Such a person is sanctified with greatest sanctity and the Lord will be his portion and his inheritance forever and ever, and he will merit what he deserves in the world to come.[32]

In this text, Maimonides undeniably left open the possibility of universal salvation ("Anyone in the world . . ."). There is no explicit reference or implicit hint of restricting the world to come to those accepting Sinaitic revelation. In fact, the text stresses that the person herein described is characterized by independent conclusions in both his spiritual dimension ("his spirit moves

---

30 Maimonides states explicitly in *MT*, Laws of Forbidden Intercourse 14:7, that resident aliens are also included in the class of righteous gentiles (and therefore merit the world to come). Kirshenbaum and Lamm, "Freedom and Constraint in the Jewish Judicial Process," 118–119, n. 78, imply that there is a crucial difference between a resident alien and a righteous gentile other than the imposition of a juridic oath: the resident alien is politically coerced to accept Noahide laws, whereas the righteous gentile accepts them freely. However, the necessity of political coercion with regard to the resident alien is not directly implied by Maimonides's text.
31 *MT*, Laws of Repentance 3:5; and *MT*, Laws of Witnesses 2:10; as well as Commentary on *Mishna Sanhedrin* 10:2 are the other references where Maimonides states that "Righteous gentiles have a share in the world to come."
32 *MT*, Laws of Jubilee 13:13.

him . . .") and in his intellectual faculties ("understands by his own knowledge"). This person is similar to Kook's wise gentile, in that his immortality results from his autonomous nature and not from his acceptance of heteronymous revelation. Other passages in Maimonides's halakhic and philosophic works also emphasize that an autonomous apprehension of theoretical and moral truths are essential characteristics of those who perfect their souls and attain salvation.[33] It seems that Kook's wise gentile would feel very much at home with those personalities in the world to come.

How does Rav Kook know that Maimonides regarded the rational and autonomously ethical person to be on a higher level than the righteous gentile? In the famous discussion found in chapter 6 of his *Eight Chapters*, Maimonides resolves the disagreement between the philosophic and rabbinic traditions regarding the status of different types of ethical personalities:

> Both (claims) are true and there is no disagreement at all between them. The evils designated by the philosophers are evils about which they state that "he who has no longing for them is more to be praised than he who desires them but conquers his passion." They are commonly held by all men to be evil, such as bloodshed, stealing, robbery, exploitation, harming someone who has done no wrong, doing evil to one's benefactor. . . . These are laws about which the Sages, peace be upon them, said, "Had they not been written (in the Torah) they should have been written." . . . There is no doubt that the soul that desires them and yearns for them is deficient and that the noble soul has no such desires at all for them. However, the things about which the sages said, "He who conquers his urges is more important and his reward is greater, they are laws from tradition." This is true, for were it not for the Torah, they would not be evil. . . . Consider the wisdom of the sages and their examples. They do not claim, "One should not say, I have no desire to kill, to steal, to lie"; rather they say, "I desire them, but what can I do? My Father in heaven has forbade them to me!" But all the examples they cite are traditional laws, such as meat and milk, the wearing of intermixed garments, forbidden sexual unions.

---

33 See *Guide* III:51; and *Qovets Teshuvot ha-Rambam*, ed. A. Lichtenberg (Leipzig, 1859), 2:23b–24a.

Maimonides stressed in this passage that someone who refrains from violating rational laws simply because such acts were prohibited by divine law has a deficient soul (*nefesh haserah*). The more complete moral personality is he who feels no internal temptation to sin and therefore has no need to rely on heteronymous law for restraint. He is someone who realizes within himself that such behavior is morally wrong.

It is no accident that Maimonides utilized the term *mefursamim*, that is, claims widely known, to denote rational moral principles and that the examples he selects are bloodshed, stealing, and violations of basic reciprocal behavior that constitutes the foundation of a just and law-abiding society. These are precisely the universally obligating Noahide laws that the wise gentile recognizes autonomously to be morally binding. In other words, it is the sage, apprehending the intrinsic moral integrity of the *mefursamim* (Noahide laws), who possesses a more complete character than the righteous gentile, who is deficient in recognizing moral truths and observes these rational moral laws only because "my Father in Heaven has forbidden them to me." Other Maimonidean passages confirm this inference.[34] When focusing exclusively on the narrow context of the passage in *Hilkhot Melakhim*, Rav Kook's reading may appear forced and idiosyncratic. Yet when we consider it against the broader background of Maimonides's other writings, it has strong logical support.

IV

As noted earlier, the debate over which version of our text is authentic and which interpretation is correct continues unabated. If Rav Kook's reading represented one extreme, utilizing the *ela* version to create a religious vision that was radically open and universal, a second twentieth-century rabbinic personality offered another interpretation presenting the opposite worldview.

---

34 See Moses Maimonides, *Introduction to Pereq Heleq* [Hebrew] (Jerusalem: Mossad ha-Rav Kook, 1965), 132–133, where he emphasizes that a necessary condition for both human perfection (*shalemut*) and entry to the world to come is moral wisdom manifested by an autonomous internal motivation to observe moral laws. This wisdom and autonomous behavior ("He is moved from within himself") is what differentiates human beings from animals, whose behavior is determined by external forces. In *Guide* III:17, Maimonides also stresses the value of the autonomously motivated personality by stating that people bear responsibility for their compliance with or violation of moral laws—even those not originating in divine commands—since each person's intelligence (*sehel*) naturally informs him of his moral obligations.

Apparently unaware of the problems cited, R. Velvel Soloveitchik read the *ve-lo* text as a strict constructionist and carried it to its logical conclusion.[35] For him 8:10 and 8:11 constituted one logical unit and all eight occurrences of the verb "to accept" (*leqabel*) in that unit indicated that identical substantive acceptance on the part of the resident alien, the righteous gentile, the wise gentile, and the Noahide. He believed that Sinaitic revelation changed the legal requirement of Noahide laws. Whereas before Sinai it was sufficient for a Noahide not to violate any of the seven commandments, after Sinai explicit positive acceptance is demanded. Most importantly, since acceptance is the same for both the righteous gentile and the Noahide, even a Noahide is now required to believe in revelation at Sinai.

Alarming logical consequences flow from this interpretation. Not only is the rational and autonomous moral person denied wisdom and a share in the world to come, he also fails to qualify as a Noahide. And as Maimonides explains in 8:10, anyone who does not accept the Noahide commandments is guilty of a capital offense and is subject to death. Hence, anyone who does not believe in Mosaic revelation at Sinai forfeits his right to life in this world!

Of course, R. Soloveitchik did not advocate that Jews actually put non-believers to death, but the religious *Weltanschauung* that naturally emerges from this interpretation pronounces axiological death upon the heterodox and non-Jewish world. It robs all non-believers and their cultures of any intellectual, religious, or even human value. R. Velvel's universe is sharply divided between traditional Judaism and paganism, between the theology of Torah and intolerable heresies, between believers in Sinai and people lacking intrinsic dignity and a right to life. In this binary universe there is no possibility for religious pluralism, interactive coexistence between Jews and gentiles, or any synthesis between the traditional understanding of Judaism and disciplines possessing secular "wisdom." Rather, religious integrity requires an exclusive parochial Jewish frame of reference—where Jews are hermetically sealed off from all outside social, intellectual, cultural, and political influences. In stark contrast to Rav Kook's religious world, Rav Velvel Soloveitchik's ideal universe was one of isolationism and rejection of modernity. Hence, Rav Velvel was quite consistent in opposing secular education as well as the State of Israel as a political phenomenon.

As we have seen, Maimonides's controversial text raises a host of philosophic, legal, and theological issues that have occupied thinkers over the

---

35 Velvel Soloveitchik, *Novellae (Hedushei) ha-Griz* [Hebrew], final paragraph.

centuries. Its urgency in our time, however, stems from its implications for Judaism's attitude toward gentiles and their culture: Can Jews accord full dignity to those who do not share their belief in revelation? Can Jews see spiritual and intellectual value in non-Jewish wisdom? Ought Jews to participate in the non-Jewish world? The same text informs diametrically opposed religious conceptions, with the *ela* version nourishing Rav Kook's open, pluralistic, and integrative religious sensibility, and the *ve-lo* version providing support for an isolationist worldview. In other words, Maimonides's text has been used to argue for both Modern/Centrist/Zionist Orthodoxy and separatist Ultra-Orthodoxy.

It is surprising, therefore, to find spokesmen identified with Centrist Orthodoxy advocating the *ve-lo* text, dismissing the seriousness of Rav Kook and citing Rav Velvel on this point.[36] These voices seem oblivious to the fact that, in doing so, they are denying essential tenets of Centrist Orthodoxy and Zionism, namely, (1) that gentile knowledge can constitute wisdom and its study has religious value, (2) that non-Jewish pluralistic society can be a spiritually significant arena of participation for religious Jews, and (3) there is religious validity to the State of Israel and political Zionism. When one denies *a priori* wisdom to a non-believer, there is no consistent way to advocate a synthesis of Torah and Western knowledge. Of course, one can continue to view secular knowledge functionally, and use it as an instrument to achieve pragmatic ends, but one cannot maintain the centrist principle that non-Jewish knowledge can have spiritual character and that its study can constitute the fulfillment of the commandments to know and to love God. When one rejects the possibilities of righteousness and spiritual integrity to autonomously motivated gentiles, there can be no religious justification for active engagement with those who do not accept revelation. That is, such a person can no longer see gentile society as a stage of possible religious sanctity, as a place where he can act out God's will and make a religiously significant contribution. Withdrawal and separation must be the operative religious imperatives.

Finally, if one denies the right to life and the essential humanity of those who do not share traditional Jewish theology, then there is no practical way to support the Jewish people organizing around the State of Israel and participating in the family of nations. Statehood implies economic, social, and diplomatic

---

36 Bleich, "Judaism and Natural Law"; Fox, "Maimonides and Aquinas on Natural Law"; and Menachem Genack, "Ambiguity as Theology," *Tradition* 25, no. 1 (Fall 1989): 79 all argue for *ve-lo*. Bleich dismisses Rav Kook's interpretation in a cavalier fashion. Genack, writing in the foremost journal of centrist Orthodox thought, omits any reference to Rav Kook and approvingly cites only the interpretation of R. Velvel Soloveitchik.

cooperation with other nations, interaction with foreign governments, and according their officials full human dignity and respect. In a word, Israel requires that the Jewish people be active in the world and establish honest dialogue with the representatives of foreign cultures. This is impossible if they are regarded as pagans, unworthy of true human status.

In arguing for *ve-lo me-ḥakhmehem*, writers in effect misappropriate Maimonides as an advocate of intellectual and social separatism. This revisionist biography robs Jewish thought of its greatest rabbinic model and ideological father. In their zeal to distance themselves from more liberal and universalistic interpretations of Judaism, some Orthodox thinkers have crossed over the line and come to idealize isolation and an *a priori* rejection of modern life. This turn is intellectually untenable, for it ultimately distorts Maimonides's worldview and religious understanding, as well as denuding Jewish intellectual and religious traditions of striving to see God in every corner of the universe and engaging with God's human creatures, all of whom are endowed with *Tselem Elokim*—God's Holy Image.

5

Idolatry Today

Some years ago a group of Jewish thinkers met at University of Scranton to discuss how to begin building a Jewish theology of other religions that would be credible in contemporary society where Jews come into frequent contact with Christians, Muslims, Hindus, Buddhists, other Asian believers, and secularists.[1] Of course, a central issue was what to do with the halakhic category of *avodah zarah*—worship often identified with idolatry. What does it mean in our world where few pray to the stars, sun or other material objects? To whom if anyone does it apply today? How can Jews today accept the unmitigated intolerance—sometimes to the point of annihilation of idolatrous persons and cultures[2]—that the Bible and *Halakhah* demand of Jews? In practice and theory, *avodah zarah* functions in rabbinic discourse as the domain of the intolerable. It defines the line at which tolerance should end and intolerance is warranted.[3]

Much to my surprise, one Orthodox professor of philosophy urged us to disregard the concept entirely: the idea of *avodah zarah* has no relevance today, and the sooner we get rid of it the better, he insisted.

To me and many others at the conference this suggestion seemed eminently reasonable. The idea of wreaking violence on other persons for their variant theological convictions, however incorrect or objectionable, seems unjustifiable today—particularly to Jews with a keen awareness of the suffering Jews endured for their dissident beliefs during the long night of our exile.

---

[1] The conference resulted in the volume *Jewish Theology and World Religions*, ed. Alon Goshen Gottstein and Eugene Korn (Portland, OR: Littman Library of Jewish Civilization, 2012), many of whose essays explore this issue in detail.

[2] "You shall not leave one soul alive" (Deut. 20:16) is the biblical command to Jews regarding the idolatrous Canaanite nations. See also *MT*, Laws of Idolatry 10.

[3] See the trenchant analysis of *avodah zarah* and its function in Moshe Halbertal and Avishai Margolit, *Idolatry* (Cambridge, MA: Harvard University Press, 1994).

Not long after the conference I discussed this issue with the progressive theologian Rabbi Irving (Yitz) Greenberg. He passionately disagreed with the idea of dropping *avodah zarah* from contemporary Jewish deliberations, insisting that we need the idea of idolatry for a healthy theological worldview. Idolatry has significance today, he claimed, and we would not be able to honestly fashion contemporary Jewish theologies toward others without considering it.

Technically, *avodah zarah* means worship deemed illicit by Jewish law, both in its idolatrous and non-idolatrous manifestations.[4] While often identified with the pagan idolatry that the Bible condemns, it is in fact a wider category that also includes some non-pagan forms of worship.

We have seen that, fundamentally, two competing conceptions are prevalent in rabbinic discourse, both inferred from the Bible. The Torah sometimes describes intolerable idolaters as people who worship celestial bodies, stars, and trees[5] (that is, any finite physical object), understanding them to be divine. At other times, idolaters are portrayed as people with abominable immoral practices.[6] Maimonides and most other rationalist rabbis have emphasized the first conception—that of intellectual error. As the greatest halakhic authority in Jewish tradition, Maimonides exerted prodigious influence over the Jewish canon, and as a rationalist philosopher steeped in Aristotelian metaphysics, Maimonides understood *avodah zarah* to be the conceptual confusion of mistaking something finite for God, Who is infinite in being and essence. Maimonides catalogued the types of this confusion in his code of Jewish law (*Mishneh Torah*) within *Sefer Madda*, the Book of Knowledge. For him, an idolater is anyone who believes that God is physical, plural, has emotions, or is subject to change, since all these properties indicate limit and imperfection.

We saw in chapter 3 that Maimonides considered Christianity to be full-fledged *avodah zarah* because of its doctrines of the incarnation and trinity, and ruled that Christians holding these beliefs were idolaters and were subject to all the same strictures of alienation and intolerance as the pagans of the biblical and Talmudic eras. He was consistent in his judgment, and also considered that Jews who harbored personalistic conceptions of God were worse offenders than gentiles who believed that God was physical.[7]

Menaḥem Meiri emphasized the other biblical identification of idolaters as primitive immoral pagans with abominable ethical, religious, and sexual

---

4 For a fuller analysis, see chapter 7.
5 Deut. 4:12 and 16.
6 Lev. 18; Deut. 12.
7 *Guide* I:36.

practices. For him, idolatry was primarily a religion that permitted wild immorality, that is, did not contain the moral Noahide commandments that constitute the foundations of orderly civilized society.[8] Thus, according to Meiri, even a polytheist and a corporealist who subscribed to fundamental moral principles belonged to the domain of valid believers—*ba'alei dat.* Meiri had no theological or practical problem with Christianity or with any other civilizing religion of which he was aware.[9] In fact, one Christian cleric even inspired him to write his book on repentance, *Hibur ha-Teshuvah*,[10] and he restricted idolatry in his day to the far-flung corners of the earth—those places where Jews did not live. In doing so, Meiri relegated Judaism's mandatory intolerance of idolators to the realm of theory.[11]

Greenberg offers a third definition of idolatry: "Idolatry is the partial, created or shaped by humans, that claims to be infinite. Idolatry mimics the Divine and claims the absolute status of the Divine, yet it is in fact finite."[12] Greenberg's definition is at once traditional, drawing on both Maimonides's and Meiri's traditional rabbinic conceptions, and modern, because it is fashioned in light of twentieth-century history, the *Shoah*, and our awareness of different religious traditions in the contemporary pluralistic world.

Greenberg's definition most obviously resembles Rambam's understanding of idolatry as cognitive error, as mistaking the finite for the infinite, the limited for the absolute. Absolutizing our own limited theological, political, or philosophical ideas betrays the infinite nature of God. Even religious beliefs based on a conviction in God's revelation are grounded in our human perception and cognition of that revelation, and hence are subject to human epistemological limitations. This awareness led rabbinic tradition to assert that revelation at Sinai had 600,000 differing interpretations, one for each male Jewish adult present.

---

8 See Katz, *Exclusiveness and Tolerance*, ch. 10; and Moshe Halbertal, *Bein Torah l'Hokhmah*, (Jerusalem: Hebrew University Press, 2000), ch. 3. For an English translation of Halbertal, see his "Ones Possessed of Religion: Religious Tolerance in the Teachings of Meiri," *The Edah Journal* 1, no. 1 (*Marheshvan* 5761), www.edah.org.
9 That is, such belief systems were not *avodah zarah* for gentiles, and perhaps even not for Jews.
10 As Meiri indicates in his introduction to the work.
11 Meiri never addressed how he would evaluate atheists, and this is an important issue for Jewish theology today. I suspect that Meiri required belief in and submission to a transcendent God because like nearly every other thinker in the Middle Ages, he assumed that any moral code lacking a punishing and rewarding divine authority could not be sustained.
12 Irving Greenberg, "Pluralism and Partnership," in *For the Sake of Heaven and Earth* (Philadelphia: Jewish Publication Society, 2004), 210.

And R. Greenberg's conception also bears a close relation to Meiri's ethical conception of *avodah zarah:*

> This pseudo-infinite cannot contain the infinity of life (or of human dignity). In fact, we know that idolatry is the god of death and that it creates a realm of death.... All human systems (even those that are given by divine revelation) that claim to be absolute, exercise no self-limitation and leave no room for the other turn into idolatry, i.e. into sources of death.... It is no accident that Nazism which sought perfection and eliminated all restrictions and limitations created a realm of total death—the kingdom of night.... All political systems and all religions that allow themselves to make unlimited absolute claims are led to idolatrous behaviors. They often generate death-dealing believers.... All social systems that "other" the other and absolutize their own host culture turn idolatrous and then degrade or destroy others.[13]

Yet more important than idolatry's cognitive error is its horrific moral consequences:

> Absolutizing our limited ideas leads to imposing them on others, which as history has shown, inevitably produces persecution, destruction and death. And this moral problem turns theological: it is theologically abhorrent because it annihilates the Image of God present in human beings and thus eliminates the presence of God in the world—literally <u>H</u>illul ha-Shem [the absence of God]. Jews understand this viscerally. As victims of the absolutist doctrines of the medieval Church, the Nazi Final Solution and Stalinist Communism, this truth has been burned into our flesh. These monistic systems sought to impose imperial truth on the world, ultimately crushing all dissenters and murdering millions of Jews.[14]

---

13 Ibid.
14 Ibid. As an absolutist, Maimonides taught similar intolerance and violence toward idolators. See *MT*, Laws of Idolatry 10, and Laws of Kings and Their Wars 8:10.

Written in 1999, Greenberg's insight was prophetic, accurately describing the jihadist slaughter wreaked by Al Qaida, ISIL, and other Islamist zealots that was to emerge in the first decades of the twenty-first century. In their absolute quest to purge the Middle East of all vestiges of non-Islamic life and culture, these extremists brought chaos, destruction, and death to the countries and peoples of the region. Their absolutism has become a savage murderous idol, and their absolutist worship has shown itself to be the enemy of the God of Creation Who brought order out of chaos and sanctified each human being with the Divine Image.

Nor are Jews immune from this modern idolatry. Some religious Jews have absolutized their beliefs and have begun to practice intolerant exclusivism in Israel. These monists deny the legitimacy of religious pluralism, advocate restricting Israeli residence to Jews, and at times physically assault Muslims and Christians in their midst—all on allegedly religious grounds.[15]

Only non-absolute systems or religions that allow room for the other can succeed in protecting the dignity of human beings and seeing the *Tselem Elokim* (Divine Image) in every person. It is our commitment to self-limitation (human *tsimtsum* that imitates God's act of creation, according to kabalistic teaching) and our awareness of the finitude of our religious and political conceptions that ensure human life can flourish. All absolutist systems are destined to produce only "oceans of blood,"[16] and violate God's love for His children as well His covenantal plan for humanity. In the end, the greatest witness to the Creator of Life is the covenantal pluralism that protects religious coexistence and promotes human partnership.

Covenantal Pluralism and Relativism

The most troubling aspects of modern culture for traditional theologians are empirical pluralism, social equality, and the expansive awareness of other cultures gained through global travel and internet communication. Three hundred years ago, a New Englander could believe that the Boston State House was the hub of the solar system and that his church had a monopoly on God's truth.[17]

---

15 See chapter 3, n. 47.
16 See statement of Isaiah Berlin, chapter 3, p. 49.
17 Abraham Joshua Heschel, "No Religion Is an Island," in his *Moral Grandeur and Spiritual Audacity*, ed. Susannah Heschel (New York: Farrar, Strauss, Giroux, 1996), 237.

Yet today our universe has expanded exponentially on scientific, cultural, and religious levels. We know there are multiple solar systems, and we regularly meet, come to value, and learn from, those who believe differently from us. No longer can a rational person believe that his or her group is the exclusive center of humanity, moral excellence, or theological truth—and returning to premodern innocence means turning one's back on God's universe and His creatures. Often this attempt at willful blindness generates cognitive dissonance, frustration and uncontrolled rage when God's real pluralistic universe inevitably intrudes.[18]

Greenberg's acknowledgement of the validity of other religions and advocacy of covenantal pluralism has led some to see him as a relativist and accuse him of violating normative Jewish belief. Evidently his recognition that other religions can also possess spiritual worth and theological truth, that Judaism does not have monopoly on God's revelation, is too much for some traditional Jews to accept.

Yet, religious pluralism is no foreign idea to rabbinic thought or *Halakhah*. Long before modernity, the rabbis of the Talmud taught covenantal pluralism: *Torat Moshe*, the Sinaitic covenant with Moses with its 613 *mitsvot* applied to the Jewish people, while the Noahide covenant containing seven *mitsvot* applied to gentiles. Importantly, the rabbis acknowledged that just as the Torah is valid and sufficient for Jews, so too is the Noahide covenant and its *mitsvot* valid and sufficient for non-Jews, and that there is no need for gentiles to enter the Mosaic covenant for them to be loved by God or to gain a share in the world to come.[19] This covenantal pluralism is simply classic Judaism and time-honored *Halakhah* devoid of any hint of relativism.

Moreover, according to many halakhic authorities the definition of *avodah zarah*, too, is pluralistic. Most *ḥakhmei Ashkenaz* accepted one definition of *avodah zarah* for Jews (the violation of absolute monotheism), and a different one for gentiles. They ruled that any *shituf* (associationism) like the trinity that includes the Creator of Heaven and Earth—which constitutes *avodah zarah* for Jews—is not *avodah zarah* for gentiles and is a valid form of belief for them.[20]

Further still, the dialectical nature of *Halakhah* also exhibits pluralistic logic. Though there exists a procedural need to decide on one halakhic position over its opposition, in fact both are considered to possess truth.

---

18 This is Bernard Lewis's explanation for current Islamic frustration and violence. See Bernard Lewis, *What Went Wrong?* (New York: Oxford University Press, 2002).

19 *Tosefta Sanhedrin* 105a; and *MT*, Laws of Kings and Their Wars 8:11. See chapter 4 of this book.

20 See chapter 6 for a fuller explanation of this point.

The Talmudic rabbis proclaimed, "*Elu v'elu divrei Elokim Hayim*" ("Both are the words of the living God"). Finally, Isaiah announces to us a pluralistic understanding of God's elect and blessed: "Blessed be my people Egypt, My handiwork Assyria and My very own Israel" (Isa. 25:19). In all these instances, traditional Judaism endorsed pluralism regarding covenant, acceptable theology, and religious standards without any vestige of impermissible relativism.

Conflating Greenberg's covenantal pluralism and relativism is simply conceptual confusion. Relativism is the doctrine that points of view have no absolute truth or validity, only subjective value according to perception. Thus, relativism easily leads to the loss of the capacity to affirm any truth or standard. Yet Greenberg makes clear that for him (and for other Jews) Judaism is absolutely true and objectively binding. Judaism is a non-subjective truth for Jews, but one that stands alongside a plurality of other absolute truths in the universe. Greenberg has not been seduced by Plato's ghost. Unlike relativism, Greenberg's theological pluralism does not give up on absolutes or undermine their authority. It limits them so that they do not turn into instruments of intellectual, political, or religious oppression. As God is infinite, so is His truth open to manifold understandings. And as human beings are unique, so are their understandings of God unique. To know God perfectly or to define God definitively is to turn God into a mere object of human cognition and subordinate Him to our finite intellects.

The difference between principled pluralism and cognitively weak relativism was demonstrated dramatically by another pluralist theologian, Abraham Joshua Heschel. He was in the forefront of building cooperation and mutual appreciation between Christians and Jews during the Second Vatican Council in the early 1960s, and saw both Christianity and Judaism as valid ways to understand and worship God. He believed that "God is a pluralist"—that God wills for people to worship Him in different ways. Yet Heschel never wavered in his commitment to Judaism as the only true way for Jews to worship the God of Abraham, Isaac, and Jacob. He even traveled to the Vatican during Catholic deliberations over the correct formulation of *Nostra Aetate*, the Church document that was to lay out the new Catholic teachings about Jews and Judaism. Heschel firmly denounced any hint of conversion to Christianity appearing in the document or in proper Jewish-Christian relations. He poignantly—and bluntly—announced to Vatican officials, "If faced with the choice of baptism or the crematoria of Auschwitz, I would choose Auschwitz."[21] Greenberg's

---

21 Judith Hershcopf, "The Church and the Jews: The Struggle at Vatican Council II," *American Jewish Yearbook* (1965): 128; Reuven Kimmelman, "Rabbis Joseph B. Soloveitchik

insistence on the absolute correctness of Judaism for Jews augers for the same choice.

Idolatry Again

Greenberg's covenantal pluralism stands, then, midway between the relativism of no absolute truths and the absolutist monism that insists on only one religious truth for everyone. As a moderating position, it functions as the corrective to the evils of both extremes that lead to either theological anarchy or brutal repression.

In *The Brothers Karamazov,* Dostoevsky claimed that "without God, all is permitted." Without one absolute God determining good and evil, morality is impossible. Analogously, today's religious thinkers should ask, "Without universal religious truth is every conception of God permitted?" Under the pluralist principle, we must allow others to form their own idea of God without imposing our own limits upon them. Yet, if every form of worship is potentially legitimate—even if only for others—do pluralists not forfeit the right to criticize those who believe differently, even when they worship the God of death and destruction? How can theological pluralism not turn on itself and deny its believers the right to reject religious intolerance and violence?

It is here that we can see the need for R. Greenberg's conception of idolatry and the centrality of *Tselem Elokim* in his religious worldview. His concept of idolatry as human systems that claim to be absolute, that exercise no self-limitation and that leave no room for the other, establishes the limit of legitimate theological pluralism. And in doing so, it saves theological pluralism from becoming a false idol of its own. Without Greenberg's concept of idolatry, there would no logical way to distinguish between a valid religious worldview promoting the sanctity of every person and one that destroys other people in the name of God. Without the idolatry-limit, a principled pluralist would have no rational grounds for critiquing the religious imperialist who strives to violently impose his intolerant views on others.

But, ultimately, it is not idolatry's logical function that makes it essential to Greenberg's religious world or ours. Rather it is its role in steering persons away from delegitimizing others and the brutal carnage that absolutism brings

---

and Abraham Joshua Heschel on Jewish-Christian Relations," *Modern Judaism* 24 (2004): 255.

in its wake. Insisting that idolatry is an evil that must be avoided directs religious people to the path of God Who loves his creatures.

In a prophetic key, idolatry's inverse of covenantal pluralism teaches us to be partners with others who work to realize the biblical vision, the one where human beings flourish, where peace and cooperation reign and where different peoples recognize the Creator of Heaven and Earth—by whatever names they call Him and in whatever forms they worship Him. Again, we do well to cite Micah's prophetic vision:

> It shall be in the end of days that the mountain of the Lord shall be established on top of all mountains and shall be exalted above the hills. And peoples shall stream onto it. Many nations shall come, and say, "Come let us go up to the mountain of the Lord and to the house of the God of Jacob; and He will teach us His ways and walk in His paths. For the Torah shall go forth from Zion, and the word of the Lord from Jerusalem." They shall beat their swords into plowshares and their spears into pruning hooks. Nation shall not lift up sword against nation, nor shall they learn war anymore. But every man shall sit under his vine and his fig tree; and none shall make him afraid. . . . For let all people walk, each in the name of his God and we will walk in the name of the Lord our God for ever and ever. (Micah 4:1–5)

Greenberg stands with four other great modern Jewish pluralists, all of whom have had a profound effect on contemporary Jewish thinking. Isaiah Berlin taught us the necessity of political pluralism for a free and open society. Abraham Joshua Heschel's poetic pluralism sensitized us to the essential role of spirituality in modern scientific material culture. Jonathan Sacks showed us the virtues of philosophic pluralism in a Jewish mode, while David Hartman detailed the necessity of pluralism for Israeli civil society.

Greenberg's covenantal pluralism is a conceptually rich, hopeful theology. It teaches us how to see the Image of God in the face of the Other and offers a way to work toward a future brighter than our dark conflicted past. With its absolute commitment to the Jewish covenant conjoined with accepting other religions affirming life and understanding, Greenberg's vision is the contemporary expression of Micah's ancient dream.

Both Micah and R. Greenberg teach that combining conviction and pluralism is no contradiction. On the contrary, it is spiritually necessary in our experience of God's diverse world, as well as in God's larger plan for sacred history.

Part Two

JUDAISM, JEWS, AND CHRISTIANITY

6

Rethinking Christianity: Rabbinic Positions and Possibilities

Introduction

One of the most pervasive conditions of modern life is empirical pluralism. Social, cultural, and religious diversities pursue us relentlessly today. The Emancipation of the eighteenth and nineteenth centuries moved most Western Jews out of their insulated ghettoes, granted them citizenship, and welcomed their participation in their mainstream national cultures, thus inevitably increasing their contact with gentile neighbors. In Europe and America, this meant closer, more harmonious, and more frequent interaction with Christians and Christianity. Even Jewish statehood, born out of the deep desire to free the Jewish people from subordination to gentiles, willy-nilly has brought about unprecedented requirements for Jewish interaction with Christians and Christianity. Israel now assumes sovereign responsibility for the welfare and rights of more than 160,000 individual Christian citizens as well as numerous churches in its midst. And as the visits to Israel of Popes John Paul II in 2000, Benedict XVI in 2009, and Francis in 2021 have demonstrated, Israelis now must interact with church officials to find respectful relations and common ground. This is true not only in the realm of *realpolitik*, but also in religious domain, as delegates of the Israeli Chief Rabbinate meet regularly with high-level Vatican and Protestant clergy from abroad to dialogue on issues of mutual spiritual and practical concern.

Of course, Jews and Christians met in medieval times also, but modernity saturates us with pluralistic interaction of a frequency, intensity, and quality not experienced in the past. The contemporary forces for social diversity are inescapable, and avoiding the religious other is impossible for a modern Jew—of any stripe.

The European Enlightenment created a vast secular space for the citizens of the new world. Since the French Revolution, Jews and Christians have been meeting, speaking, and cooperating with each other in the offices of their professions, the corridors of government, the lecture halls of universities and the public areas of their cities primarily as fraternal secularists. They have been pluralists who all too often were willing to trade their religious identities for the dream of social equality and mutual dignity. Judah Leib Gordon's famous nineteenth-century advice "Be a Jew in your home and a man outside it," was the watchword of many Enlightenment Jews even prior to Gordon. From then until today, even when they met *qua* Jews and Christians, religion was often left behind. There is more than a little truth to the quip that the founding American members of the National Conference of Christians and Jews were Christians who didn't believe in Christianity and Jews who didn't believe in Judaism. Needless to say, they agreed on much.

None of this bargain with modern secular life can work for Jewish theology or religious Jews who seek to shape their life experience into a wholistic and coherent worldview. For them there is no secular space or naked public square, no experience devoid of religious meaning or human relationship unshaped by their Jewish values and halakhic worldviews. In the words of the preeminent twentieth century Orthodox philosopher, R. Joseph B. Soloveitchik, "God claims the whole, not a part of man, and whatever He established as an order within the scheme of creation is sacred."[1] If so, a contemporary Jewish theology needs to formulate a coherent and sober understanding of Christianity and

---

1   Joseph B. Soloveitchik, "Confrontation," *Tradition* 6, no. 2 (1964), note 8. R. Soloveitchik also emphasized this in 1971 in his conversation with Cardinal Johannes Willebrands: "All dialogue between Jews and Christians cannot but be religious and theological. . . . Can we speak otherwise than on the level of religion? Our culture is certainly a religious one." *Fifteen Years of Catholic-Jewish Dialogue 1970–1985* (Vatican City: International Catholic-Jewish Liaison Committee, 1988), 273. Yet even R. Soloveitchik may have briefly fallen into the cultural trap of advocating meeting others on secular grounds. In "Confrontation," which explored the correct parameters of Jewish-Christian dialogue, he initially advocated interfaith cooperation in "secular orders." Realizing this problematic language, he qualified it as "popular semantics" in note 8 of the essay "Confrontation," found in the journal *Tradition*, and in the later "Addendum to the Original Edition of 'Confrontation'" added the following: "Rabbis and Christian clergymen cannot discuss socio-cultural and moral problems as sociologists, historians or cultural ethicists in agnostic or secularist categories. As men of God, our thoughts, feelings, perceptions and terminology bear the imprint of a religious world outlook" (*A Treasury of Tradition*, accessed April 28, 2022,

Christian belief today. What are theologically oriented Jews to make of their Christian neighbors and colleagues, particularly the pious among them who no longer seek to undermine Judaism or the Jewish people? Can Jews see the Image of God in the face of a believing Christian? And can Jewish theology understand contemporary Christianity as a positive religious and spiritual phenomenon, particularly within the context of traditional *Halakhah*?

Since religion has surged back into the forefront of contemporary culture and politics, investigating the possibility of relating to gentiles *on religious grounds* assumes added significance for Jews who are unapologetic about appreciating the pluralism and blessings of modern life, and who look to Jewish tradition, thought, and *Halakhah* to shape their attitudes and experiences. A mature Jewish theology need not feel defensive about such an inquiry. Moreover, many Christians are now actively seeking to enhance their own identity through deepening their understanding of Judaism and theological reconciliation with the Jewish people and their faith. Thus, for a variety of spiritual and empirical factors, developing an understanding of contemporary Christians and Christianity remains a compelling post-Emancipation challenge, for both contemporary Judaism and for Jews who search for God in every corner of their experience and are committed to an integrated spiritual *Weltanschauung*.

Preliminary Observations

We should bear in mind a number of points regarding a contemporary analysis of Christians and Christianity. First, Jewish consideration of Christianity today is theologically and halakhically different from the issue that faced Jewish authorities at the time of Jesus and the first century of the Common Era. This is due to the fundamental theological break that occurred among Jewish Christians sometime after the death of Jesus. During this period, a new belief arose that the teachings of Jesus no longer fit into mainstream Judaism as then practiced. Instead, the later thinking claimed that belief in Jesus *replaced* obedience to the commandments of the Torah (*mitsvot*) as the way to reach God, thus rendering the Jewish covenant no longer valid.[2] Belief in Jesus was

---

       https://traditiononline.org/confrontation-addendum). For a full analysis of "Confrontation" and his arguments relating to interfaith activity, see chapter 8.
2   This teaching later became known as "supersessionism." While traditional scholarship and teachings maintained that Paul introduced this nullification of the Jewish commandments ("the Law") for Jews, much recent scholarship claims that Paul advocated that Jews

alleged to reflect a new, more mature, covenant and constituted a different religious testimony pointing to a different revelation and path to salvation. With this development, Christian belief ceased being a tolerable deviance within the Jewish community and became an intolerable heresy for Judaism and its rabbinical authorities. Bitter feuds broke out, and Jewish Christians became *minim*, sectarian apostates to be excluded from the Jewish community.[3] At that point the two communities began to part ways and develop independent calendars, *sancta*, traditions, and theologies.

Yet something else occurred that simultaneously mitigated the strains. When Saul of Tarsus exported Christianity to the gentiles of the Roman Empire, he transformed the disagreement from an internal Jewish argument to an external one. Christianity then ceased being primarily a heretical strain of Judaism and became an independent gentile religion. Later, the conversion of Constantine and the Council of Nicea in the fourth century formally established Christianity and its doctrines as a different religion from Judaism, one predominantly for gentiles. Theoretically, this made it easier for Jews to reconsider Christianity, since, according to the Jewish law, confronting Jewish heresy is different from the logic of evaluating gentile religions. After the separation, the crucial Jewish question changed from "How shall we deal with heresy?" to "How can Judaism regard gentile Christians and their religion?"

Second, in our time most Christian churches have changed their official teachings about Jews and Judaism. Since the Second Vatican Council convened in 1962, Catholic and Protestant thinkers have generated a robust literature of new Christian theology toward Judaism and the Jewish people. The genesis of this transformation was the Holocaust and its near successful Final Solution for the Jews in Europe. For Jews, the *Shoah* was a searing physical tragedy from which the Jewish people is still recovering; and for Christians, the Holocaust caused a deep theological and moral trauma. Something in Christendom had gone undeniably wrong and Christian thinkers recoiled from what had been wrought. Reflection on this unimaginable evil that took root so easily in the

---

continue to observe the *mitsvot*, and only gentiles do not need the commandments for salvation. See Alan Segal, *Paul the Convert* (New Haven, CT: Yale University Press, 1992); E. P. Sanders, *Paul and Palestinian Judaism* (Minneapolis: Augsburg Fortress, 1977); James D. J. Dunn, *Paul and the Mosaic Law* (Grand Rapids, MI: Eerdmans, 2001); and Krister Stendahl, *Paul among Jews and Gentiles* (Minneapolis: Augsburg Fortress, 1976).

3   See James Parkes, *The Conflict of the Church and the Synagogue* (New York: Atheneum, 1969), ch. 1–3, Lawrence Shiffman, *Who was a Jew? Rabbinic and Halakhic Perspectives on the Jewish-Christian Schism* (Jersey City, NJ: KTAV, 1985), ch. 7, and Paula Fredriksen, *When Christians Were Jews* (New Haven: Yale University Press, 2018).

heart of Christian culture was the impetus for Christians to reappraise their tortured history and theology regarding Jews. Over the past sixty years, this reassessment process has spawned a discussion no less remarkable for its content than for its quantity. One Catholic religious thinker summed up this theological revolution in the Church by calling it "the six R's": (1) the repudiation of antisemitism, (2) the rejection of the charge of deicide, (3) repentance after the *Shoah*, (4) recognition of Israel, (5) review of teaching about Jews and Judaism, and (6) rethinking of proselytizing Jews.[4] Judged in light of traditional Christian teachings, current normative Christian theologies constitute a revolution with respect to their spiritual and historical Jewish patrimony. The Second Vatican Council's proclamation, *Nostra Aetate*,[5] in 1965 proved to be a point of departure for a Christian journey from which there has been no return.[6]

This profound Christian transformation opens up new possibilities for a fresh contemporary Jewish theological approach to Christianity, and has had a dramatic salutary effect in the last sixty years on how Jews can relate on an empirical level to religious Christians. This is possible because neither normative Jewish law, nor Jewish theology, nor Jewish attitudes towards Christians and their faith are wholly dogmatic or theoretical. Throughout history they have been influenced by what Christian doctrine says about Judaism and Jews and, perhaps more significantly, how Christians related to Jews in the economic, social, and political conditions of different eras. In short, Jewish theology about Christianity is partially rooted in the different experiences of the Jewish people with the Church.

---

4   Mary Boys, *Has God Only One Blessing?* (New York: Publisher, 2000), 247–266.
5   The text of *Nostra Aetate* can be found at JCRelations.net, http://www.jcrelations.net/en/?item=2552.
6   Two events dramatically indicate this change in Christian attitude about Jews and Judaism. Before the First Zionist Congress in 1897, an article appeared in the official Vatican periodical, *Civilta Cattolica*, explaining that Jews are required to live as servants in exile until the end of days, a fate to be avoided only by their conversion to Christianity. So when Theodore Herzl approached Pius X in 1904 to enlist his support for the Jewish return to Zion, the pope declined: "It is not in our power to prevent you to go to Jerusalem, but we will never give our support. As the head of the Church, I cannot give you any other answer. The Jews do not recognize our Lord, hence we cannot recognize the Jewish people. When you come to Palestine, we will be there to baptize all of you." (*The Diary of Theodore Herzl*, ed. Marvin Leventhal [New York: Dial, 1956], 429–430.) By contrast, in March 2000, Pope John Paul II made an official visit to Israel, met with the Jewish State's President and Chief Rabbis, and prayed at Jerusalem's Western Wall for the welfare of the Jewish people as his elder brothers who remain the people of God's covenant.

Third, we have seen in chapter 1 that, while the written Torah generally paints a negative picture of the gentile nations,[7] the Bible and the Talmudic rabbis expanded the idea of the stranger (*ger*) and conceptualized it into a broad legal and moral category, demanding that Jews protect people in this category and relate to them with moral responsibility.[8] As we have seen, the *ger* is a person who accepts basic morality, the seven Noahide commandments: the six prohibitions of murder, theft, sexual immorality, idolatry, eating the limb of a live animal (a paradigm for cruelty and devaluation of life), and blasphemy against the single God of the universe, as well as the one positive injunction to set up courts of law that will justly enforce these six prohibitions. All gentiles who live under these basic laws of civilization are considered to be worthy *benei Noah*.[9] Thus the Talmudic tradition split the gentile world into two subcategories: the immoral heathen practicing an illicit and intolerable religion, and the positively regarded Noahides[10] whom Jews are obligated to protect and sustain. This revolutionized the biblical view of humanity from a largely binary one, of Jews and evil gentiles, to a tripartite conceptualization of Jews, worthy gentiles (*benei Noah*), and heathens.

Judaism thus maintains a double covenant theology: Jews stand obligated as partners with God in one divine covenant containing 613 commandments, while gentiles stand under the divine covenant of the seven Noahide *mitsvot*. As we have seen, each covenant is valid for its respective adherents and there is no compelling theological or moral need for Noahides to convert and join the Jewish covenant. Noahides participate in an independently authentic covenant that prescribes a separate, valid, and religiously valuable way of life. In rabbinic tradition, they are accorded positive status—even to the extent that gentiles who faithfully keep the Noahide commandments are regarded by God as more beloved than Jews who violate the fundamentals of their covenant of

---

7 In Genesis, the gentiles are immoral pagans with whom the Partriarchs interact. In Exodus, gentiles are the brutal Egyptians and Amalekites. In Leviticus, the gentiles are those who engage in abominable practices. In Deuteronomy, the gentiles are the seven idolatrous Canaanite nations.

8 *Tosefta Avodah Zarah* 8:4; and *MT*, Laws of Kings and Their Wars 9:1. See chapter 3.

9 *MT*, Laws of Kings and Their Wars 8:10.

10 The term *benei Noah* or "Noahide" is used in rabbinic literature in two different senses. Technically, all gentiles are Noahides and stand under the seven Noahide commandments, whether they observe them or violate them. However, the term is frequently applied to only those who observe the Noahide commandments as contrasted with those who violate those commandments, that is, idolaters or *ovdei avodah zarah*.

613 commandments.[11] Rabbinic tradition paid some of these gentiles the ultimate theological compliment by teaching that "righteous gentiles have a share in the world to come."[12]

The last point is significant and presents a critically important theological asymmetry with traditional Christian teaching. As indicated, rabbinic Judaism taught that the Jewish covenant was not the sole valid religion or path to salvation. Judaism possesses a natural theological openness that flows from this double covenant theory. A gentile need not believe in Jewish theology or practice what Jews practice to be in holy relation with God. By contrast, until recently Christianity never accepted any such theory. The normative teaching was "*extra ecclesiam nulla salus*," that Christianity is the exclusive path to salvation and those not subscribing to Christian belief lack a true relationship with God.[13] Hence Christianity has been historically keen on conversion, for without conversion those outside the church are lost theologically—both in this world and in the world to come.

Jewish Law and Christianity

In the eyes of *Halakhah*, is Christianity within the category of invalid form of gentile worship or is it an authentic, licit religion that conforms to the seven Noahide commandments? Interestingly, the Talmudic rabbis do not discuss this question.[14] There is only one explicit reference to the theological status of *gentile* Christians in the Talmud, and rabbinic opinions dispute whether this text refers to Christianity or to a separate Persian cult.[15]

Yet, the theological status of Christianity was discussed at length in the Middle Ages, when two well-known and fundamentally opposing views arose. One is that of Maimonides in twelfth century Moslem Spain and North Africa.

---

11 R. Jacob Emden, *Seder Olam Rabbah*, cited in translation by Oscar Z. Fasman, "An Epistle on Tolerance by a 'Rabbinic Zealot,'" in *Judaism in a Changing World*, ed. Leo Jung (New York: Soncino, 1971).

12 BT *Sanhedrin* 105a; *MT*, Laws of Repentance 3:5, and Laws of Kings and Their Wars 8:11. For an extended discussion of the topic of salvation for righteous gentiles, see chapter 4.

13 Whereas the early interpretation of this principle was that those not subscribing to Catholic belief were disqualified from eternal salvation, the more recent normative interpretation allows for some non-Christians to be saved, as "anonymous Christians." See *Catechism of Catholic Church*, 2nd ed. (Vatican City: Libreria Editrice Vaticana, 1997), part 1, §§846–848.

14 See Louis Jacobs, "Attitudes towards Christianity in Halakhah" [Hebrew], in *Gevuroth ha-Romah*, ed. Z. Falk (Jerusalem: Mesharim, 1987), XIX.

15 BT *Avodah Zarah* 7b; and Meiri, *Beit ha-Behirah, ad loc.*

We saw previously that he believed that Christianity constituted *avodah zarah*—foreign and illicit worship, often connoting idolatry.[16] To many moderns this may sound strange, but it was quite logical to Jews in the Middle Ages who were grounded in biblical and Talmudic theology. Christianity violated the second commandment of the Decalogue, that is, the prohibition against making graven images of God. Moreover, Christians venerated saints and prayed to intermediaries such as Mary, religious characteristics largely foreign to Jewish theology and practice. Yet, for Maimonides, the deepest problems of Christianity were the doctrines of the trinity and the incarnation.[17] Maimonides insisted that monotheism must be pure, and that any understanding of God that denied the absolute unity of God violated God's essence.[18] As a student of Aristotle's metaphysics, Maimonides maintained that to predicate any division of God is to imply that God is physical, limited, and imperfect, that is, it is not God at all.[19] For Maimonides, to proclaim "Hear O Israel, the Lord our God, the Lord is One" is to understand that God is not only one, but an absolutely unique, indivisible and simple Being—and this understanding is incumbent on Jew and gentile alike. Hence, the trinitarian object of Christian worship could never be identical with the single Creator of the universe, and was necessarily some foreign concept. Since one of the seven Noahide commandments is the prohibition of *avodah zarah*, Maimonides ruled that Christians were sinful Noahides, and that their religion was illicit.

The other rabbinic opinion was that of Rabbi Mena<u>h</u>em Meiri in thirteenth- and fourteenth-century Provence. In his commentary on BT *Avodah Zarah* and elsewhere, Meiri taught that *avodah zarah* was not primarily theological or philosophical, and the negation of God's absolute unity does not *ipso facto* represent a God foreign to Judaism or constitute idolatry.[20] If seen from the perspective of the Bible rather than from Aristotelian philosophy, *avodah zarah* is cultic worship whose primary characteristic is the absence of moral demands upon its worshipers. Illicit religion is represented by those religions that do not

---

16   Commentary on *Mishna Avodah Zarah* 1:3–4; *MT*, Laws of Idolatry 9:4 (Kafih ed.).
17   For further elaboration on this, see Alon Goshen Gottstein's essay, "Encountering Hinduism: Thinking through *Avodah Zarah*," in *Jewish Theology and World Religions*, ed. Alon Goshen Gottstein and Eugene Korn (Oxford: Littman Library of Jewish Civilization, 2012), 263–298.
18   *Guide* I:50.
19   *MT*, Laws of the Foundations of Torah 1:7.
20   See recent scholarship: Katz, *Exclusiveness and Tolerance*, ch. 10; Halbertal, *Bein Torah l'<u>H</u>okhmah*, ch. 3. For an English translation of Halbertal, see his "Ones Possessed of Religion."

impose the prohibitions of murder, theft, sexual immorality, and cruelty upon its adherents, that is, they neither insist upon the Noahide commandments nor satisfy the Noahide covenant.[21] Meiri claimed that while trinitarian Christianity may violate pure monotheism, it is not *avodah zarah* because it worships the single Creator of heaven and earth and requires Christians to subscribe to the basic moral norms of civilization. Hence, Christians fulfill the Noahide covenant and Christianity is an autonomously valid religious form.

It is crucial to note the impact of experience on these opinions of Jewish law and theology.[22] Maimonides never had any positive firsthand experience with Christians to counteract his philosophical conclusions. Except for his brief stay in Crusader Palestine, he did not live with Christians and his understanding of Christianity came exclusively from books. Unlike Maimonides, Meiri lived in Christian society in an era of relatively good Jewish-Christian relations in the latter part of his life. Meiri encountered believing Christians as living human beings, discussed religion with Christian priests and understood that Christians could be moral and religiously sophisticated people.[23] It made no sense to him to categorize them as idolators, identical to the pagans to which the Bible and the Talmud refer. Also crucial were the demographic and political realities of the medieval Jewish communities in Christian Europe. Historians agree that the pressing communal, economic, and social conditions throughout Germany and France of that period influenced Meiri's legal opinion—and those of most rabbinic authorities in Ashkenaz—toward Christianity, effecting a more permissive halakhic attitude regarding Jewish contacts with Christians of that period.[24]

Life gave Meiri what it never gave Maimonides, namely the incentive to rule as a point of Jewish law that Christians did not practice idolatry or "foreign worship." Meiri understood the deep implications of his thesis, going as far as to include Christians in the biblical category of "brother."[25] In doing so Meiri achieved a conceptual transformation of *avodah zarah* within Jewish law, one

---

21 Meiri, *Beit ha-Behirah, Sanhedrin* 57a and *Avodah Zarah* 20a.
22 On this point, see also Adin Steinsalz as quoted in Goshen-Gottstein, "Encountering Hinduism," 284.
23 Menahem Meiri, *Hibur ha-Teshuvah*, ed. A. Schreiber (New York: Hotsa'at Talpiyot, 1950), 2. I thank Prof Greg Stern for calling my attention to this text. See also Katz, "The Vicissitudes of Three Apologetic Statements," 119, 124; Salo Baron, *A Social and Religious History of the Jews* (New York: Columbia University Press, 1960), IX, 5–11; and *Encyclopedia Judaica* 13:1260–1261.
24 Katz, "The Vicissitudes of Three Apologetic Statements," 116–117.
25 Meiri, *Beit ha-Behirah, Bava Metsi'a* 59a.

rich in implications for the contemporary interpretation of the Jewish understanding of Christians and their faith.

In fact, however, neither the ruling of Maimonides regarding Christianity nor the exact view of Meiri represents normative *Halakhah*. *Inter alia*, Maimonides ruled that *ab initio* a Jew is forbidden to reside in or even traverse a city where a church is located[26]—a prohibition that no Jew, however scrupulous about adhering to *Halakhah*, honors today. And we will soon see that no other authority accepts Meiri's opinion regarding the status of a Jewish convert to Christianity. In point of fact, these two authorities represent end points of the spectrum of rabbinic positions, while the majority of halakhic opinions lie within two intermediate categories. The opinions in the first intermediate category maintain that the traditional legal prohibitions regarding Jewish contact with worshippers of *avodah zarah* and the economic halakhic discriminations against those who practice *avodah zarah* do not apply to contact with Christians. This position—that Jewish law does not consider Christians to be worshippers of *avodah zarah*—is held by R. Yosef Karo (sixteenth-century Turkey and Tsefat)[27] and virtually all the great rabbinic authorities living in European Christian societies (*hakhmei Ashkenaz*) including Rashi (eleventh-century France),[28] R. Asher Ben Yehiel (also known as Rosh, thirteenth-century Germany),[29] and early modern authorities (*aharonim*).[30] These authorities left open the possibility, however, that Christianity might still be *avodah zarah* and forbidden for gentiles.[31] And they certainly believed that Christianity was wrong for Jews, such that it is incumbent upon a Jew to die rather than to convert to Christianity.

The opinions in the second intermediate category claim that Christians are not adherents of *avodah zarah* precisely *because* Christianity as a system

---

26 Rambam, commentary on *Mishnah Avodah Zarah* 1:1–3.
27 Yosef Karo, *Shulhan Arukh, Yoreh De'ah* 148:2; and Beit Yosef, *Tur Shulhan Arukh, Hoshen Mishpat* 266.
28 *Responsa Rashi*, Elfenbein ed. (New York, 1943), vol. 1, nos. 55, 155, 327.
29 Commentary on BT *Avodah Zarah* 4:7.
30 See later authorities, P'ri Megadim, Mahtsits ha-Shekel, and Hatam Sofer, on *Orah Hayyim* 156; *Responsa Minhat Eliezer*, vol. 1, 53:3; and R. Samuel Landau, *Responsa Nodeh bi-Yehudah*, no. 148, all of whom rule that gentiles are obligated to be pure monotheists.
31 The legal possibility that Christianity is *avodah zarah*, yet Christians would not be considered worshippers of *avodah zarah*, is based on the opinion of R. Yohanan found in BT *Hulin* 13b: "Gentiles outside the land of Israel are not worshippers of *avodah zarah*, but only follow the traditions of their ancestors." Although the precise meaning of this statement is unclear, its legal import is not: gentiles in the Talmudic and post-Talmudic eras are not subject to the halakhic restrictions applicable to the worshippers of *avodah zarah*.

of belief and worship does not constitute *avodah zarah* for gentiles. While Christianity is not pure monotheism, in fact it represents a valid positive belief in the same One Creator of heaven and earth that Judaism requires Jews to worship. The distinction between one standard of *avodah zarah* for Jews and another for gentiles is exegetically based on the second commandment of the Decalogue (Ex. 20:3) addressed specifically to Jews at Sinai: "There shall not be *for you* other gods before Me." According to rabbinic tradition, idolatry had already been prohibited to gentiles and Noahides in Gen. 2:16, hence the commandment in Exodus requiring pure monotheism must address Jews uniquely ("for you") and not apply to gentiles.[32] In addition to Meiri, this was the halakhic position of medieval authorities (*rishonim*) such as R. Ya'akov ben Meir (Rabbeinu Tam, twelfth-century France),[33] and later authorities (*aharonim*) such as R. Moses Isserles (Remo, sixteenth-century Poland),[34] R. Shabtai

---

32 See R. Joseph Saul Nathanson, *Sho'el u-Meshiv* I:26 and 51; also R. Dov Baer ben Judah Treves, *Sefer Ravid ha-Zahav,* Ex. 20:3. See also R. Ovadia Yosef, *Yehaveh Da'at* 4:45 (footnote), who finds textual warrant for this position in book of Ruth and BT, Yebamot 47B.

33 A number of scholars believe that believe that this position is more accurately attributed to R. Isaac (Ri), the nephew of Rabbeinu Tam. See Katz, *Exclusiveness and Tolerance*, 35. Whether Rabbeinu Tam or R. Isaac, this is based on the majority interpretation of BT *Sanhedrin* 63b, s.v. "*assur.*" See David Novak, *Jewish-Christian Dialogue: A Jewish Justification* (New York: Oxford University Press, 1989), 42–53. For a comprehensive listing of later authoritative rabbinic opinions (*aharonim*) on this issue see Moshe Yehudah Miller, "Regarding The Law that Noahides are not Admonished against Associationism" [Hebrew], in *Torat Hayyim*, ed. Avraham Y. Mirsky and Avraham N. Hartman (New York: Yeshivat Or Ha-Hayyim, 2000), 169–179. For variant interpretations maintaining that Rabbeinu Tam believes that Christianity remains in the category of *avodah zarah*, see David Berger, *The Rebbe, The Messiah and The Scandal of Orthodox Indifference* (London: Littman Library of Jewish Civilization, 2001), appendix 3; and J. David Bleich, "Divine Unity in Maimonides, the Tosafists and Me'iri," in *Neoplatonism and Jewish Thought*, ed. Lenn E. Goodman (Albany, NY: SUNY Press, 1992), 239, who concedes that this variant reading is a minority opinion among later rabbinic authorities. It is important to note that even according to these minority interpretations of the Tosafot (whether Rabbeinu Tam or R. Isaac), Christianity differs in nature from *avodah zarah* of antiquity, since it recognizes as God the One Creator of Heaven and Earth, whereas classical *avodah zarah* recognized as gods entities wholly different from the Creator (Berger has termed the former, "*avodah zarah* in a monotheistic mode"). We thus arrive at a paradox: It is precisely these restrictive minority interpretations acknowledging the difference between classical and Christian *avodah zarah* forms that create the logical opening for not applying to Christianity the halakhic requirement of intolerance toward (classical) *avodah zarah* and its worshippers in *Erets Yisrael* under Jewish sovereignty. Berger correctly sees this logical implication and suggests such a policy. See David Berger, "Jews, Gentiles, and the Modern Egalitarian Ethos: Some Tentative Thoughts," in *Formulating Responses in an Egalitarian Age,* ed. Mark Stern (New York: Rowman and Littlefield, 2005), 101. This also appears to be the position of R. Isaac Herzog. See Isaac Herzog, "The Rights of Minorities according to *Halakhah*" [Hebrew], *Tehumin* 2 (1981): 174, n. 9.

34 Moses Isserles, *Darkhei Moshe* on Tur, *Orah Hayyim* 151; gloss on *Orah Hayyim* 156:1.

ha-Cohen (Shakh, seventeenth-century Bohemia),[35] R. Moses Rivkis (Ber ha-Golah, seventeenth-century Lithuania),[36] R. Yair Bacharach (seventeenth-century Germany),[37] R. Jacob Emden (Yavets, eighteenth-century Germany),[38] R. Yehezkel Landau (Nodeh bi-Yehudah, eighteenth-century Prague),[39] R. Tsvi Hirsch Hiyyus (nineteenth-century Galicia),[40] R. Avraham Borenstein (Avnei Nezer, nineteenth-century Poland),[41] R. Samson Raphael Hirsch (nineteenth-century Germany),[42] R. David Tsvi Hoffman (nineteenth-century Germany),[43] and others.[44]

Importantly, many of these later authorities go beyond the mere denial that Christianity is *avodah zarah*, and accord positive theological status to Christian belief. Here are the words of R. Rivkis:

> The gentiles in whose shadow Jews live and among whom Jews are disbursed are not idolators. Rather they believe in *creatio ex nihilo* and the Exodus from Egypt and the main principles of faith. Their intention is to the Creator of Heaven and Earth and we are obligated to pray for their welfare.[45]

---

35 Shabtai ha-Cohen, gloss on *Yoreh De'ah* 151:4.
36 Moses Rivkis, gloss on *Shulhan Arukh, Hoshen Mishpat* 425:5.
37 Yair Bacharach, *Responsa Havot Ya'ir*, nos. 1 and 185.
38 Jacob Emden, *Seder Olam Rabbah*, 35–37; Jacob Emden, *Sefer ha-Shimush*, 15–17.
39 Some scholars mistakenly identify Yehezkel Landau with his son, Samuel. The latter explicitly claimed that Christianity is *avodah zarah* for Christians because of its doctrine of the trinity (*Responsa Nodeh bi-Yehudah, Yoreh De'ah* 148). R. Samuel signs his name to this responsum; hence its authorship is not open to question. I thank Marc Shapiro for pointing this out to me. The father, Yehezkel, had a positive evaluation of Christian belief for Christians: "Regarding the nations of our day in whose midst we live, they believe in the fundamentals of faith, in creation and in the prophecy of the prophets and all the miracles and wonders that are written the Torah and the books of the prophets" (introduction to *Responsa Nodeh bi-Yehudah, Tinyama* ed.).
40 Tsvi Hirsch Hiyyus, *The Works of Maharats Hiyyus* (Jerusalem: Mossad Ha-Rav Kook, 1948), 66 and 489–490.
41 Avraham Borenstein, *Responsa Avnei Nezer*, no. 123:9.
42 Samson Raphael Hirsch, "Talmudic Judaism and Society," in his *Collected Writings*, vol. 7 (New York: Feldheim, 1992), 225–227; Samson Raphael Hirsch, *Nineteen Letters on Judaism*, ed. Joseph Elias (Jerusalem: Feldheim, 1995).
43 See his glosses to the beginning of the *The Shulhan Arukh*; and David Tsvi Hoffman, *Responsa Melamid le-Ho'el, Yoreh De'ah* 55.
44 This is also the explicit or implicit position of R. Meir Leib Ben Michael (Malbim), commentary on II Kgs. 17:7–9 and 41:32–34; R. Tsvi Hirsch Shapira, *Darkhei Teshuvah*, gloss on *Yoreh De'ah* 151:1, R. Ya'akov Ettinger, *Binyan Tsion*, responsum 63; R. Baruch Halevi Epstein, *Torah Temimah*, Ex. 21:35 and Deut 22:3.
45 Moses Rivkis, gloss on *Shulhan Arukh, Hoshen Mishpat*, section 425.

And R. Emden:

> The Nazarene brought a double goodness to the world.... The Christian eradicated *avodah zarah*, removed idols (from the nations) and obligated them in the seven *mitzvot* of Noah so that they would not behave like animals of the field, and instilled them firmly with moral traits.... Christians and Moslems are congregations that (work) for the sake of heaven—(people) who are destined to endure, whose intent is for the sake of heaven and whose reward will not denied.[46]
>
> The goal of (Christians and Moslems) is to promote Godliness among the nations, ... to make known that there is a Ruler in heaven and earth, Who governs and monitors and rewards and punishes.... We should consider Christians and Moslems as instruments for the fulfillment of the prophecy that the knowledge of God will one day spread throughout the earth. Whereas the nations before them worshipped idols, denied God's existence, and thus did not recognize God's power or retribution, the rise of Christianity and Islam served to spread among the nations, to the furthest ends of the earth, the knowledge that there is One God who rules the world, who rewards and punishes and reveals Himself to man. Indeed, Christian scholars have not only won acceptance among the nations for the revelation of the Written Torah but have also defended God's Oral Law. For when, in their hostility to the Torah, ruthless persons in their own midst sought to abrogate and uproot the Talmud, others from among them arose to defend it and to repulse the attempts.[47]

And R. Hirsch:

> Judaism does not say, "There is no salvation outside of me." Although disparaged because of its alleged particularism, the

---

46   Jacob Emden, *Seder Olam Rabah ve-Zutah*, 35-37. *Sefer Ha-shimush*, 15-17. For a fuller explanation of R. Emden's position, see Harvey Falk, "Rabbi Jacob Emden's Views on Christianity," *Journal of Ecumenical Studies* 19, no. 1 (Winter 1982); and Moshe Miller, "Rabbi Jacob Emden's Attitude toward Christianity," in *Turim, Studies in Jewish History and Literature*, vol. 2, ed. M. Shmidman (New York: Touro College Press, 2008), 105-136.

47   Jacob Emden, *Commentary on Ethics of the Fathers* 4:11.

Jewish religion actually teaches that the upright of all peoples are headed toward the highest goal. In particular, they have been at pains to stress that, while in other respects their views and ways of life may differ from those of Judaism, the peoples in whose midst the Jews are now living [that is, Christians] have accepted the Jewish Bible of the Old Testament as a book of Divine revelation. They profess their belief in the God of heaven and earth as proclaimed in the Bible and they acknowledge the sovereignty of Divine Providence in both this life and the next. Their acceptance of the practical duties incumbent upon all men by the will of God distinguishes these nations from the heathen and idolatrous nations of the Talmudic era.[48] Before Israel set out on its long journey through the ages and the nations, ... it produced an offshoot [Christianity] that had to become estranged from it in great measure, in order to bring to the world—sunk in idol worship, violence, immorality and the degradation of man—at least the tidings of the One Alone, of the brotherhood of all men, and of man's superiority over the beast. It was to teach the renunciation of the worship of wealth and pleasures, albeit not their use in the service of the One Alone. Together with a later offshoot [Islam] it represented a major step in bringing the world closer to the goal of all history.[49]

In the twentieth century, a number of rabbinic authorities did not rule officially on the halakhic status of Christianity for gentiles or whether Christianity was a positive religious phenomenon.[50] Yet, others in the twentieth century

---

48 Hirsch, "Talmudic Judaism and Society," 225–227.
49 Hirsch, *Nineteen Letters on Judaism*.
50 It appears that the American Orthodox leader R. Joseph Soloveitchik is in this category. I argued in chapter 8 that R. Soloveitchik's essay "Confrontation" is a statement of Jewish policy and because it is devoid of any halakhic language and argumentation it lacks halakhic status. R Soloveitchik wrote "Confrontation" before *Nostra Aetate* was proclaimed and before the dramatic changes in Christian teachings about Judaism and Jews. In this essay he argued on prudential grounds against Jewish participation in theological debate or dialogue with Christian theologians, but advocated cooperation with Christians in moral, social, and political areas. To my knowledge, he never issued a formal halakhic ruling on the status of Christianity for Christians. From his behavior, however, he could not have followed Maimonides, who outlawed residing in a city with a church (see Commentary on *Mishna Avodah Zarah* 1:3–4). Living in the largely Catholic metropolis of Boston, R. Soloveitchik delivered his spiritual confession, "The Lonely Man of Faith," at St. John's Catholic seminary in Brighton. There is also anecdotal evidence that while recuperating in a hospital he tried to persuade his secular doctor to return to his Christian faith, something

such as Rabbis Yehiel Halevi Epstein (Arukh ha-Shulḥan),[51] Abraham Isaac ha-Kohen Kook,[52] R. Yehiel Ya'akov Weinberg (Seridei Aish),[53] Isaac Herzog,[54] Hayim David Halevi,[55] Joseph Messas,[56] and Yosef Eliyahu Henkin[57] who regarded Christianity positively and concluded that it does not constitute *avodah zarah* for gentiles. Still others ruled so implicitly.[58]

Thus an accurate logical map of Jewish legal opinions indicates that nearly all rabbinic authorities living in Christian societies ruled that Christians cannot be identified with the idolators of antiquity and that the legal prohibitions attaching to biblical and Talmudic gentiles do not apply to contemporary Christians. Some *rishonim*, namely Meiri and Rabbeinu Tam, and the majority of *aḥaronim* had a more positive view of Christianity itself, ruling that it was a valid religion for gentiles, but not for Jews. Hence, there exists normative halakhic precedent for ruling that Christianity, *qua* religion, is a valid faith for gentiles, one that is beneficial to the world and that Jews can appreciate and

---

that Maimonides could not have done consistent with his view of Christianity being *avodah zarah* for everyone.

51 Yehiel Halevi Epstein, *Arukh Ha-Shulḥan, Oraḥ Ḥayyim* 156:4.

52 See Kook, *Letters*, vol. 1, no. 89 (1904), where he accepts the position of Me'iri and includes Christians (and Moslems) in the category of resident aliens, who do not practice *avodah zarah*.

53 Weinberg, who advocated unqualified acceptance of Meiri's position, considers pious Christians who follow the precepts of Christianity "to be blessed." See his letter to S. Atlas, October 26, 1964, cited in Marc Shapiro, *Between the Yeshiva and Modern Orthodoxy* (Portland, OR: Littman Library of Jewish Civilization, 1999), 182. See also *Li-Frakim* (Warsaw: Hotsa'at ha-Aggadah v'ha-Derush, 1936), 384, 386.

54 Herzog, "The Rights of Minorities according to *Halakhah*," *Teḥumim* 2 (1951) 174–175.

55 Hayim David Halevi, *Make a Teacher for Yourself* [Hebrew] (Tel Aviv: Committee for the Publications of Hayim David Halevi, 1989), part 5, 65–67; and Hayim David Halevi, "Paths of Peace in Relations between Jews and Non-Jews" [Hebrew], *Teḥumim* 9 (1958): 71–81. For a fuller analysis of Halevi's position on Christianity, see David Ellenson, "Rabbi Hayim David Halevi on Christianity and Christians," in *Transforming Relations: Essays on Jews and Christians throughout History in Honor of Michael Signer*, ed. Franklin T. Harkins (Notre Dame, IN: University of Notre Dame Press, 2010).

56 Joseph Messas, *Shemesh u-Magen* (Jerusalem: Machon Keter Shalom, 2000), vol. 3; Joseph Messas, *Sefer Mayyim Ḥayyim*, vol. 2, section 66.

57 See Berger, "Jews and Gentiles and the Modern Egalitarian Ethos," 100.

58 Marc Shapiro also notes ("Of Books and Bans," *The Edah Journal* 3, no. 2 [*Elul* 5763], www.edah.org) that one rabbinic authority permits Jews to contribute to the building of a church, on the assumption that Christian worship is not sinful for gentiles: R. Marcus Horowitz, *Matteh Levi* (Jerusalem: Y. Kaufmann, 1933), vol. 2, *Yoreh De'ah*, no. 28. See also David Ellenson, "A Disputed Precedent: The Prague Organ in Nineteenth-Century Central European Legal Literature and Polemics," *Leo Baeck Institute Yearbook* 40 (1995): 251–264; R. Isaac Unna, *Sho'alin ve-Dorshin* (Tel Aviv: M. Greenberg, 1964), no. 35; R. Yehudah Herzl Henkin, *Benei Vanim* (Jerusalem: Otsrot ha-Torah, 1997), vol. 3, no. 36.

encourage gentiles to practice. Given this spectrum of halakhic opinion, the decision to adopt the rabbinic position that regards Christianity negatively or the one that regards it as a positive theological phenomenon will likely depend on sociological, historical and ideological considerations that lie outside the domain of formal *Halakhah*. The religious orientation of contemporary Jews toward Christianity is most often dispositional (based on history or memory) or prudential (based on expectation of future consequences).

There is a significant philosophical implication of the second position that demands absolute monotheism of Jews but permits non-absolute monotheism for gentiles. Because it asserts one definition of "foreign worship" for Jews—one that includes associationism, i.e., the addition of another thing to the single Creator of heaven and earth—and yet another definition of *avodah zarah* for gentiles (worship of entities that exclude the one Creator of the universe), the halakhic concept of *avodah zarah* is better understood as a legal standard of unacceptable belief and behavior rather than as a concept implying a theological truth claim. Logically, ascribing a given property to a specific object is either correct or incorrect; it cannot be different for different persons. This is also true for what one predicates of God. Were the legal concept of *avodah zarah* to imply a philosophic truth claim (that *avodah zarah* constitutes an ontological error because it misidentifies something that is in fact not divine as God), the criterion for *avodah zarah* would of necessity be universal and undifferentiated for both Jews and gentiles. But according to most *aḥaronim*, Jewish law *does* rule that the same belief may be "foreign worship" for Jews when it is not so for gentiles. Hence, *avodah zarah* should be more properly understood as representing that which is beyond the limit of the legally tolerable—a standard that can vary for Jews and gentiles without entailing any conceptual incoherence.

A simple analogy can help clarify this point: According to Jewish law, eating pork is an act that is forbidden to Jews but permitted to gentiles. This is possible because the laws of *kashrut* do not refer to any inherent characteristic of pork. They merely lay down behavioral norms. So too, the laws relating to *avodah zarah* relate to norms and do not assert any inherent characteristic of God. This conceptualization of *avodah zarah* is true to its literal meaning of the term, for something can be "foreign" (that is, unacceptable) for one person or community, while not so to another. This conclusion has a crucial implication for theological pluralism: if the halakhic category of *avodah zarah* is a legal standard rather than a claim about theological (in)accuracy, then Jewish law does not take an ultimate metaphysical position regarding the nature of God and should be able to coexist with a limited number of contrasting theologies.

Finally, it is important to recognize that although Meiri is often used as a basis for this second intermediary position, he went beyond it, ruling that Christianity was not *avodah zarah* even for Jews.[59] This aspect of his position is accepted by no other rabbinic authority and therefore plays no role in normative Jewish legal opinion.

Except for Maimonides and Messas, the aforementioned rabbinic authorities encountered Christians within their experience as real human beings, not as stereotypes or abstract legal categories. It is hardly credible that their social, moral and interpersonal experiences with living Christians did not influence their halakhic and theological opinions. As cited earlier, there is no doubt that economic factors and Jewish commercial interaction with—and dependency on—their Christian neighbors in Ashkenaz also played a significant role in permissive rabbinic judgments toward Christians and Christianity.[60]

If one looks at this map temporally, one can plot four stages in the evolution of Jewish religious thinking about Christianity under different historical circumstances:

(1) In the first and second centuries, Jewish Christians came to be regarded as heretics (*minim*) or apostates from Judaism. Jewish belief in Jesus and the "new covenant" were considered *avodah zarah*.

(2) In the Middle Ages, when Jews lived in small communities in Christian Europe and were dependent on economic interaction with Christians, most *rishonim* in Ashkenaz ruled (in accordance with the Talmudic opinion of R. Yohanan previously cited) that Christians were not idolators, but they still considered belief in Christian doctrine to be illegitimate *avodah zarah*.

(3) In the late Middle Ages and early modernity, the majority of Western *aharonim* did not consider Christianity to be *avodah zarah* for non-Jews.

(4) From the seventeenth century through the twentieth century, when Christian toleration of Jews grew,[61] a number of rabbinic authorities

---

59 Meiri, *Beit ha-Behirah, Horayot*, 219 (Sofer ed.).
60 See Katz, *Exclusiveness and Tolerance*, ch. 3.
61 Katz advances the causal thesis that it was the budding Christian tolerance during this period that significantly influenced the development of a positive halakhic attitude toward Christians held by traditionalist Orthodox rabbis of the time: "The first signs of tolerance toward Jews gave rise to a corresponding attitude on the part of Jews to Christians" (Katz, "The Vicissitudes of Three Apologetic Statements," 166). It is evident from the statements

began to appreciate Christianity as a positive historical and theological phenomenon for gentiles that helped spread fundamental beliefs of Judaism (such as the beliefs in God, revelation, and Noahide commandments) and thus advanced the Jewish religious purpose.

Two points are critical. First, Jewish law regarding Christians and Christianity has undergone an evolution with changing historical circumstances. Second, *Halakhah* and traditional Jewish theology contain the seeds for a limited theological openness by recognizing the possibility of other valid religions and forms of worship. In principle, *Halakhah* allows for a positive view of Christianity (for gentiles).

Jewish historical experience with Christians cuts both ways, however. In spite of the open halakhic and theological possibilities toward Christianity, many historically oriented Jews have been reluctant to accord Christianity positive value because of the traditional Christian supersessionist teachings about Judaism that spawned virulent *Adversus Judeaos* Christian teachings. These teachings (later labeled "The Doctrine of Contempt" by Jules Isaac) denied any continuing theological validity to Judaism and promoted demonic understandings of Jews that were the basis for hateful antisemitic behavior throughout much of the Middle Ages. Contemporary scholars have uncovered the substantive influence that the *Adversus Judeaos* teachings have played in shaping antisemitic attitudes and antisemitic persecution throughout Jewish-Christian history, into modernity and including the Holocaust.[62] And for many Jews up to today—both rabbis and laity alike—the wounds of that suffering are still too fresh to allow for any religious re-evaluation of Christianity and its believers.

---

of Rivkis, Emden, and Ya'ir Bacharach (to which Katz is referring) that this positive attitude referred not only to Christians, but also to Christianity *qua* religious belief system.

62   Boys, *Has God Only One Blessing?*, ch. 4; James Carroll, *Constantine's Sword* (Boston: Houghton Mifflin, 2001); Edward Flannery, *The Anguish of the Jews* (Mahwah, NJ: Paulist Press, 1985); Malcolm Hay, *Europe and the Jews* (Boston: Beacon Press, 1992 [1960]); Jules Isaac, *Jesus & Israel* (New York: Holt, Rinehart, Winston, 1971); Jules Isaac, *The Teaching of Contempt: Christian Roots of Anti-Semitism* (New York: Generic, 1965); Joshua Trachtenberg, *The Devil and the Jews* (Philadelphia: Jewish Publication Society, 1984); Robert Wilken, *John Chrysostom and the Jews* (Portland, OR: Wipf and Stock, 2004).

Christianity and Judaism Today

Jews who wish to preserve—or perhaps recreate—pre-Emancipation social conditions and isolate themselves from positive relations with Christians will find refuge in the halakhic attitude of Maimonides and his disciples.[63] Yet after the thicket of legal obstacles is cleared, Jews who have been touched by modernity and who value openness to Western culture, dignified relations with Christians and appreciation of Christianity's moral and spiritual values can also find ample halakhic justification for their aspirations.

Of course, safeguarding Jewish identity demands limits on interaction with Christians and Christian culture. Without such limits in an open pluralistic society, assimilation is unavoidable and both Jews and Judaism are likely to be absorbed totally by the dominant Christian population and culture. Assuming such limits can be maintained, the salient question today for Jews regarding Christianity is: "Is Christianity today still a physical and theological threat to Jews and Judaism as in the past, or is it now be a potential spiritual and political ally?" If the former, attempts at developing a positive appreciation of Christianity may well imperil distinctive Jewish survival; if the latter, then a more open Jewish theology of Christianity is possible, even desirable.

In considering this question, we must examine contemporary Christianity in more detail. With the Second Vatican Council's proclamation of *Nostra Aetate* in 1965, the Catholic Church formally repudiated antisemitism, first "deploring" it categorically, and subsequently "condemning" it in official documents.[64] Later still, Pope John Paul II repeatedly labeled antisemitism "a sin against God and humanity."[65] Moreover, the condemnation of antisemitism is a tenet of every large Protestant church today, whether liberal or conservative.[66] At a time when antisemitism is widespread in the Islamic world, again burgeoning

---

63 As indicated above, this is a practical impossibility on a consistent basis for one who lives in a city or a culture containing Christians.
64 See *Guidelines and Suggestions for Implementing the Conciliar Declaration "Nostra Aetate"* (Vatican City: Commission for Religious Relations with the Jews, 1975), preamble and section 4 (hereafter, *Guidelines*); and *Notes on the Correct Way to Present the Jews and Judaism in Preaching and Teaching in the Roman Catholic Church* (Vatican City: Commission for Religious Relations with the Jews, 1985), section 6, no. 26 (hereafter, *Notes*).
65 Papal statements in Fall 1990 and Winter 1991, cited in *Vatican City Pontifical Council on Christian Unity: Information Service* 75, no. 4 (1990): 172–178; and papal address, Hungary, August 16, 1991, cited in *Origins* 21, no. 13 (September 5, 1991): 203.
66 See, for instance, the denunciation of antisemitism by statements of the World Council of Churches in its first (Amsterdam, 1948) and third (New Delhi, 1961) assemblies, or the 1994 statement by the Evangelical Lutheran Church in America, which repudiated Martin

in Europe and America, and no longer an embarrassment in radical European leftist circles and in academia, official Christian rejection of antisemitism functions as a strong positive force throughout the world.

Nostra Aetate also formally rejected the ancient charge of deicide, which was the primary theological basis for so much violence against, and contempt for, the Jewish people. It is important to understand that the document did not "forgive" the Jews for deicide—it rejected any basis for the charge. Once again, nearly every Protestant denomination has followed suit. Nor did many churches stop at repudiating this noxious doctrine: many have issued profound statements of repentance for their role in antisemitism and the *Shoah*.[67]

The Vatican established diplomatic relations with the State of Israel in 1994 and today virtually every major Protestant church officially recognizes the right of Israel to live in safety and security. After the Holocaust, many Jews today consider Israel and its blessings of sovereignty and effective self-defense capacities to be the best security that Jews have for a future that is more hopeful than the past. Thus widespread Christian recognition of Israel increases the prospects for Jewish safety and security.

Yet, part of the Christian picture regarding Israel remains troubling. Some mainline Protestant churches' criticism of Israel and hostile liberal church actions such as divestment from companies doing business with Israel are sources of deep concern.[68] Although no government policy anywhere should be immune from moral critique—particularly from religious leaders—Jews of all political orientations cannot ignore the possibility that the vehement and unbalanced Protestant criticisms of Israel are rooted in traditional Christian biases against Jews and Judaism. Because Israel is the public face of the Jewish

---

Luther's antisemitic statements. All statements are available on JCRelations.net, www.jcrelations.net. See also Boys, *Has God Only One Blessing?*, 253–255.

67 See *We Remember: A Reflection on the Shoah*, issued by the Vatican in March 1998; *Statement of the German Catholic Bishops on the 50th Anniversary of the Liberation of the Extermination Camp at Auschwitz*, January 27, 1995; *Declaration of Repentance by the Roman Catholic Bishops of France*, September 30, 1997; and Pope John Paul II's statement in his visit to Yad Vashem Museum in Jerusalem in March 2000 (quoted later in chapter 8). All can be found on JCRelations.net, http://www.jcrelations.net. For Protestant documents, see Boys, *Has God Only One Blessing?*, 256.

68 The World Council of Churches and the Presbyterian Church USA are in the forefront of such anti-Israel campaigns. In 2014 Rev. Jerry Pillay, who was elected head of the WCC in 2022 published a paper accusing Israel of committing apartheid. In early 2022, the stated clerk of PCUSA, J. Herbert Nelson II, claimed that Israel practices "modern-day slavery" and in July 2022 PCUSA formally accepted a resolution terming Israeli policies "(racist) apartheid."

people today—indeed, the "body" of the Jewish people—unjust attitudes toward Israel often indicate a continuing underlying animus to Jews and the Jewish people.

These attitudes are most obvious when Jews possess power and lay claim to national equality. A prime offender is the politically driven school of Palestinian Liberation Theology,[69] which has found its way to sympathetic ears of many liberal Protestant churches in Europe and America. This thinking leads quickly to replacement theology that substitutes oppressed people (read: Palestinians) for the Jewish people as God's partners in the biblical covenant. Their theology assaults the Jewish covenant, the Bible, and the very legitimacy of Israel and Jewish peoplehood. Jews rightly understand this as a rejection of the recent salutary changes in Christian theology and a reversion to the traditional Christian denial of Judaism that is antisemitic at its core.[70] It is important to note that the Catholic Church has no connection to the Palestinian Liberation Theology and little enthusiasm for liberation theology of any kind.

More common are some American national Protestant Church positions on the Middle East conflict. While recognizing the right of Israel to exist, they identify nearly exclusively with Palestinian arguments and are so critical of Israeli defensive actions that it is difficult to see any serious concern for the welfare of Israel or individual Israelis. Moreover, their explicit or tacit support for the Boycott, Divestment, and Sanction movement (BDS) has encouraged antisemitism, both in attitude and action.[71] Such unjust criticisms undermine the security of Israel and raise the historical specter of Christians again striving to render Jews defenseless and celebrating Jewish victimization. Given the violent past, Jews today are particularly vigilant about this possibility. Unlike the national church leadership, the majority of Christians in America and many in Europe are strongly sympathetic to Israel and reject this hostile view.[72] Yet, all Christians need to better understand that national independence is constitutive of Judaism, that it is essential to the Jewish understanding of the Jewish

---

69 See Naim Ateek, *Justice and Only Justice* (Maryknoll, NY: Orbis, 1989); and Mitri Raheb, *I am a Palestinian Christian* (Minneapolis: Augsburg Fortress, 1995).
70 See Adam Gregerman, "Old Wine in New Bottles: Liberation Theology and the Israeli-Palestinian Conflict," *Journal of Ecumenical Studies* 41 (2004).
71 See my "BDS has Failed," *First Things*, April 2018, https://www.firstthings.com/article/2018/04/bds-has-failed.
72 See my monograph, *Divestment from Israel, the Liberal Churches, and Jewish Responses: A Strategic Analysis* (Jerusalem: Jerusalem Center for Public Affairs, 2007), http://www.JCPA.org/jcpa/JCPA/Templates/ShowPage.asp?DBID=1&LNGID=1&TMID=111&FID=254&PID=0&IID=1421.

people's biblical covenant with God, that for most Jews Israel is an existential issue rather than a mere political interest, and that serious Christian support for Israeli security is a *sine qua non* for good faith relations with the Jewish people.

Notwithstanding the liberal Christian criticism of Israel, the transformations achieved by official Catholic and Protestant renunciations of antisemitism and anti-Judaism have significance beyond politics. The Second Vatican Council radically changed the theological posture of the Catholic Church towards the Jewish people, and helped stimulate the change in Protestant theology.[73] Later, the Church rejected the old doctrine of hard supersessionism—in which Christianity entirely *replaced* Judaism—by acknowledging the living and autonomous validity of Judaism.[74] (Hence some Christians no longer speak of the "Old Testament," but of the "First Testament," "Hebrew Scriptures," or "Shared Scriptures" to ensure there is no linguistic implication that the Jewish covenant has fallen into obsolescence and is no longer valid.) Church recognition of Israel also has theological implications: it willy-nilly vitiates the doctrines of the early church fathers that the Jewish people lost all rights to their biblical homeland because they rejected Jesus as the messiah and that God decreed that Jews wander throughout Christendom in abject humiliation because Jews bear the curse of Cain as collective punishment for deicide.[75] These early teachings not only provided the basis for historical discrimination against Jews in Christian societies, but also fueled the polemic against the continuing spiritual integrity of Judaism. They are now both implicitly and explicitly repudiated by most churches. Although it is sometimes stated in nuanced or implicit fashion, some Christian theologians now appear to accept their own

---

73 For overviews of the changes in Christian doctrine, see Boys, *Has God Only One Blessing?*; Eugene Fisher and Leon Klenicki, eds., *In Our Time: The Flowering of Jewish-Catholic Dialogue* (New York: Paulist Press, 1990); and chapter 8.

74 The latest and most explicit official Church reference to this rejection of supersessionism is the Vatican's 2015 paper, *The Gifts and the Calling of God Are Irrevocable: A Reflection on Theological Questions Pertaining to Catholic-Jewish Relations on the Occasion of the 50th Anniversary of "Nostra Aetate"* (No. 4), https://ccjr.us/dialogika-resources/documents-and-statements/roman-catholic/vatican-curia/crrj-2015dec10. Most Christian Arab theologians are still pre-Vatican II hard supersessionists who reject the validity of Judaism after the appearance of Christianity.

75 This was understood early by R. Joseph B. Soloveitchik. See his *"Kol Dodi Dofek*—It is the Voice of My Beloved that Knocketh," in *Theological and Halakhic Responses on the Holocaust*, ed. Bernhard H. Rosenberg (New York: RCA, 1992), 70–71; and chapter 8 of this book.

double covenant theory, affirming the concurrent validity of the ancient Jewish *berit* alongside the Christian covenant.[76]

In 2002, delegates of the United States Conference of Catholic Bishops' Committee Ecumenical and Interreligious Affairs seemed to acknowledge this explicitly. Basing themselves on earlier papal and Vatican statements, they proclaimed "a Catholic appreciation of the eternal covenant between God and the Jewish people," and that "campaigns that target Jews for conversion to Christianity are no longer theologically acceptable in the Catholic Church."[77]

It is important to note that traditional supersessionist and "mission to the Jews" doctrines still hold theoretical sway among some influential Christian ecclesiastic officials, causing justified consternation among the Jewish people. *Reflections on Covenant and Mission* caused alarm in some traditional Catholic circles,[78] and some conservative Catholics and Evangelicals at the time promptly proclaimed the Catholic authors heretics for their limited theological pluralism. Witness also the 1999 mission statement of the Southern Baptist Board that denied the efficacy of Jewish prayer, and the debate over the proper interpretation of the 2000 Vatican document, *Dominus Iesus*,[79] written by Cardinal Joseph Ratzinger, later Pope Benedict XVI.

The discomfort regarding *Reflections on Covenant and Mission* has, apparently, continued, for in the summer of 2009 the United States Conference of Bishops felt constrained to issue a formal clarification of some of the document's ambiguities and insist on the continuing obligation of Christians to evangelize to Jews (as well as to all non-Christians), to which a number of prominent Jews

---

76 Examples are Franz Musser, *Tractate on the Jews: The Significance of Judaism for Christian Faith* (Philadelphia: Fortress, 1984), 226; Marcus Braybrooke, *Christian-Jewish Dialogue: The Next Steps* (London: SCM Press, 2000); and John Pawlikowski, "Toward a Theology of Religious Diversity," *Journal of Ecumenical Studies* 11 (Winter 1989): 138–153. See also Pawlikowski's excellent overview of these trends in John Pawlikowski, "Reflections on Covenant and Mission: Forty Years after *Nostra Aetate*," *Crosscurrents* 56, no. 4 (2007): 70–94.

77 *Reflections on Covenant and Mission*, August 12, 2002, http://www.jcrelations.net/en/?id=966.

78 See Avery Dulles, "Covenant and Mission," *America* Vol. 187/ No. 12 (October 2002). See also Korn, "The Man of Faith and Religious Dialogue," 302–303.

79 See David Berger, "On *Dominus Iesus* and the Jews," and the response of Cardinal Walter Kasper. Both papers were originally delivered at the Seventeenth Meeting of the International Catholic-Jewish Liaison Committee, New York, May 1, 2001, subsequently printed in *America* 195, no. 7 (September 17, 2001) and https://www.ccjr.us/dialogika-resources/documents-and-statements/analyses/berger01may1#ges:searchword%3DDavid%2BBerger%26searchphrase%3Dall%26page%3D1

representing Jewish organizations responded with serious concern.[80] Despite these dissenting reactions to *Reflections on Covenant and Mission*, it is important to note that today there is no office in the Catholic Church or resources spent dedicated to converting Jews specifically, nor have efforts toward conversion actually appeared in contemporary Jewish-Catholic dialogue. This is also the case in liberal Protestant churches, but not Evangelical ones.

Notwithstanding these points, it is hard to overestimate the difficulty—and the impressive character—of the changes represented by "the six R's." Every religion with a rich tradition is necessarily conservative, and anyone familiar with orthodox religious systems knows how difficult it is to effect a change in theology and policy. If any change of the fundamentals occurs at all, it is achieved most often in evolutionary fashion. However, in slightly more than forty years, a revolution has occurred in Christian theology. The transformation is incomplete and its process is continuing, yet it is undeniable that a majority of ecclesiastical authorities have now adopted the "new teaching" about Judaism and the Jewish people, and that the groundwork has been laid for an end to the spiritual and physical enmity between Christianity and the Jewish people.

A New Theology and a Different Future?

Perhaps more important than the challenge of finding a path for neutral Jewish-Christian theological coexistence is the bolder inquiry of whether there are grounds for a new *theological* relationship and mutual appreciation between the faiths. If an important religious question for Jews before modernity was whether Christians gained legitimacy by fulfilling the obligations of the Noahide covenant, the bolder and more important contemporary Jewish theological challenge is whether Jews can understand Christians and Christianity in a new way. Are there grounds for a new *theological* relationship in which Jews understand Christians as participating in a common covenant with them? And can this new

---

80   See "A Note on Ambiguities Contained in *Reflections on Covenant and Mission*," the Committee on Doctrine and Committee on Ecumenical and Interreligious Affairs, United States Conference of Catholic Bishops (USCCB), June 18, 2009, http://www.ccjr.us/index.php/dialogika-resources/themes-in-todays-dialogue/conversion/559-usccb-09june18.html; and "Letter on USCCB 'Note on Ambiguities,'" National Jewish Interfaith Leadership, http://www.ccjr.us/index.php/dialogika-resources/themes-in-todays-dialogue/conversion/574-njil09aug18.html. The United States Conference of Catholic Bishops later agreed to rescind the statements relating the evangelization of Jews, at least in the context of Jewish-Catholic dialogue.

theological relationship function as the foundation for Jews and Christians for forging an active partnership in building a future based on a common religious mission?

On practical grounds, there should be no religious objection to such partnership, for even Maimonides—the harshest rabbinic critic of Christian theology—accorded Christianity a positive instrumental role in history:

> There is no human power to comprehend the designs of the Creator of the universe.... Thus, the words of Jesus and of the Ishmaelite [Mohammed], who came after him were only to prepare the way for the messiah and to repair the whole world [*le-taqqen et ha-olam*], to serve the Lord in unison, for it is written, "I shall make all the peoples pure of speech, so that they all call upon the name of the Lord and serve him with one heart" (Zephaniah 3:9).[81]

Note that Maimonides's statement claims that Christianity as a historical phenomenon helps (however imperfectly) fulfill *the Jewish covenantal mission* by preparing the world to serve the Lord.[82] The passage implies that Christians and Jews have different roles in the same divine mission in history, rather than being members of totally independent faiths. How Christianity as *avodah zarah* can do this is surely a divine mystery for Maimonides—hence his opening explanatory confession.

On the theological level, closer to our time we have seen that Rabbis Rivkis, Emden, Hirsch and others were explicit in interpreting Christianity as going well beyond the Noahide requirements since Christianity commits Christians to believe in the Creator of the universe, the veracity of Sinaitic revelation and messianic history. In other words, there is important theological affinity between Christian belief and mission and the Jewish covenantal role

---

81 MT, Laws of the Kings and Their Wars 11:4 (uncensored edition).
82 Nahmanides of thirteenth-century Spain concurs with Maimonides on this point. Quoting Maimonides's passage at length, he emphasizes the moral and theological progress that Christianity brought to the nations of the world and distinguishes Christians and Moslems from pre-Christian practitioners of *avodah zarah*. This historical progress is a direct result of Christianity inheriting the religious and moral principles of Torah. In Nahmanides words, Christians are "inheritors of Torah." Ramban, *Writings of Ramban* [Hebrew], Chavel ed. (Jerusalem: Mossad ha-Rav Kook, 1959), vol. 1, 143–144. Simon Federbusch, *Studies in Judaism* [Hebrew] (Jerusalem: Mossad ha-Rav Kook, 1965), 224 maintains that Nahmanides agrees with those rabbinic authorities who deny that Christianity is *avodah zarah*.

in history. To quote once again the clear words of R. Emden, "Their goal is to promote Godliness among the nations . . . and to make known that there is a Ruler in heaven and earth Who governs and monitors and punishes. . . ." Similarly, R. Hirsch says, "Israel produced an offshoot [Christianity] to bring to the world . . . the tidings of the One Alone. . . . It represented a major step in bringing the world closed to the goal of all history." Although Christianity and Judaism have critical—and seemingly permanent—differences, in their eyes, Christianity has promoted fundamental aspects of Jewish theology and belief.

Catholic and Protestant doctrines have always insisted that Christianity is the extension of the Jewish covenant at Sinai, but this would constitute a radical thesis for Jewish theology. Indeed, it is difficult to see how Jews (or Christians) could logically understand Christians standing at Sinai while not being obligated to observe all the Sinaitic *mitsvot*, without at least part of Sinai covenant being invalidated or superseded. We will explore this further in chapter 9.

Yet, Christians and Christianity are closer to Judaism in history, mission, and theological content than, for example, any Asian religion that might fulfill the Noahide commandments. It is clear that Christian covenant stands theologically somewhere between Noah and Sinai. According to traditionalists Emden and Hirsch who claim that Christianity helped spread the knowledge of the Creator throughout the world, there are solid grounds for probing the possibility that Christianity has entered into the Jewish covenantal mission that began with Abraham. For numerous Jewish thinkers in medieval and modern times, it is teaching the world about God and his moral law that is precisely the purpose of the Jewish covenant. Maimonides, too, stressed that teaching the world the knowledge of the One God of Heaven and Earth was the primary vocation of Abraham,[83] and both R. Ovadiah Seforno in fifteenth- and sixteenth-century Renaissance Italy and R. Hirsch in nineteenth-century Germany interpreted the covenantal charge to the Jewish people at Sinai, "You shall be a nation of priests" (Ex. 19:6), as an imperative to teach the nations of the world the reality of God.[84] And as we saw earlier, in the nineteenth century R. Naftali Tsvi Yehudah Berliner (Netsiv) claimed that teaching the truth of God to all the nations of the earth is the ultimate purpose of Sinaitic revelation. Hence, for

---

83   MT, Laws of Idolatry 1:3, Book of Commandments, positive commandment 3; *Guide* III:51.
84   Seforno, commentary on Ex. 19:6; Hirsch, commentary on Ex. 19:6. It is because Hirsch believed that the fulfillment of God's covenant as spreading the reality of God throughout the world constituted the *telos* of sacred history that he could claim that "Christianity (and Islam) "represented a major step in bringing the world closer to the goal of all history" (*Nineteen Letters on Judaism*).

him, God's covenant at Sinai with the Jewish people was the culmination of God's creation of the world, and the book of Exodus was but a continuation of the book of Genesis.[85] And in 2015, more than 100 Orthodox rabbis and scholars publicly pronounced their understanding of the common covenantal mission of Jews and Christians.[86]

Recent history gives credence to this theological direction. From the second half of the twentieth century until today, the Holocaust has cast an enormous shadow over Western history and philosophy—and it carries substantive theological implications for Jewish theology and covenantal history. It has affected nearly all Jewish religious thinking after 1945 and has stimulated some contemporary Jewish thinkers to extend the trajectory of a positive attitude to Christianity. The two foremost post-Holocaust thinkers who argue for accepting Christianity as a positive spiritual force are Rabbis Abraham Joshua Heschel and Irving Greenberg. In light of the Nazi experience, they contend that it is not merely possible for Judaism and Christianity to cooperate with each other, it is *essential* that they do so. In his groundbreaking essay "No Religion is an Island,"[87] Heschel taught that Judaism and Christianity must now be spiritual bulwarks against a godless world that produced the Final Solution and the abandonment of morality. In the context of secularist and postmodern values, the Judaic and Christian spiritual worldviews have more commonality than difference, and it would seem that faithful Jews and Christians are natural partners.[88] Greenberg has gone further still, maintaining that Judaism and Christianity are different dimensions of the same covenant to work for messianic fulfillment and the sanctification of life in human history and culture.[89]

As we saw in chapter 5, it is a logical mistake to conflate the pluralism of Heschel and Greenberg's notion of theological pluralism with relativism that

---

85 *Ha-Emeq Davar*, introduction to the book of Exodus (cited in chapter 2).

86 See *Orthodox Rabbinic Statement on Christianity: "To Do the Will of Our Father in Heaven: Toward a Partnership between Jews and Christians,"* CJCUC, December 3, 2015, https://www.cjcuc.org/2015/12/03/orthodox-rabbinic-statement-on-christianity/.

87 Heschel, "No Religion Is an Island," 235–250.

88 Even the Modern Orthodox rabbinic opinion that officially shuns interfaith theological dialogue, understands the importance of cooperation with Christians on social, political, and ethical matters: "Communication among various faith communities is desirable and even essential. We are ready to enter into dialogue on such topics as War and Peace, Poverty, Freedom, Man's Moral Values, The Threat of Secularism, Technology and Human Values, Civil Rights, etc. . . ." R. Joseph B. Soloveitchik, *Rabbinical Council of America Record*, February 1966.

89 Irving Greenberg, *For the Sake of Heaven and Earth* (Philadelphia: Jewish Publication Society, 2004).

mocks religious truth or permanent difference, as some detractors have done. Such conflation is a thorough distortion of their faith commitment to traditional Judaism.

Heschel and Greenberg are frequently seen as visionaries who are far ahead of their communities—a polite yet unmistakably dismissive description. Yet it is not difficult to understand why they see common spiritual ground between Judaism and Christianity, possibly intimating a differentiated role in the same covenantal mission, and why there are compelling reasons for Jews and Christians to rethink their theologies regarding the other and move beyond tolerance to become allies at this point in history. Whereas sixty years ago interfaith cooperation was championed primarily by liberals of tepid religious commitment and minimalist theological conviction, today it is theologically oriented people seeking a coherent conception of God in their lives and transcendent meaning in their ethics who stand to benefit most from this new relationship. This is undoubtedly why a significant number of Orthodox Jewish leaders participate in Jewish-Christian dialogue.[90] Despite their profound theological differences, traditional Jews and faithful Christians are nearly alone today in Western culture when they assert traditional core moral values.

The 1998 Vatican document, *We Remember: A Reflection on the Shoah*, indicates this commonality of moral values. The paper asserts that Nazism was a "neo-pagan" phenomenon, suggesting that neither faithful Christians nor the Catholic faith ("the Church as such") bore direct responsibility for Nazi evil. This is simply wrong. Though Hitler, Himmler, Hess, and other high Nazi

---

90 It is noteworthy that individual Orthodox Jews in Israel, Europe, and America comprise a large percentage of those Jews engaging formal interfaith relations. The Israeli Rabbinate has official delegations appointed to hold regular dialogue with the Vatican on political, ethical, scriptural, and religious topics. Also in Israel, the Elijah Institute, headed by the Orthodox academic Dr. Alon Goshen Gottstein, and the Hartman Institute headed by Orthodox rabbis David and Donniel Hartman, have active programs in interfaith dialogue. In 2008, R. Shlomo Riskin, Chief Rabbi of Efrat, launched the Center for Jewish-Christian Understanding and Cooperation, designed to promote Judeo-Christian values and interfaith theological inquiry. I was the Academic Director of the Center, and co-director of its Institute for Theological Inquiry. In Europe, the United Kingdom's Chief Rabbi, Jonathan Sacks, has often spoken to the Church of England, and France's former Chief (Orthodox) Rabbi, René-Samuel Sirat, has long been a significant participant in Jewish-Christian dialogue. R. David Rosen is President of the International Jewish Commission on Interreligious Consultations (IJCIC). In America, R. Irving (Yitz) Greenberg has long been a leader in dialogue with Christian theologians. The Orthodox academic, Prof. Alan Brill holds a chair in Jewish-Christian relations at Seton Hall University, while Professor Lawrence Schiffman and Ms. Betty Ehrenberg have been Chairs of the International Jewish Coalition of Interreligious Consultations (IJCIC).

officials were baptized Catholics, they were not Christians in any meaningful sense. Yet, most of the people who operated the crematoria of Birkenau and implemented the grisly Final Solution were believing Christians. Moreover, the scholarship referred to earlier has demonstrated that traditional Christian anti-Judaic teachings were a substantive factor in the popular Christian acceptance of the Nazi extermination of Jews.

We Remember was correct, however, in stating that Nazism is fundamentally anti-Christian. Nazism violated in the most heinous way the sanctity of human life and rejected the fundamental biblical axiom accepted by Judaism and Christianity alike—that there exists a transcendent God who has authority over human beings. Proclaiming that human power was the ultimate value, Nazism substituted the imperative "Murder" for the biblical commandment "Thou shall not murder." This philosophy is the absolute antithesis of both Jewish and Christian ethics and an axiomatic denial of the worldviews of both those spiritual traditions. Had Hitler succeeded in completing the destruction of the Jewish people, he would have gone after Christianity and its leadership thereafter.[91] This must be so, because just as there was no way for Nazism to triumph while Jews existed to give testimony to the authority of God and His covenantal ethics, there was no way for Nazism to coexist over time with the deepest spiritual teachings of Christianity.

This common moral axiom of Judaism and Christianity is crucial today because postmodern secularism has given birth to a pervasive liberal value-orientation whose foundations contain seeds from which destructive forces can again grow. Hedonism drives much of contemporary ethos. Violence saturates our media and popular culture, sometimes appearing as merely another justified form of pleasure. This contributes to the evisceration of moral concern and the numbing of individual conscience, both essential to securing the values of human welfare and dignity. Moral utilitarian and thorough-going physicalist ideologies have also made comebacks in contemporary academia and high culture of today. In these theories, human life no longer has intrinsic value and individual human life often becomes a mere commodity to be traded and sometimes discarded. This moral philosophy shares the Nazi denial of the Judeo-Christian ethics, which insists that all persons are created in God's image, and hence each human life possesses infinite sacred value.

---

91 Recent scholarship has confirmed this theoretical conclusion. See William "Bill" Olson, "The Nuremberg Project," *Rutgers Journal of Law and Religion* (2002), which reports on Nazi plans to destroy Christianity. It is available online at https://digital.library.cornell.edu/collections/nuremberg.

Relativism has become one of the most accepted moral theories in our time, while objectivity and moral absolutes are under ferocious attack and are now on the cultural defensive. This implies that there is no objective bar by which to measure human actions, and this easily slips into the belief that there is no bar at all for valid moral judgment. It is but a small step from this conclusion to the denial of ethics entirely. In the political theater, an aggressive and imperial Islamist monism has emerged as a common threat to Judaism and Christianity. It denies Jewish and Christian legitimacy in the Middle East and by implication tolerance of all religious diversity—even within Islam itself. Finally, irrational religious extremism has become a potent force in both world politics and religious identity. Although the twenty-first century is still young, it has already seen too much violence and mass slaughter committed in the name of faith. All these phenomena constitute frightening dangers and are a call to joint action by Christians and Jews, for the Holocaust has taught us that when ethical values do not assume primary importance in human culture, radical evil results.

Can the future between Jews and Christians be better than their painful past? Does Judaism contain the seeds of a sympathetic theology to Christianity, where Christians play a complementary role to the Jewish people as part of God's covenant with Abraham? Will Jews have the courage to do so? Critical theological differences exist between Judaism and Christianity, yet both faiths demand belief in messianic history, obligating Jews and Christians to trust in the ultimate moral progress of humanity. Each of these religions teaches that their faithful have a common divine task to make the world a better place, where each person possesses sacred value because every person is created in the Image of God.

We return to the stunning vision of Micah that encompasses both the ideal of moral perfection and religious tolerance:

> Come, let us go up to the mountain of the Lord and the God of Jacob, that He teach us His ways, and we will walk in His paths. . . . Let the peoples beat their swords into plowshares and their spears into pruning hooks. Nations shall not lift up sword against nation, nor shall they learn war anymore. Let every man sit under his vine and under his fig tree; and no one shall make him afraid. . . . Let all the people walk, each in the name of his God; and we shall walk in the name of our Lord our God for ever and ever. (Micah 4:2–5)

This is the fulfillment of the Jewish covenantal mission and the messianic goal of sacred human history, the repaired world to which Maimonides refers when speaking about Christianity and Islam. For Micah it was indeed possible—perhaps desirable—for different peoples to call God by different names and worship the same Creator of Heaven and Earth in different modes.

Maimonides also offers a full messianic vision as the culmination of his magisterial code of Jewish law, *MT*:

> At that time, there will be neither hunger, nor war; neither will there be jealousy, nor strife. Blessings will be abundant and comfort within the reach of all. The single preoccupation of the entire world will be to know the Lord. Therefore there will be wise persons who know mysterious and profound things and will attain an understanding of the Creator to the utmost capacity of the human mind, as it is written, "The earth will be filled with the knowledge of God, as the waters cover the sea" (Isa. 11:9).[92]

Dare Jews and Christians believe that they can overcome the historical enmity in favor of mutual theological appreciation and religious harmony? Now that Christianity and Judaism are no longer physical and spiritual enemies, the future is open to such reconciliation. Can our future be brighter than our past? It will require mutual understanding and reappraisal, and above all a joint commitment to the messianic dream of the biblical prophets and Jewish tradition. Time will determine whether Jews and Christians have the courage to do so.

---

92 *MT*, Laws of Kings and Their Wars 12:5 (according to the Yemenite manuscript). See chapter 1 for explanation of emendations to this text.

7

Esau Hates Jacob

Christians as Esau

Jewish children learn early in their traditional Torah education that "Esau hates Jacob" (*Esav soneh l'Ya'aqov*). This rabbinic statement is found originally in *Midrash Tana'im* (*Sifri, parashat B'ha'alotkhah, pisqah* 61), but it was Rashi (Rabbi Shlomo ben Yitshaq), the great eleventh-century commentator, who etched this assertion in the minds of young Jews when he quoted it in his commentary on Gen. 33:4. In that chapter, the Bible describes the fateful confrontation between the twin brothers, Esau and Jacob. When they met Esau kissed Jacob, but the dots on top of the Hebrew word *va-yishakehu* ("He kissed him") in the Masoretic Torah text raise a question: was Esau's kiss sincere or was he only pretending and masking his deep longtime hatred for Jacob?

    The original statement *"Esav soneh l'Ya'aqov"* was made by Rabbi Shimon bar Yohai during the Roman Empire's subjugation of the Jews. Rashi tells us that Rabbi Shimon believed Esau's hatred of Jews to be "a well-known law" (*halakhah b'yadu'ah*)—a seemingly unchangeable eternal truth of the universe.[1] For the rabbis of that time, Esau was the code for the Roman Empire, which had issued a death verdict on Rabbi Shimon for disparaging Rome, had executed his beloved teacher Rabbi Akiva, and was cruelly oppressing the Jewish people. That was during the first and second centuries of the Common Era, but later Jewish writers used Esau as a symbol for Christians and Christianity. This was an easy transition, since like the ruddy Esau, the official color of both Rome

---

1   For contemporary examples of the assertion that the hatred of Esau for Jacob constitutes an eternal, unchangeable law of the universe, see Moshe Feinstein, *Iggerot Moshe, Hoshen Mishpat*, vol. 2, section 77, and the internet site of former Chief Rabbi Shlomo Amar, at http://haravamar.org.il/ (*parashat Va'yishlah*).

and Christianity was red, and in the fourth century Emperor Constantine established Christianity as the official religion of the Empire.

From the eleventh to fifteenth century, Jacob and Esau became the popular symbols of Jews and Christians in their hateful polemics against each other.[2] In those times, Jews had very good reason to believe Shimon bar Yoḥai's statement, since Christians persecuted, forcibly converted, and often killed Jews in the name of Christianity. Judaism and Christianity were bitter implacable enemies whose uncompromising theological battles utilized the images of Esau and Jacob. Christian theologians claimed that Jacob represented Christianity, since it was the "younger brother" of Judaism, and in the time of Jesus, Jews tried to defeat Christianity. Shimon bar Yoḥai's claim rang true for the Jews who understood themselves to be the descendants of Jacob. They had every reason to see Christians as living models of the evil Esau who was committed to killing Jacob, his faith, and his descendants, the Jewish people.

As mentioned in chapter 7, early Christian theologians developed terrible teachings about Judaism and Jews—that God's covenant with the Jewish people was replaced by the new covenant with the Church, or that Jews were blind to God's truth because they rejected Jesus as the messiah. Worse still, Jews were responsible for murdering Jesus, and because Jews were collectively guilty of deicide, they bore the curse of Cain and suffered his punishment. God took away their rights to their biblical homeland and condemned them to wander the earth in humiliation and insecurity. This "Teaching of Contempt" fueled antisemitism throughout Christian Europe for more than 1,500 years. Both Jewish and Christian scholars after the Holocaust found that these teachings prepared Europeans for the Nazi plan to exterminate the Jewish people, and were the reason that the Final Solution was so easily accepted by Christians in Germany, Poland, and Eastern Europe. The anti-Judaism Christian teachings were not a sufficient condition for this wide acceptance by European Christians—but they surely were a necessary condition.

As we also noted in the last chapter, after the *Shoah* most Christian churches began to realize the terrible role their teachings played in allowing Hitler to kill six million Jews, understanding that they needed to radically change their conceptions of Jews and Judaism to have moral credibility. Moreover, the miraculous return of the Jewish people to its biblical homeland and the establishment

---

2   Gerson D. Cohen, "Esau as Symbol in Early Medieval Thought," in *Jewish Medieval and Renaissance Studies,* Alexander Altmann, ed., (Cambridge, MA: Harvard University Press, 1967), 19–48.

of the State of Israel empirically falsified the Augustinian teaching and normative Christian theology, which stated that God had punished the Jews by forcing them to wander the earth.

Most churches in Europe and America began honest soul searching in the 1950s, seeking to revisit their guilt and traditional Christian doctrines about Jews. The Copernican revolution in Christian theology of the Jews became official with the Second Vatican Council's 1965 document *Nostra Aetate* ("In our Time") that officially rejected the Church's old teaching of contempt. It condemned all forms and displays of antisemitism and officially rejected the idea that Jews were collectively responsible for the death of Jesus. It also completely transformed the Catholic teaching about the faith of Judaism, now insisting that the covenant between God and the Jewish people was still a living covenant and that "the Jews remain most dear to God." The Church proclaimed that Jews remain God's elected people, and *Nostra Aetate* insisted that the roots of the Church lay in Judaism, and that "the glory and the covenant and the promise" of the Church come from the Jewish people. *Nostra Aetate* was only the first of six long official theological and practical documents that the Catholic Church has issued beginning with the Second Vatican Council to explain its teachings about Judaism and the Jewish people and to demonstrate its sincere desire to reconcile with the Jewish people and their faith.[3]

This transformation in Church teachings created the possibility of new relationships with the Jewish people. The six R's (repudiation of antisemitism, rejection of deicide, repentance for the *Shoah*, recognition of Israel, review of Christian teachings about Jews and Judaism, and rethinking of converting Jews) constituted a reversal of Christian thinking about and relations toward Jews.[4] Pope John Paul II had a number of Jewish friends as a high school student in Poland, and later during his papacy he exhibited great sympathy and closeness to the Jewish people. In 1986 he visited the Great Synagogue in Rome, warmly embracing his colleague, Chief Rabbi Elio Toaff. John Paul II repeatedly taught that antisemitism "is a sin against man and God," as did Popes Benedict XVI and Francis who followed him. One of the first things that the current Pope Francis

---

3   The others are *Guidelines and Suggestions for Implementing the Conciliar Declaration "Nostra Aetate"* (1974), *Notes on the Correct Way to Present the Jews and Judaism in Preaching and Catechesis in the Roman Catholic Church* (1985), *We Remember: A Reflection on the Shoah* (1998), *The Jewish People and Their Sacred Scriptures in the Christian Bible* (2001), and *The Gifts and the Calling of God are Irrevocable* (2015).

4   Boys, *Has God Only One Blessing?*, 248, and 247–266. A more detailed description of the changes in Christian theology related to Jews and Judaism appears in chapter 7.

said after becoming pope was, "No (good) Christian can be an antisemite," since he too recognizes that the Church is based on Jewish roots. He also publicly declared in October 2016 that God gave the Promised Land to the Jewish people, when this biblical truth was challenged by a resolution of UNESCO's World Heritage Committee.[5] Today, when there is so much hatred of the Jewish people around the world and when so many deny the Jewish people's right to sovereign independence in Israel, the repeated papal public condemnations of antisemitism and assertion of the Jewish rights to their homeland, proclaimed to more than two billion Christians around the world, are a major influence in battling both antisemitism and antizionism.

The majority of antisemitism around the world today comes from extremist Muslims and radical left-wing secularists—groups that vehemently reject current Christian teachings and the authority of the Church. Unlike the past, when poisonous antisemitism came from Christian theology and Christian leaders, most of today's antisemites are people who want to destroy the influence of Christianity as well as the Jewish people. Islamic domination poses a mortal threat to Christianity in Europe, and the few dissident old-world Catholics in the West who insist on holding on to the old anti-Judaic teachings and rejecting *Nostra Aetate* have been excommunicated.[6] As a result it is simply false to claim that today's antisemitism is Christian in any sense. Quite the opposite is true: both the Jewish people and faithful Christians are fighting the same enemies, not each other.

In 2000, Pope John Paul II visited Israel and met with government officials and the Chief Rabbis. At Israel's official Holocaust Memorial Yad Vashem he joined with Jews to mourn for the six million exterminated and he prayed at Jerusalem's Western Wall, where he honored Jewish tradition by inserting this prayer in the wall:

> God of our fathers, you chose Abraham and his descendants to bring your Name to the Nations. We are deeply saddened by the

---

5   Pope Francis is reported to say, "The people of Israel, who from Egypt, where they were enslaved, walked through the desert for forty years until they reached the land promised by God." Lahav Harkov and Tovah Lazaroff, "Pope Francis: 'God promised the land to the people of Israel,'" *Jerusalem Post*, October 26, 2016, https://www.jpost.com/Arab-Israeli-Conflict/Pope-Francis-God-promised-the-land-to-the-people-of-Israel-470918. This statement was also repeated by the Jewish News Service on October 26, 2016.

6   It should be noted that many if not most Arab Catholics—in particular Palestinian Catholics—still cling to old supersessionist views, perhaps because of their political rejection of the State of Israel.

behavior of those who in the course of history have caused your children to suffer, and asking forgiveness we wish to commit ourselves to genuine brotherhood with the people of the covenant.[7]

These are the sincere words of a repentant (*ba'al teshuvah*) and a friend of the Jewish people. Liberal Protestant churches have followed this theological change. In addition, John Paul's successors, Popes Benedict XVI and Francis, each have made official visits to the Jewish State of Israel, and established a tradition that will likely continue with future popes.

Another major change from the past is that today no Catholic institution and only very few Protestant churches try to convert Jews. As the high-ranking Cardinal Walter Kasper of the Vatican said in 2001, "There is no mission *to* the Jews; there is only mission *with* the Jews. In 2015, the Vatican issued an official document entitled, "The Gifts of God are Irrevocable" proclaiming that God's covenant with the Jewish people is eternal. To foster understanding and scholarship, many universities in America and Europe under the aegis of churches now employ Jewish scholars to teach Christian students about Judaism and Jewish history, because many Christians are now eager to learn about the Jewish origin of their faith.

Due to these dramatic changes in Christian teachings about the Jewish people, many Christians are the best friends of Israel. More than two million Christians come to Israel every year, many to celebrate not only the birthplace of Christianity but also the return of the Jewish people to their biblical homeland. A small number of Catholic and Protestant theologians are beginning to develop theologies emphasizing the religious significance for Christianity of the State of Israel.[8] Along with Catholics, Protestant Christians are the strongest gentile supporters of the Jewish State, lobbying for Israel in Washington and donating tens of millions of dollars every year to help Israel's poor and hungry

---

7 John Paul II, Prayer of the Holy Father at the Western Wall, *John Paul II Travels 2000*, https://www.vatican.va/content/john-paul-ii/en/travels/2000/documents/hf_jp-ii_spe_20000326_jerusalem-prayer.html.

8 See Gavin D'Costa, *Catholic Doctrines on Jews after the Second Vatican Council* (Oxford: Oxford University Press, 2019); Philip Cunningham, "Toward a Catholic Theology of the Centrality of the Land of Israel for Jewish Covenantal Life," in Phillip Cunningham, Ruth Langer and Jesper Svartvik, eds., *Enabling Dialogue about the Land* (New York: Paulist Press, 2020), 303–334; Robert Jenson, "The Prophet's Double Vision of the Return to Zion," in *Returning to Zion: Christian and Jewish Perspectives*, ed. Robert W. Jenson and Eugene Korn (Jerusalem: Center for Jewish-Christian Understanding and Cooperation in Israel, 2015), 20–33. John Paul II, Prayer of the Holy Father at the Western Wall, *John Paul II Travels 2000*, https://www.vatican.va/content/john-paul-ii/en/travels/2000/documents/hf_jp-ii_spe_20000326_jerusalem-prayer.html

and to support Jewish immigration to the Jewish State. All these Christians revere the Bible and see themselves as partners with the Jewish people in teaching about the worship of God and creating a world filled with justice and righteousness (*tsedaqah u'mishpat*) as Gen. 18:19 teaches.

Jews also have something in common with Christians on the political level. Like Jews, Christians today are a persecuted minority and the victims of Islamist extremism, hatred, and violence. They are suffering from the same persecutions of forced conversion, eviction, humiliation, and massacres that Jews experienced for millennia in Europe. It is no exaggeration to say that today "Christians are the Jews of the Middle East"—vulnerable minorities with no government to protect them.

For both religious and political reasons, therefore, God has thrown Jews and Christians together to appreciate the Bible and to be allies against common enemies that want to destroy Jews and Christians, particularly in the Middle East.

Some religious Jews find it difficult to accept the new ideas: that Christians no longer hate Jews or are trying to destroy Judaism, that Jews have common interests with Christians, and that many Christians are eager to learn about their Jewish roots. Jews are a history-oriented people, and we have the obligation to honor to the lives of our parents and grandparents. The scars that Christians inflicted on Jews are still fresh, and our national memory is filled with pain. But our trauma from the past should not blind us to the fact that Christians have largely changed their attitudes and teachings about Jews and Judaism. Today, when most Christians wish reconciliation with the Jewish people and to support Jews as their elder brothers, there is no longer any reason to fear or hate them.

Does Esau Hate Jacob?

Yet what of "Esau hates Jacob"? While this may have been true in days of Shimon bar Yoḥai, the Talmudic era, and the time of Rashi in the Middle Ages, it is no longer true today. We are in a new era and it is important for Jews—particularly religious Jews—to understand this monumental change. The Jewish people still have real enemies today, but Christians are not among them. Jews should better focus their energies on fighting those who are actively trying to destroy us as a people and our faith.

It is important to note that the rabbinic statement "Esau hates Jacob" was never the consensus of the Talmudic sages, nor a *halakhah* in the proper sense. The statement does not imply any positive or prohibited action demanded by Jewish law. It merely expresses the political attitude and worldview of one sage,

Rabbi Shimon bar Yohai. Even though some post-talmudic rabbis interpreted this statement to be an eternal and unchanging law, even Shimon bar Yohai did not think this was the case.

The recent scholarship of the Israeli scholar Menachem Kahana has revealed that most of the early manuscripts of this text in the *Sifri* did not contained the word "law" (*halakhah*).[9] Those manuscripts read, "Is it not known [*ha-lo b'yadu'ah*] that Esau hates Jacob?" instead of "It is a known law [*halakhah b'yadu'ah*] that Esau hates Jacob." Only the French manuscript (the one Rashi used) contained the words "*halakhah b'yadu'ah*." Kahana also showed that the phrase "*halakhah b'yadu'ah*" does not appear in any other place in all of Talmudic literature, while "*ha-lo b'yadu'ah*" appears frequently. This is strong evidence that the manuscript Rashi used was a corrupt one.

Moreover, Rabbi Shimon bar Yohai is not an acceptable model for contemporary Zionist Jews. The Talmud (BT *Shabbat* 33b) teaches that Shimon bar Yohai angrily denounced Jews who let any worldly or political activity interfere with his study of Torah, even for one moment. Like Haredi (fervently Orthodox Jews), R. Shimon refused to believe that tilling and harvesting the land had any religious value. He also rejected engineering and general culture, and he certainly would have thought that devoting time to building a Jewish state was a waste of time in worthless politics. For both factual and philosophical reasons, therefore, Jews have every right to reject R. Shimon's attitude today.

Other rabbis interpreted the meeting between Esau and Jacob differently. Today the interpretation of Rabbi Naftali Tsvi Yehudah Berliner (Netsiv) describes our situation more accurately. Netsiv also used the figure of Esau as a symbol for Christians, and in his commentary *Ha-Emeq Davar* on Gen. 33:4 he observed that when the Bible describes Esau kissing Jacob, it also teaches us that both brothers wept. Here is how Netsiv understood that dramatic poignant reunion:

> "'Both of them wept': Jacob also wept and felt brotherly compassion when Esau recognized the descendants and merits of Israel."

Netsiv insisted that when Christians will come to appreciate the merits of Jews and their faith, then the people of Israel will also recognize that Christians are indeed their brothers.

---

9   Menachem Kahana, *Sifri on Numbers: An Annotated Edition* [Hebrew] (Jerusalem: Magnes, 2011–2015), vol. 1, 167, and vol. 4, 474.

Changing old Jewish attitudes toward Christians does not necessarily pose any halakhic problem. As we saw in the previous chapter, a number of authoritative traditional rabbis like Moses Rivkis, Yaakov Emden, and Samson Raphael Hirsch expressed appreciation toward Christianity. They also noticed that it was Christianity that brought the seven Noahide commandments to the nations of the world and that Christians believe in many essentials of Judaism, such as creation, the exodus from Egypt, and the revelation at Sinai.

Even Maimonides, the harshest rabbinic critic of Christian theology, admitted that it is permitted to study Torah with Christians and, quite surprisingly, that Christianity is preparing the world for the messianic era by introducing the nations to divine commandments, morality and bringing them closer to worshipping the one Creator of heaven and earth.[10]

Not long ago, a number of rabbis and I saw these truths come alive when we experienced a touching moment at a conference in Salerno, Italy. There, Orthodox rabbis and Catholic priests and bishops spoke to more than 400 people for three days. Before the priests and bishops left for home, they requested, "Rabbis, will you bless us?" These pious Christians understood the holiness of Jewish tradition and recognized that the Jewish people is still dear to God and remains His chosen people. Following the present teachings of the Catholic Church, these priests and bishops believed that Jews are indeed a *mamlekhet kohanim*, a kingdom of priests, and they wanted the rabbis to bestow God's blessings upon them. They believed the Bible's first promise to Abraham and his descendants that "All the families of the earth shall bless themselves by you" (Gen. 12:3).

Today Jews are privileged to live in a time of positive Jewish-Christian relations that Netsiv could only dream about more than one hundred years ago. God has blessed the Jewish people by giving them the State of Israel, as well as the friendship of Christians. Many Christians have gone from being enemies of the Jewish people to being true friends. It is in both the religious and physical interests of Jews to realize that they no longer live in the Talmudic era of Shimon bar Yoḥai or in the hateful Middle Ages. Jews only help themselves, Judaism, and the State of Israel when they learn more about who today's Christians really are. With this knowledge, Jews will understand that Christians can be allies against the physical and religious challenges before the Jewish people and the Jewish State.

---

10   Rambam, *Teshuvot ha-Rambam*, ed. Joshua Blau (Jerusalem: Maas, 1960), vol. 1, 284–285; MT, Laws of Kings and Their Wars 11:4 (uncensored edition).

8

The Man of Faith and Religious Dialogue

Introduction

Rabbi Joseph B. Soloveitchik (1903–1993) was the undisputed leader of Modern Orthodoxy for more than forty years. As the scion of an elite Lithuanian rabbinic family, he became the brilliant carrier of the analytic method of Talmud study pioneered by his grandfather, R. Hayim of Brisk; and as a recipient of a doctorate in neo-Kantian epistemology from University of Berlin, he developed a mastery over the classics, philosophy and theology of Western literature. R. Soloveitchik's remarkable intellectual biography combined with his personal charisma enabled him to shape Modern Orthodoxy's ideology, religious philosophy, rabbinic education, law, and politics. He taught both Talmud and Jewish philosophy at Yeshiva University, the intellectual center of the movement, where he is said to have ordained more rabbis than any person in Jewish history. For the Modern Orthodox community, he functioned as the master of both the philosophy of *Halakhah* and its practical decisions. He left such a potent legacy of students and writings that even thirty years after his death, he remains today the unrivaled spiritual guide of Modern Orthodox Jews.

No writing or oral discourse by R. Soloveitchik achieved more practical impact than his essay "Confrontation," first delivered at the 1964 Mid-Winter Conference of the Rabbinic Council of America. The work was formally published later that year as an article in the spring edition of *Tradition*, the official journal of the RCA. As a result of the conference lecture, the Rabbinical Council adopted a statement stressing the uniqueness and incommensurability of each religious community (in this case, Jews and Christians) and rejecting any interreligious discussion not based on "the full independence, religious liberty and freedom of conscience of each faith community." Since this statement was largely confined to philosophical principle, the Council adopted a more concrete statement in February 1966 stating that Jewish-Christian cooperation be confined to "universal problems" that are "economic, social, scientific and ethical." Again stressing that faith is a unique, private and intimate experience for each community, it asserted the RCA's opposition to dialogue in areas of "faith, religious law, doctrine and ritual." To ensure this nuanced position was not misconstrued, it concluded: "To repeat, we are ready to discuss universal religious problems. We will resist any attempt to debate our private individual (faith) commitment."

What prompted R. Soloveitchik (and the RCA) to delve into the complex matter of interfaith relations? The date and context are critical. In the early 1960s, The Second Vatican Council took upon itself the challenge of *aggiornamento*, that is, the updating of the Roman Catholic Church and its doctrines. A good part of this modernization entailed rethinking Catholic teachings about Judaism and the Jewish people. The Holocaust demonstrated for all who were honest that something had gone horribly wrong in Christendom, and many Catholics from Pope John XXIII downward deemed reconsideration of their Jewish spiritual patrimony and the Church's relations with the Jewish people to be urgent necessities.

The Vatican turned to religious representatives of Jewry, inviting them to dialogue and join the process of reconciliation. Many non-Orthodox rabbinic figures in America welcomed the gesture, but this development posed both a cultural and theological problem for Orthodox Jews—that sector of the Jewish people whose character has been largely forged in the fire of historical experience and traditional attitudes. Taken aback by the bold innovation of cordial relations with its perennial enemy, yet not wishing to be impolite by rejecting the offer out of hand, Modern Orthodox leaders looked to R. Soloveitchik, the one theologically sophisticated traditionalist with sufficient authority to craft an appropriate and politically acceptable response. His position rejecting any participation in interfaith theological dialogue was immediately accepted as both the *de jure* and *de facto* policy of the Modern Orthodox community, and has remained as such until today.[1]

---

1   Interestingly, the community accepted this "resistance" to theological debate, but largely ignored R. Soloveitchik's counsel for better interfaith understanding and communication on ethical, social, scientific and political issues, which he viewed as "desirable and even essential." See "Addendum to the Original Edition of 'Confrontation.'"

Almost sixty years have elapsed since R. Soloveitchik wrote "Confrontation."[2] For Jews living in twenty-first century, it is worthwhile reexamining his thesis for its meaning, wisdom, and correct application as a guide for future Jewish-Christian relations. Thankfully, in the intervening years we have witnessed a partial healing and a critical transformation in the tortured history of the Church and Jewish people. While Jews and Catholics may not be warm partners in broad cooperation, neither are these faith communities any longer implacable enemies.

The Logical Status of "Confrontation"

"Confrontation" is divided into two parts: the first, a twelve-page philosophical description of three levels of human existence that draws heavily on the biblical account of the creation of the human being; the second, a thirteen-page discussion of Jewish responsibilities to humanity, and specifically how faithful Jews should relate to other faith communities. Part theological reflection, part biblical exegesis, and part existential statement, "Confrontation" bears R. Soloveitchik's spiritual signature of bold eclectic integration and noble vision. Given its practical impact and R. Soloveitchik's multifaceted *persona* in the Orthodox community, it is important to understand correctly the nature and function of the essay. R. Soloveitchik often spoke as the community's chief halakhic authority—a kind of "rabbi's rabbi"—and many have understood the essay to constitute a formal legal opinion (*pesaq halakhah*) that formally obligated his followers and that could only be overridden by an authority greater than R. Soloveitchik.[3]

It is difficult to sustain such a categorization of "Confrontation". The traditional language of halakhic *responsa* is Hebrew, not English. Second, the essay is devoid of any classic material that all *responsa* rely upon as basis for legal analysis, that is, formal biblical imperatives, Talmudic opinions and commentary, and post-Talmudic rabbinic legal decisions. Conspicuously absent in the essay is any citation of the great rabbinic authorities such as Maimonides, R. Menaḥem Meiri, R. Yosef Karo, or R. Moshe Isserles, or of any halakhic

---

2   Given R. Soloveitchik's well-known perfectionist impulses that prevented him from going on record with anything not well thought-out and fully edited, it is reasonable to assume that he formulated the thesis of "Confrontation" well before its public delivery in early 1964.

3   David Hartman appears to accord "Confrontation" with halakhic status in his *Love and Terror in the God Encounter* (Woodstock, VT: Jewish Lights, 2001), 132.

codes, even though, as we have seen, they had significant legal opinions regarding Christianity. Lastly, the method of argumentation bears no resemblance whatever to classic halakhic analysis: no legal principles are articulated, no halakhic reasoning appears, no precedent is cited, and no legal conclusion is stated. The formal halakhic terms "forbidden" (*assur*) and "permitted" (*mutar*) never appear, nor is there any mention of the terms *Halakhah* or *mitsvah* (commandment).

The contrast between "Confrontation" and halakhic *responsa* is very evident when comparing the essay to what indeed is a formal *responsum* on the question of meeting Catholics for the purpose of interfaith dialogue, that offered by R. Moshe Feinstein.[4] It took R. Feinstein not twenty-five pages but merely one column to close the issue. In two paragraphs he ruled that interfaith dialogue violated a Torah commandment and stressed the absolute prohibition of such activities for Jews. It is instructive to note that shortly after R. Feinstein's 1967 *responsum*, he beseeched R. Soloveitchik to sign a statement formally "declaring an absolute and clear prohibition" for Jews to participate in interfaith dialogue. R. Soloveitchik never responded to R. Feinstein's request.[5] The crucial difference is not one of style or argumentation, but function. R. Feinstein penned a classic *responsum* in halakhic terms, while R. Soloveitchik argued discursively on philosophical, historical and prudential grounds regarding the correct parameters of Jewish-Catholic dialogue. The essay is more a philosophic disquisition (part 1) with a direct political application (part 2). Most assuredly, therefore, R. Soloveitchik wrote "Confrontation" as a thesis that argues for a particular Jewish policy on interfaith dialogue, not as a *pesaq halakhah*.

The Arguments of "Confrontation"

R. Soloveitchik's substantive arguments regarding interfaith dialogue appear in part 2 of the essay to which I now turn. In that section he advances three different types of arguments that are interwoven throughout the discussion: (1) a philosophic argument about the nature and limits of human communication,

---

4   Feinstein, *Iggerot Moshe, Yoreh De'ah*, no. 43, March 1967. For an excellent comparative analysis of the two opinions, see David Ellenson, "A Jewish Legal Authority Addresses Jewish-Christian Dialogue: Two Responsa of Rabbi Moshe Feinstein," *American Jewish Archives Journal* 52, nos. 1–2 (2000): 113–128.

5   Feinstein, *Iggerot Moshe, Yoreh De'ah*, no. 43; Ellenson, "A Jewish Legal Authority Addresses Jewish-Christian Dialogue," 121, 123–125.

(2) a doctrinal argument that assumes faithful Catholics are bound by specific theological claims regarding Jews and Judaism when engaging in interfaith dialogue, and (3) a historical argument based on Jewish attitudes conditioned by the painful historical experiences that Jews endured in their troubled relations with the Church.

The philosophic argument rests on the alleged intrinsic character of communication, and therefore seems independent of contingent empirical conditions or social context. That is, if the argument is valid, it is eternally so because its conclusion follows from the very nature of human communication. The doctrinal argument, however, is different in that it depends primarily on the validity of its assumptions about the limits of Catholic and Jewish doctrinal commitments, as well as presuppositions about the function and dynamics of dialogue. These are variables, for both doctrine and the nature of dialogue can change at different points in history. As such, the argument is contingent, depending upon whether these assumptions are correct at any given time. The historical argument, rooted in reactions to the past, is similarly contingent since attitudes can change over time—particularly when historical, social, and intellectual conditions undergo fundamental shifts. In other words, the validity of these latter arguments during the Middle Ages or first half of twentieth century is no assurance that they are valid for the twenty-first century or for a different understanding of the dialogical encounter.

A. The Philosophic Argument

R. Soloveitchik contends that each faith community is unique and therefore any attempt to equate them is "absurdity." From this uniqueness he concludes that:

> The word of faith reflects the intimate, private and paradoxically inexpressible cravings of the individual for his Maker, . . . which is totally incomprehensible to the man of a different faith community. (23–24)
>
> The great encounter between God and man is a wholly personal private affair incomprehensible to the outsider—even to the brother of the same community. The divine message is incommunicable since it defies all standardized media of information and all objective categories.

As a result, theological dialogue—as opposed to discussion on social, ethical, or political matters—between Jews and gentiles is futile.

Readers of R. Soloveitchik have claimed that this position is incoherent.[6] First and foremost, he spent his entire life teaching Torah and *Halakhah*—Judaism's divine *logos*. His conception of God's word assumes it is logical and communicable to finite humans. In the tradition of Maimonides,[7] we shall see that he believed that the Torah of God can be taught not only to Jews but also to Christians.

Second, according to his logic, it would seem that a Jew can no more successfully communicate his religious experience to another Jew than to a Christian. Yet, R. Soloveitchik in fact attempted to communicate his religious experience to both Jews and Christians. His most famous and perhaps most personal theological confession, "The Lonely Man of Faith" was delivered to an interfaith audience at St. John's Catholic Seminary in Brighton, Massachusetts.[8] In that work, he takes up the generic human problem of interpersonal communication and concludes that Adam and Eve were able to communicate with each other because they formed a universal covenantal community with God—well before there was any idea of a particular covenant that separated Jews from gentiles.

The final argument of his critics notes that R. Soloveitchik read Christian and heterodox Jewish philosophers and theologians. He was deeply influenced by the Scholastics, Duns Scotus, Kant, Schleiermacher, Scheler, Kierkegaard, Bergson, Barth, and Otto, among others.[9] His language and philosophy clearly indicate that these thinkers helped shape his experience of *qedushah* (holiness), *teshuvah* (repentance), and the texture of his religious life. How then could R. Soloveitchik claim in "Confrontation" that Jews and Christians should not talk to each other about the faith experience and *logos* because such dialogue was impossible, even "absurd"? Of course, it is a truism that subjective experience, be it of faith, of love, of beauty, or of awe, can never be totally captured by

---

6   Hartman, *Love and Terror*, 138; David Singer and Moshe Sokol, "Joseph Soloveitchik: Lonely Man of Faith," *Modern Judaism* 2, no. 3 (1982): 227–272.

7   Rambam, *Teshuvot ha-Rambam*, no. 364 (Blau ed.).

8   See Walter Wurzburger, "Rav Joseph B. Soloveitchik as *Posek* of Post-Modern Orthodoxy," *Tradition* 29, no. 1 (Fall 1994): 16, and Shalom Carmy, "His Master's Voice," *First Things*, June–July 2000, 68–71. Both writers fail to identify the seminary, but R. Soloveitchik's daughter, Dr. Atarah Twersky, verified that it was St. John's, which was the only Catholic seminary in Brighton at that time.

9   See Joseph B. Soloveitchik, *Halakhic Man*, trans. Lawrence Kaplan (Philadelphia: Jewish Publication Society, 1983), 110–117; and Yitzchak Twersky, "The Rav," *Tradition* 30, no. 4 (Summer 1996): 31.

language. Religious language is, at best, only inexact metaphor, a finite approximation of infinity or of numinous experience. Yet surely linguistic expression is valuable as a helpful intimation. As R. Soloveitchik admits, just as a lover cannot stop attempting to describe his love feelings, the religious person is compelled to express his religious experience, however inadequately.[10]

I believe that these critiques are unfounded. R. Soloveitchik's dismissal of religious dialogue as absurd does not refer to the personal expression of faith, but to proof or refutation of faith. As an existentialist who believed that the deepest yearnings and satisfactions of human life were not intellectual, he maintained that the foundations of Jewish faith were located in the experience of the Jewish people, in the traditions of our patriarchs, and in the passional life of individual Jews. What was absurd to him was any attempt at rational demonstration, scriptural analysis or logical deduction to prove or disprove faith. Perhaps this is why he frequently talked of Kierkegaard, but rarely of Anselm.

More to the point of "Confrontation," any interfaith discussion that utilized arguments to refute the faith of another is hostile and dishonest, not merely logically confused. The essay makes clear that R. Soloveitchik's primary objection—on both logical and moral grounds—was to *doctrinal disputation* between Christians and Jews regarding the validity of Judaism, that is, to the traditional Christian-Jewish debates imposed on Jews by the Church from Medieval times onward. This conclusion is strengthened by the list of topics "deemed improper" for dialogue that appeared in the 1966 statement formulated by R. Soloveitchik and adopted by the RCA. It is no accident that the list consists of the very subjects that were debated in medieval disputations.[11]

His sense resentment at this arrogant and unequal form of dialogue is palpable:

> Any intimation, overt or covert, on the part of the community of the many that it is expected of the community of the few to shed its uniqueness and cease existing because it has fulfilled its mission by paving the way for the community of the many must be rejected as undemocratic and contravening the very idea of religious freedom. (23)

---

10 R. Soloveitchik often rhapsodized about Song of Songs and The book of Psalms, seeing their poetry as essential expressions of authentic religious experience. See Joseph B. Soloveitchik, *Worship of the Heart*, ed. Shalom Carmy (Jersey City, NJ: KTAV, 2003), 61–68.
11 I thank Professor Lawrence Kaplan for pointing this out.

> ... We must always remember that our singular commitment to God and our hope and indomitable will for survival are non-negotiable and non-rationalizable and are not subject to debate and argumentation. (24)

R. Soloveitchik's assumption that these traditional objectives would continue to be the Catholic goals for theological dialogue was historically warranted. It was 1963–1964, almost two years before *Nostra Aetate* was written and the Church still adhered to its age-old theological posture toward Jews and Judaism. The Church held that Jews were guilty of deicide, that Christianity had superseded the "Old" Covenant of Judaism, that "*extra ecclesiam nulla salus*," and that conversion and contempt were the religiously correct Christian policies toward Jews. It was therefore logical to assume that modern Catholic-Jewish dialogue would not depart essentially from the assumptions and logic of medieval disputations. These disputations were designed to prove, in the words of one scholar, that "the truth of Christianity would be rendered manifest to destroy the errors of the Jews, that Jesus was the messiah, and that Jewish legal and ceremonial rules were discontinued and (were) never to be resumed after Jesus."[12] In other words, it was not dialogue of respect and equality at all, but a theological duel to the death that Jews could not afford to win or lose. Hence, R. Soloveitchik rejected Jews entering into theological discussions under this Catholic "frame of reference," since at best it would render Judaism only a "satellite in (Christianity's) orbit."[13]

It is this critical distinction between respectfully hearing the religious voices of others and doctrinal disputation that untangles the paradox of R. Soloveitchik's private conversation with Christian religious thinkers whose insights he integrated into his religious *weltanschauung*, and his rejection of formal interfaith dialogue on theological subjects.[14] The former posed no threat to the validity of his faith, while he assumed the latter was targeted at

---

12 See Gilbert Dahan, *The Christian Polemic Against the Jews in the Middle Ages* (Notre Dame, IN: University of Notre Dame Press, 1991), 36–37.

13 Soloveitchik, "Confrontation," 21.

14 This distinction also eliminates the alleged Achilles's heel of the essay raised by his critics, namely that Rav Soloveitchik implied that ethical, social, and political issues were part of a secular order, and therefore interfaith dialogue could proceed in those areas without invoking theology. For the faithful Jew, this is impossible. Indeed, how can one discuss Jewish ethics without utilizing its axiomatic premise, that human beings are created in God's Image, and without reference to its endpoint or *summum bonum*, that is, the messianic era, both of which are theological to their core? (See Soloveitchik, "Confrontation," n. 8, 24.) The distinction between disputation and dialogue allows Jews and Catholics to confer and

undermining Jewish faith commitment. To employ the favorite technique of R. Soloveitchik's Brisker tradition, there are two concepts of theological discourse: one is authentic dialogue, which is free religious expression that is governed by legitimacy of difference and mutual respect; the other is polemical disputation, which is futile in its illogic and objectionable in its triumphalism.

B. The Doctrinal Argument

R. Soloveitchik's understanding of traditional Catholic doctrine brought to light the "incommensurate" frames of reference that rendered Catholic-Jewish theological discussion "an absurdity."[15] He believed that the Catholic faithful would necessarily bring supersessionist assumptions to their conversation with Jews: they would assume that Christianity had replaced Judaism, that Judaism had lost its continuing spiritual vitality, that it no longer had a divine mission for the future of humanity, and that contemporary Jews who refused to accept Christian doctrine were blind to the fulfillment of God's covenant. By virtue of this "frame of reference" and their conviction in the truth of Christian mission, Catholics would have no choice but to view Judaism as inferior and incomplete and hence attempt to convert Jews to Christianity. Trying to harmonize this worldview with the Jewish commitment to the living validity of Judaism and Torah, and with pride in Jewish survival, was indeed a futile—and dangerous—exercise from which no good could come.

As a result, in "Confrontation" (23–25) R. Soloveitchik stipulated four specific preconditions for Jewish-Christian dialogue:

(1) There must be an acknowledgement that the Jewish people is an "independent faith community endowed with intrinsic worth to be viewed against its own meta-historical backdrop without relating to the framework of another (that is, Catholic) community.

(2) The Jewish "singular commitment to God and . . . hope for survival are non-negotiable and not subject to debate or argumentation."

---

cooperate on ethical issues of human dignity, respect, and welfare precisely *because* they both hold dear these theological principles.

15 I speak of Catholic "frame of reference" and Catholic-Jewish dialogue because R. Soloveitchik was responding to the Vatican's overture for dialogue. Some of "the doctrinal argument" analysis may apply, *mutatis mutandis*, to Protestant churches, but the appropriateness of theological dialogue must be examined individually for each Protestant church based on each church's doctrinal posture regarding Jews and Judaism.

(3) Jews should refrain from recommending changes to Christian doctrine, for such recommendations would lead to reciprocal Christian recommendations for changes to Jewish belief. Change must emerge autonomously from within, for "non-interference is a *sine qua non* for good will and mutual respect."

(4) Each community must articulate its position that the other community "has the right to live, create, and worship God in its own way, in freedom and dignity." Both communities have "the right to an unconditional commitment to God that is lived with a sense of pride, security, dignity and joy in being what they are." This precludes "trading favors on fundamental matters of faith" or "reconciling differences" out of an obligation to compromise.

Some have claimed that these preconditions pertain only to non-theological interfaith dialogue (that is, social, ethical, and political discussion) and that the rejection of theological discussion is non-contingent. This position runs afoul of the text, which explicitly mentions "doctrine" and "matters of faith" in its articulation of the conditions.

When R. Soloveitchik crafted "Confrontation" in 1963, he could not have foreseen the transformation of Catholic doctrine and radical shift in Christianity's "frame of reference" that was to follow. Almost two years later, the Vatican's proclamation of *Nostra Aetate* began a theological journey that continues until this day and from which Christianity will likely never return. The transformation of the Catholic frame of reference can be evaluated by examining current Catholic teaching on the previously cited six R's enunciated by Mary Boys:[16] (1) the repudiation of antisemitism, (2) the rejection of the charge of deicide, (3) repentance after the *Shoah*, (4) review of teaching about Jews and Judaism, (5) recognition of Israel, and (6) rethinking of proselytizing Jews.[17] *Nostra Aetate* achieved two explicit changes in Catholic theology that were later reinforced and expanded upon by two other authoritative Vatican documents, *Guidelines and Suggestions for Implementing the Conciliar Declaration "Nostra Aetate"* (*Guidelines*) of 1974 and *Notes on the Correct Way to Present the Jews and Judaism in Preaching and Teaching in the Roman Catholic Church* (*Notes*) of 1985.

---

16 Boys, *Has God Only One Blessing?*, 248 and 247–266.
17 This chapter attempts to give only a brief overview of the Church positions on these issues. For fuller analysis see Fisher and Klenicki, *In Our Time*; and Boys, *Has God Only One Blessing?*, 245–278.

The first point of *Nostra Aetate*, so critical to Jewish-Catholic relations, was the repudiation of antisemitism. The Church's statement on antisemitism found in *Nostra Aetate* is one of the most categorical rejections made by any institution or group:

> Remembering, then, her common heritage with the Jews and moved not by any political consideration, but solely by the religious motivation of Christian charity, she deplores all hatreds, persecutions, displays of anti-Semitism leveled at any time or from any source against the Jews.[18]

The latter two Church documents strengthened the rejection by changing the verb "deplore" to "condemn."[19] Later still, Pope John Paul II repeatedly stated that antisemitism is no mere political crime, but "a sin against God and humanity."[20]

Secondly, *Nostra Aetate* officially put to rest the noxious idea that the Jewish people is collectively guilty of deicide, a charge that was the primary theological source of Christian antisemitism throughout history and that led Christians to shed so much Jewish blood:

> What happened in his [Jesus's] passion cannot be charged against all the Jews, without distinction, then alive, nor against the Jews of today. Although the Church is the new people of God, the Jews should not be presented as rejected or accursed by God. (*Nostra Aetate*, 4)

This point was also strengthened in *Notes*, which stated that "Christians are more responsible than those few Jews because we sin knowingly."[21]

It is important for Jews to recognize that *Nostra Aetate* represents the highest teaching authority in the Catholic Church—all the worlds' bishops (including the bishop of Rome) speaking in solemn council—and that most

---

18   *Nostra Aetate*, 4, at https://www.vatican.va/archive/hist_councils/ii_vatican_council/documents/vat-ii_decl_19651028_nostra-aetate_en.html. Accessed July 21, 2021.
19   *Guidelines*, preamble; and *Notes*, section 6, no. 26.
20   Papal statements in Fall 1990 and Winter 1991, cited in *Vatican City Pontifical Council on Christian Unity: Information Service* 75, no. 4 (1991): 172–178; and papal address, Hungary, August 16, 1991, cited in *Origins* 21, no. 13 (September 5, 1991): 203.
21   *Notes*, section 4, no. 22.

of the other documents that I cite are official teaching of the Catholic magisterium, or formal teaching authority. I am certain that there are still Catholic traditionalists—some even in Rome who may wear red skullcaps—who dissent from the "new" Church teaching, but they cannot be correctly said to represent Catholic doctrine today. Their dissenting opinions carry little ecclesiastical weight, and do not determine Church policy toward Jews or Judaism.

The rejection of both antisemitism and deicide are addressed explicitly and unequivocally in *Nostra Aetate*. While these points are undergoing continual conceptual and theological development, the main challenge today is not clarification of these two above points, but their broad promulgation and implementation throughout in the Catholic community. Unfortunately, antisemitism is still present in some quarters of the Catholic community, and many Catholics still believe in the deicide charge, despite its repudiation from the highest Catholic authorities. Significantly, the condemnation of antisemitism is repeated in nearly every subsequent Catholic document addressed to Jews, as well as nearly every address to a Jewish audience by a high-ranking Catholic cleric. It is also a central feature of contemporary Jewish-Catholic dialogues. Nevertheless this teaching needs to be brought more effectively to the Catholic faithful, not only by papal and Vatican statements from Rome, but in local parishes, local Catholic media, and local Catholic educational centers.

The *Shoah* was the catalyst for the transformation of Christian teaching about Jews and Judaism. Reflection on the unimaginable evil of the Holocaust became the seed for Christian reappraisal of its tortured history and theology regarding Jews. Many Christian thinkers recoiled from the horror of the *Shoah* and sensed a causal connection between it and centuries of anti-Jewish Christian teachings. *Nostra Aetate* does not mention the Holocaust, but *Guidelines* refer to it as the "historical setting" of *Nostra Aetate*, while *Notes* mandate the development of Holocaust curricula in Catholic education to "help in understanding the meaning for Jews of the extermination [*Shoah*] . . . and its consequences." This has become a reality in some aspects of Catholic curricula, yet the wider educational mandate of *Notes* could be implemented more broadly within the Catholic community, clergy, and leadership.[22]

The most direct admission of Catholic guilt and responsibility for the Church's role in the *Shoah* came in a remarkable statement by the Catholic

---

22   Among the best sourcebooks for this are Phillip Cunningham, *Educating for Shalom* (Collegeville, MN: The Liturgical Press, 1995); Phillip Cunningham, *Proclaiming Shalom,* (Collegeville, MN: The Liturgical Press, 1995); Boys, *Has God Only One Blessing?*, 245–278; and Mary Boys, *Within Context* (Morristown, NJ: Silver, Burdett and Ginn, 1987).

bishops of Germany in 1995 and the French bishops' statement, *Declaration of Repentance*, in 1997.[23] The Vatican issued its formal statement, *We Remember*, in March 1998. This document is far from perfect, and has been justly—and unjustly—criticized by Jews and Catholics alike. It expresses itself with classic Vatican diplomatic ambiguity (what Boys has termed "churchspeak"[24]) and, unlike the statements of the German and French bishops, I believe it equivocates on the critical issue of the Church responsibility in the *Shoah*. Notwithstanding these problems, it marks a clear recognition of the complicity of Christian authorities in the Holocaust. Utilizing the Hebrew term, *teshuvah*, so dear to Jews, it states the need for Christian repentance and sincerely appeals to the Jewish people for forgiveness:

> ... the Catholic Church desires to express her deep sorrow for the failures of her sons and daughters in every age. This is an act of repentance (*teshuva*), since, as members of the Church, we are linked to the sins as well as the merits of all her children. The Church approaches with deep respect and great compassion the experience of extermination, the Shoah, suffered by the Jewish people.... It is not a matter of mere words, but indeed of binding commitment. "We would risk causing the victims of the most atrocious deaths to die again if we do not have an ardent desire for justice, if we do not commit ourselves to ensure that evil does not prevail over good as it did for millions of children of the Jewish people.... Humanity cannot permit all that to happen again."[25]

Pope John Paul II later reinforced the Catholic recognition of guilt when he visited the Yad Vashem Memorial and the *Kotel ha-Ma'aravi* (Western Wall) in March 2000 and offered the heart-felt prayer cited in the previous chapter.

We Remember is but the beginning of the official Church confrontation with its role in the Holocaust, not its last word. Continued discussion, reflection and soul searching about this horrific tragedy are necessary. The Jewish people

---

23 *Statement of the German Catholic Bishops on the 50th Anniversary of the Liberation of the Extermination Camp at Auschwitz*, January 27, 1995; *Declaration of Repentance by the Roman Catholic Bishops of France*, September 30, 1997. Both statements can be found on JCRelations.net, http://www.jcrelations.net.
24 Boys, *Has God Only One Blessing?*, 248 and 250.
25 *We Remember*, section 5.

knows that one cannot make any sense—historical, religious, or moral—of the *Shoah* without a sustained period of silence and mystery that leads to initial clumsy articulation, theological searching, and, finally, recognition of moral responsibility and spiritual purification. This is a long painful process, but one that the Church has embarked upon.

Already in 1956 R. Soloveitchik articulated the theological implications of the State of Israel for both Judaism and Christianity.[26] The return of the Jewish people to their biblical homeland and the permanent existence of the State forced a *de facto* recognition upon the Christian world that Jews were not destined to be cursed and humiliated because of their rejection of Christianity. The existence of Israel constituted an empirical refutation of Augustine's doctrine of wandering Jews functioning theologically as negative witnesses to the truth of Christianity. When the Vatican refused to recognize the State of Israel until 1994, Church officials claimed that its position was political: recognition would endanger the welfare of Christians in Arab lands and Vatican policy was to withhold recognition to states that lacked fixed borders. These political claims were undoubtedly true, but R. Soloveitchik understood that something deeper than politics was at stake. Lack of recognition was tantamount to denying that Jews had *the right* to go to their biblical homeland because the doctrines of contempt and supersessionism that nullified continuing Jewish covenantal integrity were still operative Church theology. It took twenty-nine years after *Nostra Aetate* for the Church to recognize the State of Israel in June 1994. However late, such recognition constituted *de jure* recognition of the Jewish people's right to its biblical homeland. As such, it is an implicit affirmation of the validity of the Jewish covenant and a repudiation of the Augustinian doctrine with its supersessionist denigration of Judaism. The existing Vatican recognition of Israel is now official Church policy and testifies to another monumental shift in the Catholic frame of reference.

Theologically, *Nostra Aetate* opened the door to new thinking not merely about Jews, but about how Catholics should understand Judaism. In a remarkable exegetical move that required rejecting the plain meaning of Paul's Epistle to the Romans 11—and prior Catholic doctrine—*Nostra Aetate* affirmed the continuing validity of God's biblical covenant with the Jewish people: "Jews still remain most dear to God because of their fathers, for He does not repent of the gifts He makes nor of the calls He issues."[27]

---

26   Soloveitchik, "*Kol Dodi Dofek*—It Is the Voice of My Beloved that Knocketh," 70–71.
27   *Nostra Aetate*, 4. See also the 2015 Vatican Document, *The Gifts and the Calling of God Are Irrevocable*, which takes its title and theme from Rom. 11. I am grateful to Professor Philip Cunningham for pointing out this exegetical boldness to me.

A strict reading of this statement might yield a salutary claim about Jews alone, and not their covenant with God, that is, Judaism. Moreover, *Nostra Aetate* explicitly presents the Church as "the new people of God." One could continue clinging to the doctrine of supersessionism as meaning that the Jewish covenant is no longer valid. Pope John Paul II foreclosed this logical possibility, however, in an explicit statement of 1980 that later became official doctrine when it was incorporated into *Notes*: "Jews are the people of God of the Old Covenant, which has never been revoked by God. . . . The permanence of Israel is a historic fact to be interpreted within God's design. It remains a chosen people."[28] The Pope's words imply that "the permanence of Israel" is a positive theological value, not merely a neutral fact of history. In other words, it is God's design that Israel's chosenness has not been cancelled or superseded. This theological reversal from prior Catholic teachings was asserted explicitly in the Church's December 2015 document, *The Gifts and the Calling of God Are Irrevocable*, which reaffirmed "the enduring role of the covenant people of Israel [sic] in God's plan of salvation,"[29] that "the permanent elective fidelity of God expressed in earlier covenants [with the Jewish people] is never repudiated,"[30] and that "the New Covenant does not revoke the earlier covenants."[31]

This reading can be explosive for traditional Christian theology. How far reaching are the implications? Does it mean that for Jews, Judaism is the highest fulfillment of God's design, much as Christianity is the highest fulfillment for the rest of humanity? If so, does Judaism have the same power of saving grace as does Christianity? Does it follow that attempts to convert Jews no longer are necessary or even desirable in fact and in theory? Is Christianity universal for all except Jews who remain in the covenant of Abraham?

Allow me to map out three distinct positions that try to answer these questions. Following the trajectory of recent Church statements about Judaism, a number of American Catholic theologians have gone just that far by answering "yes" to these questions. In their August 2002 paper, *Reflections on Covenant and Mission*,[32] they asserted that Judaism is salvific for Jews and that campaigns that target Jews for conversion to Christianity are no longer theologically acceptable

---

28 *Notes*, section 6, no. 25.
29 *The Gifts and the Calling of God Are Irrevocable*, section 6, no. 43.
30 Ibid., section 4, no. 27.
31 Ibid.
32 *Reflections on Covenant and Mission*, Consultation of the National Council of Synagogues and the Bishops Committee for Ecumenical and Interreligious Affairs, United States Conference of Catholic Bishops, August 12, 2002, accessed April 20, 2022, https://ccjr.us/dialogika-resources/themes-in-today-s-dialogue/conversion/cassidy2005#ges:searchwor

in the Catholic Church. In effect, they have proclaimed that Judaism is in some way theologically equal to Christianity.

This caused controversy inside the Church, for other Catholic theologians were by no means prepared to grant equivalent legitimacy to Judaism. Cardinal Walter Kasper, an ardent supporter of Catholic-Jewish theological dialogue, who as President of the Commission for Religious Relations with the Jews is the highest Vatican authority in charge of Catholic-Jewish relations, has equivocated on whether Judaism is salvific for Jews in the way that Christianity is for Christians. In a speech in Montevideo, Uruguay, in July 2001 as well as in a speech at Boston College in November 2002 he stated that Judaism was in fact "salvific" for Jews.[33] Tellingly, this important statement was omitted from the official transcript of his Montevideo speech. Perhaps he had gone too far for some in Rome—and even for himself, for he later distanced himself from the position espoused in *Reflections on Covenant and Mission*, announcing that that paper did not represent his position. Most importantly, however, Cardinal Kasper has consistently renounced any attempt at proselytizing Jews to Christianity—both in fact and theory. In Jerusalem and Boston, he argued forcefully that Christianity must approach Judaism with equality and respect for "differences" and as mentioned he has proclaimed publicly that there is "no mission *to* the Jews," either in dialogue or outside of it. There is only "mission *with* the Jews." In his own words:

> There is dialogue with Jews; no mission in the proper sense. Dialogue implies personal commitments and witness of one's own conviction and faith. Dialogue communicates one's faith and at the same time requires profound respect for the conviction and faith of the partner. It respects the difference of the other and brings mutual enrichment.[34]

The third and less equivocal position was held by Cardinal Joseph Ratzinger, prefect for the Congregation for the Doctrine of the Faith at the Vatican, before he became Pope Benedict XVI. He adamantly rejects the

---

d%3Dreflections%2Bon%2Bcovenant%2Band%2Bmission%26searchphrase%3Dall%26page%3D1.

33 Walter Kasper, Address of November 6, 2002, accessed April 21, 2022, https://ccjr.us/dialogika-resources/documents-and-statements/roman-catholic/kasper/kasper02nov6-2.

34 Walter Kasper, "Welcoming Address to the 2001 ILC Meeting," delivered at Seventeenth meeting of the International Catholic-Jewish Liaison Committee, New York, May 1, 2001, and published in *America* 195, no. 7 (September 17, 2001): 3.

notion of theological equality or pluralism. He denies any limitation on the "unicity and universality of the salvific mission of Jesus," or any implication that Christianity is not the highest fulfillment of God's word to all on earth: "The Sinai covenant is indeed superseded."[35] Yet, as David Berger has ably demonstrated,[36] Cardinal Ratzinger maintains that "theological unification [the conversion of Jews to Christianity] is hardly possible within our historical time, and perhaps not even desirable."[37] In other words, Cardinal Ratzinger is an eschatological supersessionist, maintaining that the replacement of Judaism with Christianity will not take place in our lifetimes before the *eschaton*—*aḥarit ha-yamim*. If so, Cardinal Ratzinger's form of supersessionism should play no part in the dynamic of pre-messianic relations. This means that it should pose neither a threat to Jews today, nor to Catholic-Jewish dialogue that respects the profound theological differences between Judaism and Christianity.

As I read the Catholic documents, faithful Catholics are called upon to appreciate the theological richness and value of Judaism that Jews believe and practice today. One example of this is the 2002 Pontifical Biblical Commission document, *The Jewish People and Their Sacred Scriptures in the Christian Bible*, whose preface was written by the then Cardinal Ratzinger. It recognizes that Jewish Sacred Scriptures (TaNaKH) are the word of God and therefore of the highest value for Catholics. Moreover, it admits that the traditional Jewish understanding of Scriptures is a legitimate one from which Christians have much to learn.[38] This is quite telling of the transformation, for it indicates that in dialogue the Church is striving to understand Jews "by what essential traits they define themselves in light of their own religious tradition," and that "dialogue demands respect for the other as he is; above all respect for his faith and religious convictions ... (and for) maintaining the strictest respect for religious liberty," as per official Vatican guidelines.[39] This is the very opposite of what R. Soloveitchik feared and resisted, namely that dialogue would *per force* be an exercise in which Christians view Jews as "objects of observation" in order to make Judaism a "satellite in (Christianity's) orbit" ("Confrontation," 21), that is, to deny the intrinsic value of Judaism itself.

---

35 Joseph Ratzinger, *Many Religions, One Covenant*, trans. Graham Harrison (San Francisco: Ignatius, 1999), 70–71.
36 Berger, "On *Dominus Iesus* and the Jews."
37 Ratzinger, *Many Religions, One Covenant*, 109.
38 *The Jewish People and Their Sacred Scriptures in the Christian Bible*, https://www.vatican.va/roman_curia/congregations/cfaith/pcb_documents/rc_con_cfaith_doc_20020212_popolo-ebraico_en.html, section 2, A, 7–22.
39 *Guidelines*, preamble and section 4, no. 1.

Traditional Jews should find neither difficulty nor discomfort with Cardinal Ratzinger's eschatological supersessionism. And to the disciples of R. Soloveitchik, it should sound familiar. It is a near exact parallel orthodoxy of R. Soloveitchik's eschatological convictions presented in "Confrontation":

> Only a candid, frank and unequivocal policy reflecting our unconditional commitment to God ... believing with great passion in the ultimate truthfulness of our views, praying fervently for and expecting confidently the fulfillment of our eschatological vision when our faith will rise from particularity to universality will impress our peers of the other faith community. (25)

R. Soloveitchik, too, believed that the truthfulness of his faith will spread universally at the end of time.[40] Thus, we arrive at an important (and comforting) divine paradox: Cardinal Ratzinger's supersessionism forms not a dialogical threat, but a protector of the right of Jews to articulate their own creed. When dialogue is conducted with equal rights and respect, the "Orthodoxy" of Catholic faith logically entails the validity of Orthodox Jews expressing their own parallel dreams and convictions.

Whatever the proper trajectory of current Catholic thought regarding supersessionism—be it the wide arc of the American Catholic theologians or the more acute angle of Cardinal Ratzinger's position—the most important facts for Catholic-Jewish dialogue and R. Soloveitchik's legitimate concerns are that today there is no Catholic missionary organization for Jews, and that conversion has no place in the contemporary Catholic approach to dialogue with Jews. Again, in the words of Cardinal Kasper:

---

40 This statement can be understood in at least three ways. The first, that the particularistic and nationalistic elements of Judaism will fall away and be replaced by universalizable elements, echoes traditional Christian replacement theology of Judaism. It is inconceivable to me that Rav Soloveitchik would ever countenance such an idea. The second, that in the *eschaton* all humanity will recognize the truth of Judaism and adopt current Jewish practices and creed, is a more likely reading, but one that finds no normative consensus in biblical or classical rabbinic sources. The third—and I believe most likely—interpretation is that humanity will accept the pre-Sinaitic Abrahamic religion, namely, belief in the one Creator of heaven and earth Who is a transcendent authority, Who ensures a moral order (reward and punishment), and Who continues to relate to human beings. This is what Maimonides may have meant when he referred to *dat emet* (true religion) in his discussions of the messianic age and is certainly akin to Meiri's conception of valid religion (*dat*).

> Dialogue implies witness of my deepest faith, a witness which *proposes* but by no means *imposes* one's own faith; on the contrary, it implies respect for every other conviction and every other faith.... In dialogue Jews give witness of their faith and Christians give account of the hope they have in Jesus Christ. In doing so, both are far away from any kind of proselytism.[41]

C. The Historical Argument

In 1964, barely two decades separated Jews from the centuries of Christian contempt that culminated in the European Holocaust. The wounds were still raw. Whatever theological or philosophic issues stood in the way of rapprochement with Christendom, the Jewish people were in no existential condition to overcome the problematics of the past. Indeed, the Jewish people had then yet to come to grips with the full impact of the Holocaust for themselves and with the full implications of the permanence of the State of Israel. Lastly, I add that the traditional religious community was uncertain of its fate and ability to withstand the onslaught of modern values and sociology. In other words, it was a time of internal healing of the Jewish people, introspection for the community and guardedness for Orthodoxy. In this state of existential and historical pain, R. Soloveitchik alludes to the problems of dialogue for Jews at his time:

> Non-Jewish society has confronted us throughout the ages in a mood of defiance, as if we were part of the subhuman objective order separated by an abyss from the human.... As long as we were exposed to such a soulless impersonal confrontation on the part of non-Jewish society, it was impossible for us to participate to the fullest extent in the great universal confrontation between man and the cosmic order, Heaven knows that we never encouraged the cruel relationship which the world displayed toward us. (19–20)

---

41 Walter Kasper, "The Jewish-Christian Dialogue: Foundation, Progress and Difficulties," lecture in Jerusalem, November 21, 2001, http://www.jcrelations.net/en/displayItem.php?id=818.

> ... We have not been authorized by our history, sanctioned by the martyrdom of millions, to even hint to another faith community that we are mentally ready to revise historical attitudes, to trade favors pertaining to fundamental matters of faith and to reconcile "some" differences. (25)

It is now fifty-nine years later, and as in all human relationships, timing is critical. Perhaps we still cannot make theological or moral sense of the *Shoah* in greater retrospect, but our historical and existential position has changed. The wounds of the Holocaust are still with us, yet we have begun to rehabilitate ourselves physically and spiritually.

The survival of State of Israel has gone far in leveling the playing field between Christianity and the Jewish people. Israel gives the Jewish people a sense of pride, reality, and potency. We are no longer exilic "ghosts," as Leon Pinsker maintained. Jews have political *gravitas* that gives them spiritual confidence and that forces the Church to dignify Jewish presence in the world. And in Israel itself, where Jews are the majority culture and Christianity is a marginal religion, there is no longer a Jewish sense of inferiority or disadvantage when dealing with the Vatican. Perhaps this is why the Israeli Rabbinate has already decided to engage in theological dialogue with Vatican officials, without the fear present in the American Orthodox rabbinate.

Since Christianity is no longer an aggressive physical or ideological enemy and Jews and Christians face the same mortal threat from radical Islam, perhaps the Jewish people is better able to relate to those Christians who display no triumphalist posture toward us. In "Confrontation" (24–25), R. Soloveitchik speaks of two separate problems: "trading favors on matters of faith" and "revising historical attitudes." Being precious, faith must never be sacrificed on the altar of social acceptance or Western etiquette—and any such demand by others to do so is the paragon of arrogance and disrespect. Historical attitudes towards Christendom are quite another matter. Here there is no timeless standard of "correct." Of course, some Jews may feel that the pain is still too great for venturing out into the world, but many feel otherwise. Ultimately, this is a matter of subjective judgment, and there is no objective method to determine whether it is too soon to redeem the past by attempting to build a better future through positive engagement with the Christian world.

Conclusion

Rav Soloveitchik and the RCA were correct in rejecting any debate of private religious commitment. All argumentation, disputation, and attempted refutation of faith are zero-sum games between antagonists, and are exercises that Jews must shun. This position was true in 1964 and is true today. Yet, a different concept of dialogue has emerged. It focuses on the phenomenological expression of one's spiritual experience and convictions in the presence of others committed to mutual respect and forswearing proselytizing motive. It does not attack the logical grounds of faith. Some categorize it as the expression of a religious anthropology.[42] Such a conception satisfies R. Soloveitchik's conditions for theological engagement, namely, (1) acknowledgement of the Jewish people as a vital faith community, (2) non-negotiability of the Jewish commitment to God, (3) mutual respect and non-interference in the faith of the other, and (4) agreement that each community has the right to live, create, and worship God in its own way, in freedom and dignity. I see no reason why Jews who venture into theological dialogue with others should not lay down these as preconditions, and no reason why, given the transformation in the Catholic frame of reference, the Church should not agree to them.

If we follow Cardinal Kasper's understanding, dialogue is not at all the antagonistic confrontation of Jacob and Esau of which Rav Soloveitchik spoke in 1964, but an expression of natural human needs for sharing, for catharsis of one's deepest religious beliefs, and for spiritual clarification with understanding and empathic listeners. I believe this is in fact what occurred that afternoon in Brighton when R. Soloveitchik first presented "Lonely Man of Faith" to faithful Catholic and Jews. None of the objections presented in "Confrontation" applied to that special event, nor, I believe, do they belong to current theological dialogue that is conducted with authentic yet respectful frames of reference.

The Value of Theological Dialogue

The loss of one third of our people in the *Shoah*, the security of Israel, assimilation, antisemitism, and the alienation of so many Jews from their spiritual heritage weigh heavily upon the Jewish people today. With these issues that imperil our survival still raging, should Jews add theological dialogue with Christians

---

42   Hartman, *Love and Terror in the God Experience*, 155–157; see also David Hartman, *A Living Covenant* (New York: Free Press, 1985), 21–40.

to our already crowded list of religious challenges? Confronting the religious "Other" is surely a difficult and problematic task. Even when permissible, should they divert limited Jewish energies from these internal survivalist goals?

For religious Jews, there are objective and subjective answers to these questions. In making an eternal covenant, God demands that the Jewish people strive for more than survival. The Torah asks us to bear testimony to God's presence and His authority on earth. Like our forefathers Abraham and Jacob, we are no less charged "to call the name of the Lord"[43] and make known God's name wherever we can. "Calling the name of the Lord" is not a common phrase in the lexicon of religious Jews, but that does not mean that it is not a central *mitsvah* in our lives. The important imperative of *Qiddush ha-Shem* (sanctification of God's Name) may be the rabbinic formulation of this biblical charge. God has challenged us to not be a mute people, or as R. Soloveitchik phrased it, "to be a message-bearing people, charged with *kerygma*,"[44] that is, a charismatic people that articulates its faith. As we have seen in the opening chapters, Jews are challenged to be more than a sect, more than a historical curiosity relegated to a footnote in human history. We are bidden to be a people who "teach righteousness and justice" to the world[45] and who influence the great drama of history. As God proclaimed through Isaiah (43:10), "You are my witnesses." This is the meaning of the election of Israel and the very *raison d'etre* of Judaism.

How can we "call the name of the Lord" today? Postmodern culture is skeptical, positivist, anthropocentric, and autonomy-driven in its essence. It ridicules the concept of objective truth. It sees the human being as a material or exclusively biological phenomenon, one with little hope of self-transcendence or contact with eternity. The secular people, who create their "reality" via a Cartesian proclamation of *cogito* or a Nietzschean assertion of will, are denied a natural rootedness in tradition or a world greater than themselves. The mainstream contemporary culture adores moral utilitarianism and axiological relativism. And now, religious fanaticism has become so common that, for many, it is difficult to distinguish between religious legitimacy and idolatry that manifests itself in violence and extremism.

All religions have been traumatized by modern and postmodern culture, and each traditional believer today stands as a "lonely man of faith" in the face of predominant Western thinking. In this cultural milieu, how can we "call the name of the Lord?" Jews who wish to do so must speak seriously about our

---

43 Gen. 12:8, 13:4, 22:33, 28:16.
44 Soloveitchik, *Worship of the Heart*, 73–86.
45 Gen. 18:19.

fundamental conviction in *Torah min ha-shamayim*—that our holy texts come from a transcendent authority Who is the Creator of heaven and earth and not some anonymous sage of antiquity. But who will listen to Jews of faith when we proclaim our commitment to an ageless tradition that claims us *a priori*, one that we cannot cavalierly dismiss when it is at odds with popular culture? Who will believe that Jews live in covenant with God because the Divine chose the Jewish people for a sacred mission, and who understands us when we discuss our ethical commitments based upon the metaphysical axiom that each person is created in God's Holy Image and therefore all human life has intrinsic sanctity? To whom can we express our conviction that human history will be redeemed at the end of time, even though "natural" historical analysis seems to undermine any warranted belief in moral progress? And finally, as R. Soloveitchik so eloquently put it, who will appreciate our religious trials and dilemmas, the meaning of our spiritual challenges that derive from our commitment to infuse the world with holiness through a creed that has no technical potential, that cannot be evaluated by rules of formal logic or be measured by functional utilitarian society?[46]

My experience is that once Jews leave the safe intimacy of their synagogues, religious Catholics, who have renounced triumphalism and accepted what Pope John Paul II has called their "shared spiritual patrimony with Judaism," will be among the few who understand Jewish religious and spiritual dilemmas. Although they function in distinct and sometimes radically different categories, members of both faiths face the same loneliness and many similar problems that arise from striving to live a hallowed tradition and struggling to find God in the post-modern world.

As indicated, Jews have a religious task to give testimony, to express the truths of our faith and the dilemmas of our spiritual experience. R. Soloveitchik felt existentially and spiritually compelled to express himself on these matters: "All I want is to follow the advice given by Elihu the son of Berachel of old who said, 'I will speak that I may find relief,'—for there is redemptive quality for an agitated mind in the spoken word."[47] In a later work, he put it this way:

> The Torah's message is the translation of the numinous into the kerygmatic, the translation of the non-sensical and absurd into the vernacular of the teleological and rational. The Torah aims

---

46 Soloveitchik, "The Lonely Man of Faith," 8.
47 Ibid.

to discover *caritas* in *majestas*, kindness in beauty and familiarity in strangeness.[48]

Can we not attempt to express these religious impulses with Christians who share our quest for eternity, who relate to us as subjects, who acknowledge the permanent differences between us and who sense our spiritual loneliness?

Perhaps this is what R. Soloveitchik believed we could, and attempted to do so when he revealed his inner spiritual life as a "lonely man of faith" to Catholic and Jews alike during his existential confession in Brighton. This assumption also helps explain the purpose of part 1 of "Confrontation." Part 2 was sufficient to articulate the dangers and set the policy for interfaith discussion. What did R. Soloveitchik wish to achieve in the philosophic part 1?

Part 1 of "Confrontation" outlines three levels of existence. The first is the natural, "non-confronted" person, whose individuality is submerged in the natural order, the "is," and who knows no moral norms, the "ought." Clearly, this is the pagan of antiquity and the hedonistic, power-driven aesthete of our time. The second level is the reflective person, who feels confronted by an objective order standing in opposition to the individual. Out of this confrontation, the identity, a singular "I" is born. The individual senses the disparity between reality and perfection, between fact and value. So, recognizing that one who knows has power, the individual exploits human intellect as an instrument of conquest over the environment. At this level, the human being lives a life of power-relations: the individual relates to others in Sartre-like fashion, as vanquished objects, not personal subjects. This being knows no true communication, only the depersonalized relationship of Adam to the beasts of the field, as found in Gen. 1. The third level is the redemptive person who forgoes domination and thereby achieves human relationships with others as equals. In the process of approaching Eve as a peer and helpmate, Adam of Gen. 2 discovers in-depth communication, his human identity, and God. Though Adam and Eve remain distinct and retain their independent existential integrities, together they achieve a spiritual community with God.

To whom is this philosophic excursus addressed? Its invocation of two Adam types echoes Christian scriptures,[49] its typological reading of holy texts

---

48   Soloveitchik, *Worship of the Heart*, 85.
49   Rom. 5 and I Cor. 15.

is a classic Catholic exegetical technique, and its celebration of "the word" as a mysterious creative—almost cosmic—force[50] also calls to mind the *logos* of the New Testament. For R. Soloveitchik, who was *au courant* with Christian theology, these are not coincidences. Evidently, R. Soloveitchik wrote part 1 with Christian theologians in mind.[51] He clearly viewed traditional Christianity with its historic drive to conquer Judaism and depersonalize Jews as functioning on the second level of being. If so, then it may be that R. Soloveitchik was inviting the Church to ascend to the third level of existence, by recoiling from its position of domination *vis-à-vis* Judaism and its historic treatment of Jews as objects of contempt, and to consider treating Jews as dignified subjects.[52] If he could not have predicted the revolution started by *Nostra Aetate*, perhaps he was able to dream of its possibility. Such an elevated level of existence would enable in-depth communication and comradeship, even if not "existential union" or dissolution of the profound differences between Jews and Christians. When two faith communities meet each other as the level of redemption, dialogue is logically possible and even spiritually desirable.

I have argued that for the last sixty years the Catholic Church has undergone a profound transformation regarding Jews and Judaism, a transformation from R. Soloveitchik's second to third level of existence. This transformation continues, and it may now be sufficiently developed to allow Jews and Catholics, like Adam and Eve, to begin forging a subject-to-subject relationship as faith community to faith community.[53]

Some final caveats. Because of our troubled history and disparate theologies, Jewish-Christian theological dialogue is filled with pitfalls and problems. To guard against them, we should exercise care and explicitly agree on the preconditions and protocols of dialogue before beginning the precarious journey. It is important to remember that dialogue does not progress linearly, and it is likely that Jews and Christians will experience both forward movement and

---

50   Soloveitchik, "Confrontation," 14–15.
51   This nexus is strengthened by the fact that R. Soloveitchik developed the double Adam typology more fully in "Lonely Man of Faith," directed to an interfaith audience.
52   For more on this argument, see Murray Johnston, "Rabbi Joseph B. Soloveitchik's Unexpected Contribution: Towards a Theology of Jewish-Christian Dialogue," in *Confrontation to Covenantal Partnership*, ed. Jehoschua Ahrens, Irving Greenberg, Eugene Korn (Jerusalem: Urim Publications, 2021), 263–296.
53   Religious thinkers have done much work recently discussing the evolving concept, purpose, dynamics, and topics of interfaith theological dialogue. Much still remains to be explored regarding Jewish opinion in these areas. The present chapter, however, is confined to explicating the justification for interfaith dialogue and the preconditions that would render it acceptable to traditional Jews.

withdrawal, as R. Soloveitchik was so fond of describing the spiritual life. Lastly, traditional Jews are largely unfamiliar with dialogue and few are trained in theology. Therefore, we need to proceed slowly, meticulously, and with consummate honesty.

Theological dialogue is no experience for those who lack deep conviction or pride in their faith, for those who have little knowledge of their sacred traditions, or for those who have political or social goals that eclipse theological integrity. Such persons will only achieve a polite "trading of favors" or a dangerous syncretism that both Judaism and the Church must resist. As Abraham Heschel said, "the first prerequisite of interfaith dialogue is faith"[54]—to which I would add that the second prerequisite is religious knowledge, and the third, spiritual integrity.

The above caveats are critical to Jews wishing to defend their ancient faith, and cannot be minimized. Nevertheless, if my analysis is correct, the prime issue for religious Jews is not *whether* they should engage in theological dialogue, but who should participate, how the dialogue should be structured, what should be the pace of the dialogue, and what are fruitful subjects that do not threaten the integrity of each's convictions. If Jews and Christians take the necessary precautions and approach interfaith dialogue with religious strength and spiritual humility, they can both "call the name of the Lord."[55] When they do so, they help create a world in which God is present, a world closer to the eschatological dream of R. Soloveitchik's great spiritual teacher, Maimonides:

> In that time there will be neither war, nor jealousy, nor rivalry. But goodness will pervade the earth. The entire world will be involved in the knowledge of God, as it is said, "The earth will be filled with the knowledge of God as waters cover the sea" (Isa. 9:11).[56]

---

54 Heschel, "No Religion Is an Island," 241.
55 This follows the halakhic position of R. Menaḥem Meiri, the Tosafist Rabbeinu Tam found in BT *Sanhedrin* 63b, s.v. "*assur*," and the seventeenth-century authority, R. Shabbetai ben Meir ha-Kohen (Shakh) found in *Yoreh De'ah* 151:7, who all maintained that when Christians speak of God, they have in mind the one Creator of heaven and earth. See chapter 6.
56 *MT*, Laws of Kings and Their Wars 12:5. As was explained, Maimonides ruled that Christian trinitarianism is beyond the pale of legitimate theology, but given R. Soloveitchik's statements about positive relations with Christians and his appearances at Christian institutions, it is likely that he agreed with other rabbinic authorities who reject Maimonides's position. See Ellenson, "A Jewish Legal Authority Addresses Jewish-Christian Dialogue," 117–121.

9

The People Israel, Christianity, and the Covenantal Responsibility to History

We have seen that to be a member of God's covenant with the Jewish people is to live in the unfolding of sacred history: "All the families of the earth shall bless themselves by you" (Gen. 12:3). That history began when God created Adam and Eve with holiness, endowing them with the holy Divine Image, *Tselem Elokim*. Progressing through Noah, Abraham, and the revelation at Sinai, it continues until today and will end in the messianic era, when all people recognize the reality of God and His moral authority. Only then, when the world lives with peace and blessing, will the Jewish people fulfill the sacred covenant that God made with Abraham and his descendants. Gen. 12–18 teaches us that God's covenant calls Jews to be an essential actor in the story of humanity, to partner with God in completing creation.

Jews, then, understand themselves as historically a covenantal people. The covenantal blessings given to Abraham and the covenantal commandments given at Sinai form one theological unity. As indicated in chapter 1, these covenantal responsibilities constitute the core of Jewish identity; our liturgy tells us they "are our lives and the length of our days."

We also saw that, for God to be a truly benevolent Father, the covenant must be part of the divine rational economy with an overarching objective transcending the mere fulfillment of the individual commandments.[1] The God of the Torah is not arbitrary when he commands his children. And it is Israel's universal role in sacred history, repeated to Isaac and Jacob, that gives

---

1   See chapter 1; also *Guide* III:25–26 and III:31; and Sa'adya Gaon, *Book of Beliefs and Opinions* III:1–3.

the Jewish people both eternal theological significance beyond mere ethnic survival.² As "a kingdom of priests," it is Israel's priestly role to bring God's blessings to all humanity.

Jewish Covenants and Christianity

As we saw earlier in chapters 3 and 4, the Sinai covenant is particularistic, restricted to the Jewish people at least until the end of history. This is in marked contrast to Christianity's "new covenant," whose domain is in principle universal. Yet this is not the end of the Jewish view of God's covenants with His children. At least as early as the Talmudic era (200–500 CE), Jewish thinkers found a way to establish God's enduring relationship with gentiles and grant them theological legitimacy through God's covenant with Noah and his descendants, i.e. gentile humanity. While gentiles who do not accept the moral Noahide commandments are considered unworthy pagans, all gentiles who live under these basic laws of civilization are considered to be worthy Noahides, *benei Noah*.

How can we understand Christianity against the background of this Jewish covenantal theology? As we saw in chapter 8, there are four stages in the evolution of rabbinic thinking about Christianity in different historical eras. (1) For most of the first and second centuries, Jewish Christians were a tolerated sect. (2) In the Middle Ages most rabbis in Germany, France, and Italy still considered Christian belief in the trinity and the incarnation to be an illicit form of worship (*avodah zarah*), but Christians were already seen as observing Noahides who—for technical reasons—did not violate the prohibition against idolatry. (3) In the late Middle Ages and early modernity, most rabbis living in Christian Europe (*aharonim*) did not consider Christianity to be *avodah zarah* for gentiles. They ruled that gentiles were not obligated by the Noahide

---

2   Interestingly, Michael Wyschogrod pointed out the universalist implications of God's particular election of Abraham and Israel. For him, only God's preferential love for Abraham could guarantee the possibility that every individual person can have a genuine personal relationship with God: "Chosenness expresses to Jew and Gentile alike that God also stands in relation with them in the recognition of their uniqueness." In other words, it is God's choosing of Abraham the individual that ensures that God relates personally to each individual, not merely to humanity as an impersonal collective. Moreover, "when we grasp that the election of Israel flows from the fatherhood that extends to all created in God's image, we find ourselves tied to all men in brotherhood, as Joseph, favored by his human father, ultimately found himself tied to his brothers." Michael Wyschogrod, *Body of Faith* (Lanham, MD: Rowman & Littlefield, 1996). See also Meir Y. Soloveichik, "God's First Love: The Theology of Michael Wyschogrod," *First Things*, November 2009.

covenant to be strict monotheists, and hence Christianity was a valid belief system for gentiles. (4) From the seventeenth century through the twentieth century, when Christian toleration of Jews grew, a number of rabbinic authorities began to appreciate Christianity as a positive historical and theological phenomenon that popularized many fundamental principles of Judaism (such as the existence of God, *creatio ex nihilo*, Noahide morality, and the fact of Sinai revelation) and thus advanced the Jewish religious mission. Prominent among them were Rabbis Moses Rivkis (Be'er Hagolah), Rabbi Jacob Emden (Yavets), and Shimshon Raphael Hirsch and Ya'ir Bacharach.[3]

On the Christian side, Catholic and Protestant theologies have always insisted that Christianity is the heir to the Jewish covenant. As Paul explains in the Epistle to Galatians, "There is neither Jew nor Greek, there is neither slave nor free, there is neither male nor female—for all of you are one in Christ Jesus. If you belong to Christ, then you are Abraham's descendants, heirs according to the promise" (Gal. 3:28–29).

The church is part of the unfolding history of Israel—indeed, it is "*the* new Israel." Unfortunately, for many Christians this means replacement of the old Israel.[4] Christians see themselves as the contemporary recipients of the divine blessing given to Abraham and members of the covenantal chain from Abraham to Moses that culminated in the new covenant established with the blood of Jesus.[5] In other words, Christians see themselves as the contemporary chosen people, not merely *b'nai Noah*, or people following the Noahide covenant.

This is an unacceptable thesis for Jewish theology, and traditional Jewish thinkers have consistently maintained that Jews and Christians do not share any covenant. (Of course, both are obligated by the Noahide covenant, but Jews do not identify themselves as Noahides.) Jews have resisted acknowledging the Christian claim for historical and theological reasons to be discussed in the next section. Yet the matter cannot remain settled with this denial, for it is clear that Christianity is closer to Judaism in history, mission, and content than, for example, an Asian religion that might fulfill the Noahide commandments.

---

3   See chapter 8.
4   Apparently, Paul did not share this position. See Rom. 11:17–24, 29. I thank Gerald McDermott for pointing my attention to this text.
5   This is the formulation of Irenaeus of Lyon, in *Heresies* III.11.8. See *Irenaeus of Lyons*, trans. Robert M. Grant (New York: Routledge, 2007), 132. More recently, Cardinal Dario Castrillon Hoyos put it this way: "Abraham is the father of faith, but in a chain of salvation in which the Messiah is expected. And the Messiah has arrived." See Mary Boys, "Does the Catholic Church Have a Mission 'with' Jews or 'to' Jews?," *Studies in Christian Jewish Relations* 3 (2008): 9, https://ejournals.bc.edu/index.php/scjr/article/view/1482/1335.

For whatever reasons, God has closely intertwined Jews and Christians historically, and Judaism and Christianity theologically. For Judaism, then, Christians cannot be mere Noahides. Christianity must stand theologically somewhere between the Noahide religion and the Judaism of the Sinai covenant.

When we combine the modern rabbinic appreciation of Christianity cited above with the recent Christian theological ideas that express sympathy toward Judaism, we open up fresh possibilities for rethinking a Jewish covenantal relationship with Christianity and for fashioning new Jewish-Christian cooperation in pursuit of common values.

We have seen that medieval and modern Jewish biblical commentators understood Abraham's covenantal mission as teaching the world about God and bearing witness to his moral law. And in the philosophic eyes of Maimonides, spreading the knowledge of the One God of Heaven and Earth throughout the world was the primary vocation of Abraham.[6] We have also seen in chapter 8 that this understanding of Abraham's mission is how Rabbis Rivkis, Emden and Hirsch described the mission and historical impact of Christianity.[7] In effect, these rabbis viewed Christianity as playing a role in the covenant of Abraham. If so, Jews can view Christians as partners in that covenant.[8] This may be a common assumption in Christian theology, but it is a new claim for Jewish theology. It means that Christianity qualifies as an Abrahamic religion covenantally, not merely historically.[9] Jewish thinkers have always assumed that gentile nations could be genealogically descended from Abraham, but no gentile could

---

[6] *MT*, Laws of Idolatry 1:3, Book of Commandments, positive commandment 3; *Guide* III:51.

[7] See chapter 6. It is because Hirsch believed that the fulfillment of God's covenant as spreading the reality of God throughout the world constituted the *telos* of sacred history that he could claim that Christianity (and Islam) "represented a major step in bringing the world closer to the goal of all history." See his commentary on Ex. 19:6.

[8] Although counterintuitive, the modern Jewish theologian Steven Schwarzschild and the noted contemporary Maimonides scholar Menachem Kellner have argued that Maimonides believed that some theologically advanced gentiles were included in the designation "Israel" as "Israel of the Mind." See Menachem Kellner, *Maimonides' Confrontation with Mysticism* (London: Littman Library of Jewish Civilization, 2006), chap. 7. This confirms the idea that non-Jews could also be members of the same covenant God made with the Jewish people. However, it is obvious that Maimonides would not have included Christians in that category because of their belief in the trinity, a belief tantamount to idolatry for Maimonides.

[9] Old-new problems remain with this claim, foremost among them that circumcision was an obligatory sign for members of Abraham's covenant. How uncircumcized Christians could be members of the covenant needs to be addressed. The Jews' right to the land of Canaan, which was promised to Abraham's covenantal descendants, is less problematic, as that can be understood as limited to the biological descendants of Isaac (see Gen. 21:10–12).

be within the particular covenant that God made with Abraham. That was reserved for the Jewish people alone.

If this is so, then Jews and Christians can see each other as sharing Abraham's covenant. They can understand themselves to be working toward the same spiritual goals of sacred history, but under different systems of commandments and with differentiated functions.

The Problematics of Sharing the Covenant

There are two principal reasons why Jews have rejected the Christian claim to be included in the covenant of Israel. The first problem was the exclusive and supersessionist character of traditional Christian theology. Christianity's claim to the same covenantal promises God made to the Jewish people was the very source of intense theological rivalry, the delegitimization of Judaism, and Christian persecution of Jews over the course of Jewish-Christian history.

"Hard" supersessionism[10] (the doctrine that the new covenant replaced the Jewish covenant and that after Jesus, God rejected the Jews in favor of the church) was the longstanding Christian teaching regarding Judaism and Jews. The "new Israel" invalidated the "old Israel," and the new covenant of the spirit rendered the Jewish people's Mosaic covenant limited temporally, that is, to the time when the Temple stood in Jerusalem. The concurrent validity of the Mosaic covenant and the new covenant (also known as "soft" supersessionism, the idea that the church has been grafted onto the still living tree of the Jewish people and that the new covenant represents the ultimate fulfillment of the still living Jewish covenant) with its implication that there could be concurrent validity to both the Mosaic and the new covenants, was entertained by very few early Christian thinkers. It was ultimately rejected by early normative Christian theology, which was heavily shaped by Augustine's hard supersessionist understanding of covenantal history.[11] With the advent of the new covenant of the spirit, the Mosaic covenant became meaningless, even an obstacle to future salvation history. And as Gal. 3:28 was traditionally been interpreted, there is no

---

10 David Novak makes the useful distinction between "hard" and "soft" supersessionism in "The Covenant in Rabbinic Thought," in *Two Faiths, One Covenant*, ed. Eugene Korn and John Pawlikowski (Oxford: Rowman and Littlefield, 2005), 65–80.

11 See Steven McMichael, "The Covenant in Patristic and Medieval Christian Theology," in *Two Faiths, One Covenant*, ed. Eugene Korn and John Pawlikowski (Oxford: Rowman and Littlefield, 2005), 49–51.

room left for the continued distinct existence of the Jewish people or its independent covenantal mission.[12]

Thus, according to hard supersessionism, if Christianity is true, post-Temple Judaism must be dead. The rival claim to the same covenant was a theological duel to the death, and since Jews were never inclined toward physical or spiritual suicide they have consistently rejected the Christian claim.

The second obstacle to Jews seeing Christianity sharing a covenantal identity with Judaism is rooted in the doctrines of the trinity and the incarnation, as we saw in chapter 8. Jews understand the second of the Ten Commandments, "There shall be no other gods for you besides Me" (Ex. 20:2),[13] as demanding absolute monotheism that excludes a trinitarian concept. Any denial of God's absolute unity would violate the divine essence. Also, Jews see the incarnation as a violation of the second half of that same commandment: "You shall not make for yourself a sculptured image, or any likeness of what is in the heavens above or on the earth below or in the waters under the earth" (Ex. 20:3). Philosophically inclined Jewish theologians saw these two restrictions as logically identical: predicating any division of God implies that God is physical, limited, and imperfect, that is, not God at all.[14] Thus, prior to the sixteenth century, most Jewish thinkers understood Judaism and Christianity as worshiping

---

[12] A number of contemporary Christian scholars have argued that Paul wanted Jewish followers of Jesus to continue to observe Torah, as he himself did, and hence Jewish Christians would follow Jesus in a way that is different from gentile followers. See, for example, Krister Stendahl, *Paul among the Jews and the Gentiles* (Minneapolis: Augsburg Fortress, 1976); Krister Stendahl, *Final Account: Paul's Letter to the Romans* (Philadelphia: Fortress Press, 1995); Mark Nanos, "The Myth of the 'Law-Free' Paul Standing between Christians and Jews," 6, http:// www.marknanos.com/Myth-Lawfree-12-3-08.pdf. John Gager, *Reinventing Paul* (London: Oxford University Press, 2002), also argues that Paul's audience in Galatians is entirely gentile. Gerald McDermott has pointed out that just as Paul's statement in Gal. 3:28–29 does not imply the elimination of the permanent differences between males and females, it does not imply the eradication of differences between Jews and Christians. He also notes that Rom. 4 counts Christians as "the children of Abraham"—not the children of Israel. Gerald McDermott, "Anti-Zionists Misread the Bible," *Public Discourse*, https://www.thepublicdiscourse.com/2015/11/16021/. Hard supersessionists distort these New Testament passages.

[13] Interestingly, it was the literal reading of this verse that opened up the logical possibility for many early modern rabbinical authorities to consider Christianity non-idolatrous for gentiles, while remaining idolatrous for Jews. They understood that the prohibition "There shall be no other god *for you*..." was addressed exclusively to the Jewish people at Sinai ("for you"), and thus the Christian concept of a trinitarian deity that included the one Creator of the universe along with other divine images to be permitted to gentiles. This became known in Jewish legal and theological parlance as *shituf* ("partnership" or "associationism") and is based on the commentary of the Tosafists on BT *Sanhedrin* 63b, s.v. "*assur.*" See chapter 8.

[14] *Guide* I:50.

different gods, and if so, Jews and Christians could hardly share membership in the same divine covenant.

Today, however, we have the means to overcome these problems. The change in Christian thinking about Jews and Judaism that occurred after the Holocaust has significant implications for the Jewish understanding of Christianity and its relationship to the covenant. This is possible because Jewish theology is neither dogmatic nor derived exclusively from theoretical "first principles." Jewish theology is vitally influenced by the experiences of the Jewish people through history. As God's living witnesses, Jews understand God and providence mediated through their historical experiences as a people.

As noted, after the moral and physical devastation of the Holocaust, a number of Christian thinkers understood where the traditional hard supersessionist teachings led: directly to Christian complicity in the Final Solution and indirectly to Auschwitz.[15] Christians developed more tolerant teachings about Jews and Judaism in soft supersessionist teachings maintaining that God's covenant with the Jewish people was never revoked, that Judaism continued to occupy a role in salvation history, and that Jews were not a rejected people.[16] This is the normative Catholic teaching today, which has appeared as a result of *Nostra Aetate* and the theological approach to Judaism that has grown out of the Second Vatican Council. Major Protestant churches have followed suit, and a number of Evangelical theologians make a similar argument.[17] In most of their views, however, Christianity and the new covenant remain the highest fulfillment of the old covenant, and Jewish conversion to Christianity is still a theological *desideratum*—for God, the church, and for Jews themselves. Yet, this normative soft supersessionist teaching decreases the urgency and imperative nature to convert Jews. As noted, even the eschatological supersessionism of Cardinal Ratzinger undermines active attempts to convert Jews today, since "theological unification [i.e., Jews converting to Christianity] is hardly possible within our historical time, and perhaps not even desirable."[18] In this version, the full return of Jews to the church is a matter for God at the end of time, not for Christians today.

---

15   See chapter 6, n. 62.
16   *Nostra Aetate* (1965) is only the first articulation of the soft supersessionist teaching, which was reiterated more recently in the 2015 Vatican document, *The Gifts and the Calling of God Are Irrevocable*. For Protestant statements, see Boys, *Has God Only One Blessing?*
17   Documented in Boys, *Has God Only One Blessing?*
18   See Ratzinger, *Many Religions, One Covenant*, 109.

Rightly understanding that Christians are closer to Judaism than are Noahides, the prominent non-supersessionist Catholic theologian Mary Boys has suggested to me that Christians should somehow be seen as having stood with Jews at Sinai. Yet, it is difficult to see how Jews (or even contemporary non-supersessionist Christians) can logically understand Christians as partners in the Sinaitic covenant when they are not obligated to observe all the Sinaitic *mitsvot*, without at least part of the Sinai covenant being superseded.[19] As obvious illustrations, the Decalogue at Sinai prohibits making images of God and requires Sabbath observance on the seventh (and not the first) day of the week—two commandments that Christianity does not observe.

Churches long ago lost their temporal power and their capacity for physically threatening the Jewish people, and the recent emergence of soft supersessionist, eschatological supersessionist, and non-supersessionist theologies renders Christian theology less threatening to Judaism and to Jewish covenantal integrity. These recent Christian theologies remove or at least significantly lessen the Christian theological attack on the continuing integrity of the Jewish covenantal mission in history. Understanding this, Jews need not be defensive about adopting a positive new theological approach to Christianity. Jewish and Christian theologies are no longer engaged in a zero sum game for survival, and Jews need not fear a sympathetic covenantal understanding of Christianity that is true to the Bible, Jewish thought, and values.

It is important to note that this new covenantal understanding does not require either Jews or Christians to give up their eschatological convictions. Both soft supersessionism and eschatological supersessionism still maintain that Christianity is the highest fulfillment for everyone, including Jews, and that all will join the church when truth is revealed at the end of time. Orthodox Jews, too, are free to continue "believing with great passion in the ultimate truthfulness of our views, praying fervently for and expecting confidently the fulfillment of our eschatological vision when our faith will rise from particularity to universality,"[20] should they wish.

The new covenantal relation does require, however, that Christians and Jews give up intense rivalry in their pre-messianic activities and that they begin to view each other as partners in carrying out God's covenant instead of striving

---

19 Indeed, Josef Ratzinger (Pope Benedict XVI) asserts the supersession of the Sinai covenant in the very same passage in which he insists on Christian participation in that covenant. See Ratzinger, *Many Religions*, 70–71.
20 Soloveitchik, "Confrontation," 25.

in the here and now to triumphantly convert the other.[21] Mary Boys is surely correct: God has more than enough blessings to bestow upon each of his covenantal children.

The second formal theological problem of the unacceptable status of the trinity and incarnation according to Jewish law has also been resolved by the late rabbinic distinction between what Jews are required to believe about God (absolute monotheism) and what is permitted for gentile belief (belief in the One Creator of the universe with additional associated elements). We saw in chapter 8 that this difference in legal requirements leads to a philosophic problem and points to the avoidance of theology by formal *Halakhah*, but the significant covenantal point for us is that this distinction allows acceptance of legitimately differing Jewish and Christian beliefs about God, and that it is consistent with Jews and Christians retaining their differences in worship, their fidelity to their respective faith communities, and their viewing each other as mutual partners in God's covenantal mission. Lastly, it is crucial to note that under this distinction there are limits to theological pluralism. The doctrines of the trinity, incarnation and messiahship of Jesus of Christian belief remain strictly prohibited for Jews.

The Meaning of Abraham's Covenant in the Twenty-First Century

Reconsideration of Abraham's covenant offers a rich theological agenda and new practical challenges for Jews and Christians both. Jews will need to learn how to successfully navigate between their commitment to their exclusive Sinaitic covenant and the more open covenant with Abraham. And if they share covenantal membership with Christians, what will be the theological and

---

21 It seems that the Roman Catholic Church is still working out how this dialectic can be achieved in practice, and is caught in what some scholars have called a "contradictory pluralism" and a "bipolarity of tendencies" entailed by the soft supersessionism with its struggle to work out a coherent theology about Jews and the need for their conversion to the Church after *Nostra Aetate* and the Second Vatican Council. See Boys, "Does the Catholic Church Have a Mission 'with' Jews or 'to' Jews?" Boys documents the "bipolarity" of official Catholic documents and statements regarding the need for converting Jews. The issue has become even more controversial since 2008, with the 2009 statements of the USCCB on this issue regarding evangelization toward Jews and its place in Catholic-Jewish dialogue and relations. See USCCB's "Note on Ambiguities" and its subsequent revision of *Notes*.

practical borders of this partnership that will ensure the enduring particularism of the Jewish people and their mission?

I suspect that Christians will still have to grapple with the issue of supersessionism, but in a new form. Has Christianity superseded not only the covenant of Moses, but Abraham's covenant? If not, how does Abraham's more open covenant relate to traditional Christology and ecclesiology, both past and present? And of course, the conundrum of the universality of the church coexisting with the continuing validity of the particularist Jewish covenant still cries out for resolution. Is it a virtuous divine mystery that is cause for humble reflection and celebration,[22] or a vicious logical inconsistency to be eliminated?

If we are true to the biblical account of Abraham and his covenant, we will admit that the Bible does not portray Abraham as a theologian, but as a man of faith, action, and morality. His covenant, then, should above all entail a commitment to practical action in sacred history. And it is precisely today that the practical teachings of Abraham's covenant assume particular urgency.

In the twenty-first century, human beings face awesome and terrifying possibilities. We have the tools to improve and protect human life as never before, as well as the means to destroy all human life and God's creation. Human civilization as we know it stands on the edge of a precipice: our values, choices, and behavior will be the difference between a future of blessing or the world descending into its primordial chaos. After witnessing the Holocaust and the genocides and democides of the twentieth century, any naïveté or complacency are religious sins. These horrors should have taught us that radical evil was a reality then and remains an ever-present potentiality for today and the future. As covenantal partners, the moral imperative needs to be foremost in both our behavior and theology, and there is no justification for any teleological suspension of the ethical—be the *telos* theological, political, financial, or personal.

A number of powerful troubling signs dominate our contemporary cultural and political landscapes. Postmodern secularism has created a pervasive value-orientation whose foundations contain the seeds from which destructive forces can again grow. As noted earlier, hedonism drives much of contemporary life and ethics, and the glorification of violence is commonplace. These phenomena weaken the importance of moral character and individual conscience, both

---

22 See Richard Sklba, "New Beginnings: Catholic-Jewish Relations after 40 Years," *Origins* 35, no. 31 (January 19, 2006): 509–514, who argues that the tension between the universal theological claim of Christianity and the enduring particular validity of the Jewish covenant is a mystery to be appreciated.

of which are so critical to human flourishing and dignity. Physicalism,[23] relativism, and moral utilitarianism have all become fashionable, if not dominant, in contemporary academia and high culture. These ideologies promote the idea that human life has no intrinsic value or dignity to be respected and protected. In other words, they forcefully reject the starting points of both Jewish and Christian ethics, namely that each person is created in God's image, and hence that each person is intrinsically sacred.

Nor do these ideologies reject only theologically based ethics. When all values are merely "relative," objectivity and truth are questionable notions, and a denial of all ethical constructs easily follow. Finally as we also noted earlier, political extremism, violent religious intolerance, and radicalism have surged in our young century—and much of these hostile movements take direct aim at Judaism and Christianity.

Jews and Christians play an essential role in God's sacred plan for human progress in history—indeed, for the survival of humanity. As partners in Abraham's covenant, Jews and Christians are both spiritually obligated to heed the divine call of bringing blessing to the world. We can do this together by publicly bearing witness to the following covenantal values that God bequeathed to the world.[24]

1. There is a spiritual center to the universe because the world was created by a loving God, who is intimately involved in human lives and who yearns to redeem his children. Jews and Christians should be unembarrassed about teaching this reality, as was Abraham who made God known as the "God of Heaven and Earth."
2. As Creator, God is the transcendent authority over human life, and establishes the validity of moral values. Although sometimes difficult to apply, moral values are neither relative nor human conventions, but intrinsic parts of the universe and essential for human flourishing. The fundamental Noahide moral values must remain primary to all human endeavors.
3. All persons are created in the Image of God, and each person has intrinsic sanctity that derives from this transcendent quality. All

---

23 The set of theories asserting that persons have no spiritual, non-empirical transcendent characteristics. In addition to denying a human soul, physicalism also leaves no room for morality and ethical values.

24 For a similar enumeration of our covenantal responsibilities today, see *Orthodox Rabbinic Statement on Christianity*.

persons therefore possess inherent dignity and must be treated according to this notion. Because human life has this transcendent character, human worth cannot be measured solely in utilitarian or materialistic terms. The spiritual essence of each person ensures that individual human life is not a process of biological decay toward death but a journey of spiritual growth toward life. And because every person is created in the Divine Image, any assault on innocent human life is an assault on God that diminishes the divine presence in the world.

4. Abraham learned from the binding of Isaac that God loves human life and abhors death. Thus, Abraham's covenantal children must teach that killing in the name of God is contrary to the God of Abraham, and all forms of religious violence[25] are idolatries that the world must reject.

5. As Abraham defended and taught justice and righteousness before the destruction of Sodom and Gomorrah, his children are duty bound to teach social justice and display individual righteousness. It was Abraham's moral protest to God and concern for the moral treatment of others that distinguished his righteousness from the self-righteousness of Noah, and that earned him the privilege to be the father of the covenant. Our commitment to justice and righteousness for all human creatures is the test of our fidelity to God's covenant that is designed to bring peace and harmony to the world.

6. As faithful Christians and Jews believing in messianic history, we must teach the eternal possibility of human progress and moral reform as part of human history. We may not fall prey to pessimism, nihilism, or a Malthusian acceptance of war, disease, and oppression as permanent features of human destiny. Hope in the possibility of a peaceful humanity is the meaning of our messianic belief.

Can Jews liberate themselves from the image of being a victim and seeing the rest of humanity as an intractable enemy? Can the long story of Jewish-Christian enmity be transformed into covenantal partnership? Critical theological differences must remain between Judaism and Christianity, yet both faiths demand belief in messianic history and action to create a place in the world for God to enter. We share the covenantal task to make the world a better place,

---

25 I exclude from this category capital punishment, which draws its justification from biblical and theological sources according to many religious theories of legal justice.

one where each person possesses infinite value because we are all created in the Divine Image, where moral values are real, where human affairs reflect a spiritual center to the universe and where every human life is endowed with meaning.

So we end where we began: God asks us to complete His creation and continually perfect His world through the covenant. Even Maimonides—Judaism's harshest critic of Christianity—admitted that realizing the covenant requires Christian help.[26] Neither Jews nor Christians can achieve this on their own. Maimonides ends his *Mishneh Torah* with a magnificent vision of the perfected world representing the culmination of God's mission for the Jewish people. His noble dream merits repeating:

> At that time, there will be neither hunger, nor war; neither will there be jealousy, nor strife. Blessings will be abundant and comfort within the reach of all. The single preoccupation of the entire world will be to know the Lord. Therefore there will be wise persons who know mysterious and profound things and will attain an understanding of the Creator to the utmost capacity of the human mind, as it is written, "The earth will be filled with the knowledge of God, as the waters cover the sea" (Isa. 11:9).[27]

Both Maimonides and the biblical prophets remind us that despite violence, suffering and hatred, human peace and understanding are achievable. That peace and understanding would be our most powerful witness to God's presence in human history and to our religious responsibility to bring God's blessing to the world. This task is the very mission of Abraham's covenantal children, indeed, all of God's children.

---

26 *MT*, Laws of Kings and Their Wars 11:4 (uncensored edition). Although repairing the world (*tiqqun olam*) is sometimes dismissed by traditionalists and scholars as an inauthentic popular invention, in this passage Maimonides insists on the human responsibility to repair the world (*l'taqqen ha-olam*) as essential to sacred history.

27 *MT*, Laws of Kings and Their Wars 12:5 (according to the Yemenite manuscript). See end of chapter 1 for an explanation of the emendation to this text.

Bibliography

Books

Ahrens, Jehoschua, Irving Greenberg, and Eugene Korn, eds. *From Confrontation to Covenantal Partnership*. Jerusalem: Urim Publications, 2021.

Altmann, Alexander. *Moses Mendelssohn: A Biographical Study*. Tuscaloosa, AL: University of Alabama, 1973.

Ateek, Naim. *Justice and Only Justice*. Maryknoll, NY: Orbis, 1989.

Baron, Salo. *A Social and Religious History of the Jews*. New York: Columbia University Press, 1960.

Ben Asher, Yaakov. *Tur Shulhan Arukh*.

Berger, David. *The Rebbe, the Messiah and the Scandal of Orthodox Indifference*. London: Littman Library of Jewish Civilization, 2001.

Berlin, Isaiah. *Liberty*. Oxford: Oxford University Press, 2002.

Berman, Josh. *Created Equal*. London: Oxford University Press, 2008.

Berthelot, Katell, Menachem Hirshman, and Josef David, eds. *The Gift of the Land and the Fate of the Canaanites in Jewish Thought*. Oxford: Oxford University Press, 2014.

Blau, Joshua, ed. *Teshuvot ha-Rambam*. Vol 1. Jerusalem: Maas, 1960.

Boys, Mary. *Has God Only One Blessing?* New York: Paulist Press, 2000.

Braybrooke, Marcus. *Christian-Jewish Dialogue: The Next Steps*. London: SCM Press, 2000.

Carroll, James. *Constantine's Sword*. Boston: Houghton Mifflin, 2001.

Catechism of Catholic Church. 2nd ed. Vatican City: Libreria Editrice Vaticana, 1997.

Chavel, Charles. *Writings of Ramban* [Hebrew]. Jerusalem: Mossad ha-Rav Kook, 1959 [5719].

Cohen, Hermann. *Religion of Reason out of the Sources of Judaism*. Translated by Simon Kaplan. New York: Oxford University Press, 1972.

Cordovero. Moses. *The Palm of Deborah*. Translated by Louis Jacobs. London: Vallentine, Mitchel, 1960.

Crocker, Richard L. "Early Crusader Songs." In *The Genesis of the Crusades in Holy War* by H. E. J. Cowdrey, 96–97. City: Ohio State University Press, 1976.

Cunningham, Phillip. *Educating for Shalom*. Collegeville, MN: The Liturgical Press, 1995.

———. *Proclaiming Shalom*. Collegeville, MN: The Liturgical Press, 1995.

D'Costa, Gavin. *Catholic Doctrines on Jews after the Second Vatican Council*. Oxford: Oxford University Press, 2019.

Dahan, Gilbert. *The Christian Polemic against the Jews in the Middle Ages*. Notre Dame, IN: University of Notre Dame Press, 1991.

David Halevi, Hayim. *Make a Teacher for Yourself* [Hebrew]. Tel Aviv: Committee for the Publications of Hayim David Halevi, 1989.

De Vaux, Roland. *Ancient Israel: Its Life and Institutions*. New York: McGraw-Hill, 1997.

Dunn, James D. J. *Paul and the Mosaic Law*. Grand Rapids, MI: Eerdmans, 2001.

Duns Scotus. *Oxford Commentary on the Four Books of the Sentences*. In his *Opera Omnia*, 2nd ed. Paris: Vives, 1891–1895.

Elazar, Daniel. *Covenant and Polity in Biblical Israel*. New Brunswick, NJ: Routledge, 1994.

Elimelekh of Lizhensk. *Noam Elimelekh*.

Elitsur, Yosef, and Yitshaq Shapira. *Torat Hamelekh* [The teaching of the king]. Lev Ha-Shomron: Yeshivat Od Yosef Hai, 2009.

Emden, Jacob. *Seder Olam Rabbah*.

Encyclopedia Judaica, 2nd ed. 1948.

Epstein, Baruch Halevi. *Torah Temimah*.

Ettinger, Ya'akov. *Binyan Tsion*.

Federbusch, Simon. *Studies in Judaism* [Hebrew]. Jerusalem: Mossad ha-Rav Kook, 1965.

Feinstein, Moshe. *Iggerot Moshe*. Vol. 2.

Fifteen Years of Catholic-Jewish Dialogue 1970–1985. Vatican City: International Catholic-Jewish Liaison Committee, 1988.

Fischer, Shlomo. "State Crisis and the Potential for Uncontrollable Violence in Israel-Palestine." In *Plowshares into Swords? Reflections on Religion and Violence—Essays from the Institute for Theological Inquiry*, edited by Robert W. Jenson and Eugene Korn, 61–99. Jerusalem: Center for Jewish-Christian Understanding and Cooperation, 2014.

Fisher, Eugene, and Leon Klenicki, eds. *In Our Time: The Flowering of Jewish-Catholic Dialogue*. New York: Paulist Press, 1990.

Flannery, Edward. *The Anguish of the Jews*. New York: Paulist Press, 1985.

Fredriksen, Paula. *Augustine and the Jews*. New Haven: Yale University Press, 2010.

———. *When Christians Were Jews*. New Haven: Yale University Press, 2018.

Gikatilla, Joseph ben Abraham. *Gates of Righteousness* [Hebrew].

Goshen-Gottstein, Alon, and Eugene Korn, eds. *Jewish Theology and World Religions*. Oxford: Littman Library of Jewish Civilizations, 2012.

Green, Ronald M. *Religion and Moral Reason*. New York: Oxford University Press, 1988.

Greenberg, Irving. *For the Sake of Heaven and Earth*. Philadelphia: Jewish Publication Society, 2004.

Halbertal, Moshe, and Avishai Margolit. *Idolatry*. Cambridge, MA: Harvard University Press, 1994.

Halbertal, Moshe. *Bein Torah L'Hokhmah*. Jerusalem: Hebrew University Press, 2000.

Halevi, Yehudah. *The Kuzari* [Hebrew].

Hartman, David. *Love and Terror in the God Encounter*. Woodstock, VT: Jewish Lights, 2001.

Hay, Malcolm. *Europe and the Jews*. Chicago: Chicago Review Press, 1992.

Henkin, Yehudah Herzl. *Benei Vanim*. Vol. 3. Jerusalem: Otsrot ha-Torah, 1997.

Herzl, Theodore. *The Diary of Theodore Herzl*. Edited by Marvin Leventhal. New York: Dial, 1956.

Heschel, Abraham Joshua. *Moral Grandeur and Spiritual Audacity.* Edited by Susannah Heschel. New York: Farrar, Strauss, Giroux, 1996.

Hirsch, Samson Raphael. *Nineteen Letters on Judaism.* Edited and annotated by Joseph Elias. Jerusalem: Feldheim, 1995.

Hiyyus, Tsvi Hirsch. *The Works of Maharats Hiyyus* [Hebrew]. Jerusalem: Mossad ha-Rav Kook, 1948.

Hoffman, David Tsvi. *Responsa Melamid le-Ho'el.*

Horowitz, Marcus. *Matteh Levi.* Jerusalem: Y. Kaufmann, 1933.

Ibn Shem Tov, Yosef. *Kavod Ha-Elokim.*

Irenaeus. *Irenaeus of Lyons.* Translated by Robert M. Grant. New York: Routledge, 2007.

Isaac, Jules. *The Teaching of Contempt: Christian Roots of Anti-Semitism.* New York: Holt, Rinehart and Winston, 1964.

———. *Jesus & Israel.* New York: Holt, Rinehart, Winston, 1971.

Jenson, Robert W., and Eugene Korn, eds. *Plowshares into Swords? Reflections on Religion and Violence—Essays from the Institute for Theological Inquiry.* Jerusalem: Center for Jewish-Christian Understanding and Cooperation in Israel, 2014.

———. *Returning to Zion: Christian and Jewish Perspectives.* Jerusalem: Center for Jewish-Christian Understanding and Cooperation in Israel, 2015.

Juergensmeyer, Mark. *Terror in the Mind of God.* Berkeley, CA: University of California Press, 2000.

Karo, Yosef. *Shulhan Arukh.*

Katz, Jacob. *Exclusiveness and Tolerance.* Jerusalem: Schocken, 1962.

Kellner, Menachem. *Maimonides' Confrontation with Mysticism.* Oxford: Littman Library of Jewish Civilization, 2006.

———. *Must a Jew Believe Anything?* Oxford: Littman Library of Jewish Civilization, 2006.

———. *Gam Hem Qeruyim Adam: Ha-Nohkri be-Einei ha-Rambam* [They also are called Adam: The gentile in the eyes of Maimonides] [Hebrew]. Tel Aviv: Bar-Ilan University Press, 2016.

Kierkegaard, Soren. *Fear and Trembling.* Princeton, NJ: Princeton University Press, 1954.

Kook, Rabbi Abraham. *Letters* [Hebrew]. Vol. 1. Jerusalem: Mosad ha-Rav Kook, 1923.

Koren Siddur. American edition. Jerusalem: Koren Publishers, 2009.

Korn, Eugene. *To Be a Holy People; Jewish Tradition and Ethical Values.* Jerusalem: Urim, 2021.

Landau, Yehezkel. *Responsa Nodeh bi-Yehudah* [Hebrew].

Levenson, Jon. *In The Death and Resurrection of the Beloved Son.* New Haven: Yale University Press, 1993.

Lewis, Bernard. *What Went Wrong?* Oxford: Oxford University Press, 2002.

McKim, Robert, ed. *Religious Perspectives on Religious Diversity.* Boston: Brill, 2017.

McTernan, Oliver. *Violence in God's Name.* Maryknoll, NY: Orbis, 2003.

Meiri, Menahem. *Hibur ha-Teshuvah.* Edited by A. Schreiber. New York: Hotsa'at Talpiyot, 1950.

Mendelssohn, Moses. *Jerusalem.* Translated by Allan Arkush. Hanover: Brandeis University Press, 1983.

Moses Maimonides. *Book of Commandments* [Hebrew].

———. *Shemonah Peraqim.*

———. *Qovets Teshuvot ha-Rambam*. Edited by A. Lichtenberg. Leipzig: A. Lichtenberg, 1859.
———. *The Guide of the Perplexed*. Translated by Shlomo Pines. Chicago: University of Chicago Press, 1963.
———. *Introduction to Pereq Heleq* [Hebrew]. Jerusalem: Mossad ha-Rav Kook, 1965.
———. *Mishneh Torah*. Edited by Shabse Frankel. New York: Congregation Benei Yosef, 1998.
Musser, Franz. *Tractate on the Jews: The Significance of Judaism for Christian Faith*. Philadelphia: Fortress Press, 1984.
Nathanson, Joseph Saul. *Sho'el u-Meshiv*.
Novak, David. *The Image of the Non-Jew in Judaism*. Oxford: Littman Library of Jewish Civilization, 2011.
Parkes, James. *The Conflict of the Church and the Synagogue*. New York: Atheneum, 1969.
Raheb, Mitri. *I am a Palestinian Christian*. Minneapolis: Augsburg Fortress, 1995.
Rashi. *Responsa Rashi*. Edited by I. Elfenbein. New York: Schlesinger Bros., 1943.
Ratzinger, Joseph. *Many Religions, One Covenant*. Translated by Graham Harrison. San Francisco: Ignatius, 1999.
Rosenberg, Bernhard H., ed. *Theological and Halakhic Responses to the Holocaust*. New York: KTAV, 1992.
Sa'adyah Gaon. *Book of Beliefs and Opinions*. New Haven: Yale University Press, 1989.
Sacks, Jonathan. *The Dignity of Difference*. London: Continuum, 2002.
Sanders, E. P. *Paul and Palestinian Judaism*. Minneapolis: Augsburg Fortress, 1977.
Schneerson, Menachem Mendel. *Torat Menahem*.
Segal, Alan. *Paul the Convert*. New Haven: Yale University Press, 1992.
Shapiro, Marc. *Between the Yeshiva and Modern Orthodoxy*. Oxford: Littman Library of Jewish Civilization, 1999.
———. *The Limits of Orthodox Theology*. Oxford: Littman Library of Jewish Civilization, 2004.
Shiffman, Lawrence. *Who was a Jew? Rabbinic and Halakhic Perspectives on the Jewish Christian Schism*. New Jersey: KTAV, 1985.
Soloveitchik, Joseph. *Halakhic Man*. Translated by Lawrence Kaplan. Philadelphia: Jewish Publication Society, 1983.
———. *Worship of the Heart*. Edited by Shalom Carmy. Jersey City, NJ: KTAV, 2003.
———. *Abraham's Journey, Reflections on the Life of the Founding Patriarchs*. Edited by David Shatz, Joel B. Wolowelsky, and Reuven Zeigler. Jersey City: KTAV, 2008.
Soloveitchik, Velvel. *Novellae (Hedushei) ha-Griz* [Hebrew].
Spiegel, Shalom. *The Last Trial: On the Legends and Love of the Command to Abraham to Offer Isaac as a Sacrifice: The Akedah*. New York: Jewish Theological Seminary, 1950.
Spinoza, Baruch. *Theological-Political Tractatus*. Translated by R. H. M. Elwes. New York: Dover Publications, 1951.
Sprinzak, Ehud. *Brother against Brother*. New York: Free Press, 1999.
Stendahl, Krister. *Paul among the Jews and the Gentiles*. Minneapolis: Augsburg Fortress, 1976.
———. *Final Account: Paul's Letter to the Romans*. Philadelphia: Fortress Press, 1995.
Trachtenberg, Joshua. *The Devil and the Jews*. Philadelphia: Jewish Publication Society, 1984.
Twersky, Isadore. *Introduction to the Code of Maimonides*. New Haven: Yale University Press, 1980.

Wilken, Robert. *John Chrysostom and the Jews.* Portland, OR: Wipf and Stock, 2004.
Wyschogrod, Michael. *Body of Faith.* Lanham, MD: Rowman & Littlefield, 1996.
Yosef, Ovadia. *Yehaveh Da'at.*

Articles

Berger, David. "On *Dominus Iesus* and the Jews." *America* 195, no. 7 (September 17, 2001).
———. "Jews, Gentiles, and the Modern Egalitarian Ethos: Some Tentative Thoughts." In *Formulating Responses in an Egalitarian Age,* edited by Mark Stern, 83–108. New York: Rowman and Littlefield, 2005.
Bleich, J. David. "Divine Unity in Maimonides, the Tosafists and Me'iri." In *Neoplatonism and Jewish Thought,* edited by Lenn E. Goodman, 237–254. Albany, NY: SUNY Press, 1992.
Bleich, J. David. "Judaism and Natural Law." *Jewish Law Annual* 6 (1987): 5–42.
Blidstein, Gerald. "Maimonides and Me'iri on Non-Judaic Religion." In *Scholars and Scholarship: The Interaction between Judaism and other Cultures,* edited by Leo Landman, 27–35. New York: Yeshiva University Press, 1990.
Boys, Mary. "Does the Catholic Church Have a Mission 'with' Jews or 'to' Jews?" *Studies in Christian Jewish Relations* 3 (2008): 1–19. https://ejournals.bc.edu/index.php/scjr/article/view/1482/1335.
Carmy, Shalom. "His Master's Voice." *First Things* 104 (June/July 2000).
Cohen, Gerson D. "Esau as Symbol in Early Medieval Thought." In *Jewish Medieval and Renaissance Studies,* edited by Alexander Altmann, 19–48. Cambridge, MA: Harvard University Press, 1967.
Cucarella, Diego Sarrio, and Daniel Madigan. "Thinking Outside the Box: Developments in Catholic Understandings of Salvation." In *Religious Perspectives on Religious Diversity,* edited by Robert McKim, 63–119. Boston: Brill, 2017.
Cunningham, Phillip. "Toward a Catholic Theology of the Centrality of the Land of Israel for Jewish Covenantal Life." In *Enabling Dialogue about the Land,* edited by Phillip Cunningham, Ruth Langer, and Jesper Svartvik, 303–334. New York: Paulist Press, 2020.
David Halevi, Hayim. "Paths of Peace in Relations between Jews and Non-Jews" [Hebrew]. *Tehumim* 9 (1958): 71–81.
Dienstag, Jacob. "Natural Law in Maimonidean Thought and Scholarship." *Jewish Law Annual* 6 (1987): 72–74.
Dulles, Avery. "Covenant and Mission." *America* 187, no. 12 (October 2002).
Ellenson, David. "A Jewish Legal Authority Addresses Jewish-Christian Dialogue: Two Responsa of Rabbi Moshe Feinstein." *American Jewish Archives Journal* 52, nos. 1–2 (2000): 113–128.
———. "A Disputed Precedent: The Prague Organ in 19th-Century Central European Legal Literature and Polemics." In *Leo Baeck Institute Yearbook* 40 (1995): 251–264.
———. "Rabbi Hayim David Halevi on Christianity and Christians." In *Transforming Relations: Essays on Jews and Christians throughout History in Honor of Michael Signer,* edited by Franklin T. Harkins, 340–362. Notre Dame, IN: University of Notre Dame Press, 2010.

Falk, Harvey. "Rabbi Jacob Emden's Views on Christianity." *Journal of Ecumenical Studies* 19, no. 1 (Winter 1982).

Fasman, Oscar Z. "An Epistle on Tolerance by a 'Rabbinic Zealot.'" In *Judaism in a Changing World*, edited by Leo Jung, 128–136. New York: Soncino, 1939.

Gellman, Jerome. "The Akedah and Covenant Today." In *Two Faiths, One Covenant?*, edited by Eugene Korn and John Pawlikowski, 35–44. Oxford: Rowman and Littlefield, 2005.

———. "Jewish Chosenness and Religious Diversity: A Contemporary Approach." In *Religious Perspectives on Religious Diversity*, edited by Robert McKim, 21–36. Boston: Brill, 2016.

Genack, Menachem. "Ambiguity as Theology." *Tradition* 25, no. I (Fall 1989): 79.

Goshen-Gottstein, Alon. "Concluding Reflections." In *Jewish Theology and World Religions*, edited by Alon Goshen Gottstein and Eugene Korn, 317–328. Oxford: Littman Library of Jewish Civilizations, 2012.

———. "Encountering Hinduism: Thinking Through *Avodah Zarah*." In *Jewish Theology and World Religions*, edited by Alon Goshen Gottstein and Eugene Korn, 263–298. Oxford: Littman Library of Jewish Civilizations, 2012.

———. "A Kingdom of Priests and a Holy Nation." In *Judaism's Challenge: Election, Divine Love, and Human Enmity*, edited by Alon Goshen-Gottstein, 13–49. Boston: Academic Studies Press, 2020.

Greenberg, Irving. "Pluralism and Partnership." In his *For the Sake of Heaven and Earth*, 198–212. Philadelphia: Jewish Publication Society, 2004.

Gregerman, Adam. "Old Wine in New Bottles: Liberation Theology and the Israeli-Palestinian Conflict." *Journal of Ecumenical Studies* 41 (2004): 313–340.

Harkov, Lahav, and Tovah Lazaroff. "Pope Francis: God Promised the Land to the Jewish People." *Jerusalem Post*, October 26, 2016. Accessed July 22, 2012. https://www.jpost.com/Arab-Israeli-Conflict/Pope-Francis-God-promised-the-land-to-the-people-of-Israel-470918.

Herzog, Isaac. "The Rights of Minorities according to *Halakhah*" [Hebrew]. *Teḥumin* 2 (1981): 169–179.

Heschel, Abraham Joshua. "No Religion Is an Island." In his *Moral Grandeur and Spiritual Audacity*, edited by Susannah Heschel, 235–250. New York: Farrar, Strauss, Giroux, 1996.

Hirsch, Samson Raphael. "Talmudic Judaism and Society." In his *Collected Writings*, vol. 7, 209–244. New York: Feldheim, 1992.

Hirshman, Marc. "Rabbinic Universalism in the Second and Third Centuries." *Harvard Theological Review* 93 (2000): 101–115.

Horowitz, Elimelech (Elliot). "From the Generation of Moses to the Generation of the Messiah: Jews against Amalek and His Descendants" [Hebrew]. *Zion* 64 (1999): 425–454.

Jacobs, Louis. "Attitudes towards Christianity in Halakhah." In his *Judaism and Theology: Essays on the Jewish Religion*, 102–116. London and Portland, OR: Vallentine, Mitchell, 2005.

Jenson, Robert W. "What Kind of God Makes a Covenant?" In *Covenant and Hope: Christian and Jewish Reflections*, edited by Robert W. Jenson and Eugene Korn, 3–18. Grand Rapids, MI: Eerdmans, 2012.

———. "The Prophet's Double Vision of the Return to Zion." In *Returning to Zion: Christian and Jewish Perspectives*, edited by Robert W. Jenson and Eugene Korn, 20–33. Jerusalem: Center for Jewish-Christian Understanding and Cooperation in Israel, 2015.

Johnston, Murray. "Rabbi Joseph B. Soloveitchik's Unexpected Contribution: Towards a Theology of Jewish-Christian Dialogue." In *From Confrontation to Covenantal Partnership*, edited by Jehoschua Ahrens, Irving Greenberg, and Eugene Korn, 263–296. Jerusalem: Urim Publications, 2021.

Kant, Immanuel. "The Conflict of the Faculties." In *Religion and Rational Theology*, translated and edited by Allen W. Wood and George DiGiovanni. Cambridge: Cambridge University Press, 1996.

Katz, Jacob. "The Vicissitudes of Three Apologetic Statements" [Hebrew]. *Zion* 23–24 (1958–1959): 174–193.

Kellner, Menachem. "*Farteicht un Farbessert*: Comments on Tendentious Corrections to Maimonidean Texts" [Hebrew]. In *Be-Darkei Shalom: Iyyunim be-Hagut Yehudit Mugashim li-Shalom Rosenberg* [In the paths of peace: Topics in Jewish thought in honor of Shalom Rosenberg], ed. B. Ish-Shalom. Jerusalem: Beit Morasha of Jerusalem Press, 2006, 255–263. In English: "*Farteicht un Farbessert* (On Correcting Maimonides)." *Meorot* 6, no. 2 (*Marheshvan* 5768). https://library.yctorah.org/files/2016/07/Kellner-on-Rambam-FINAL.pdf.

———. "Maimonides' 'True Religion': For Jews or All Humanity? A Response to Chaim Rapoport." *Meorot* 7, no. 1 (September 2008): 2–28. Accessed July 19, 2021. https://library.yctorah.org/journals/september-2008/.

———. "We Are Not Alone." In *Radical Responsibility: Celebrating the Thought of Chief Rabbi Lord Jonathan Sacks*, edited by Michael J. Harris, Daniel Rynhold, and Tamra Wright, 139–154. London: School of Jewish Studies; New York: The Michael Scharf Publication Trust of Yeshiva University Press, 2012.

Kimmelman, Reuven. "Rabbis Joseph B. Soloveitchik and Abraham Joshua Heschel on Jewish-Christian Relations." *Modern Judaism* 24, no. 3 (October 2004): 251–271.

Kirschenbaum, Aaron, and Norman Lamm. "Freedom and Constraint in the Jewish Judicial Process." *Cardozo Law Review* 1 (1979).

Korn, Eugene. "Divestment from Israel, the Liberal Churches, and Jewish Responses: A Strategic Analysis." Jerusalem Center for Public Affairs, 2007. Accessed July 21, 2021. https://jcpa.org/article/divestment-from-israel-the-liberal-churches-and-jewish-responses-a-strategic-analysis/.

———. "BDS has Failed." *First Things*, April 2018. Accessed July 21, 2021. https://www.firstthings.com/article/2018/04/bds-has-failed.

———. "On Liberty and *Halakhah*." In his *To Be a Holy People: Jewish Tradition and Ethical Values*, 125–154. Jerusalem: Urim Publications, 2021.

———. "Moralization in Jewish Law: Divine Commands, Rabbinic Reasoning and Waging a Just War." In his *To Be a Holy People: Jewish Tradition and Ethical Values*, 103–124. Jerusalem: Urim Publications, 2021.

———. "Reflections on a Jewish Tragedy: The Image of God and Jewish Morality." In his *To Be a Holy People: Jewish Tradition and Ethical Values*, 77–102. Jerusalem: Urim Publications, 2021.

Lamm, Norman. "The Sage and the Saint in the Thought of Maimonides" [Hebrew]. In *Samuel Belkin Memorial Volume*, edited by Norman Lamm, Moshe Sokolow, Gershon Churgin, Moshe Carmilly, and Hayim Leaf, 11–28. New York: Yeshiva University Press, 1981.

Leaman, Oliver. "Maimonides and Natural Law." *Jewish Law Annual* 7 (1988): 78–93.

Leighton, Christopher M. "An Unfinished Story: Contending with God, Cain and Abel." In *Plowshares into Swords? Reflections on Religion and Violence—Essays from the Institute for Theological Inquiry*, edited by Robert W. Jenson and Eugene Korn, 132–162. Jerusalem: Center for Jewish-Christian Understanding and Cooperation, 2014.

Levenson, Jon D. "The Universal Horizon of Biblical Particularism." In *Ethnicity and the Bible*, edited by Mark R. Brett, 143–169. Leiden: Brill, 2002.

McDermott, Gerald. "Anti-Zionists Misread the Bible." *Public Discourse*. https://www.thepublicdiscourse.com/2015/11/16021/.

McMichael, Steven. "The Covenant in Patristic and Medieval Christian Theology." In *Two Faiths, One Covenant*, edited by Eugene Korn and John Pawlikowski, 45–64. Oxford: Rowman and Littlefield, 2005.

Mendelssohn, Moses. Letter 154. In *Gesammelte Schriften Jubilaeumsausgabe*, vol. 19. In *Moses Mendelssohn: A Biographical Study*, by Alexander Altman. Tuscaloosa, AL: University of Alabama, 1973.

Miller, Moshe Yehudah. "Regarding the Law that Noahides are not Admonished against Associationism" [Hebrew]. In *Torat Ḥayyim*, edited by Avraham Y. Mirsky and Avraham N. Hartman, 169–179. New York: Yeshivat Or Ha-Ḥayyim, 5760/2000.

———. "Rabbi Jacob Emden's Attitude toward Christianity." In *Turim, Studies in Jewish History and Literature*, vol. 2, edited by M. Shmidman, 105–136. New York: KTAV, 2008.

Novak, David. "Natural Law, Halakhah, and the Covenant." *Jewish Law Annual* 7 (1988): 5–42.

———. "The Covenant in Rabbinic Thought." In *Two Faiths, One Covenant*, edited by Eugene Korn and John Pawlikowski, 65–80. Oxford: Rowman and Littlefield, 2005.

Pawlikowski, John. "Reflections on Covenant and Mission: Forty Years after *Nostra Aetate*." *Crosscurrents* 56, no. 4 (2007), 70–94.

———. "Toward a Theology of Religious Diversity." *Journal of Ecumenical Studies* 11 (Winter 1989): 138–153.

Rackman, Emmanuel. "Secular Jurisprudence and Halakhah." *Jewish Law Annual* 7 (1988): 45–63.

Rapoport, Chaim. "*Dat Ha-Emet* in Maimonides' *Mishneh Torah*." *Meorot* 13 (2008). Accessed July 19, 2021. https://library.yctorah.org/journals/september-2008/.

Riskin, Shlomo. "Selling Land in Israel to Gentiles." *Meorot* 9 (2011). Accessed July 21, 2021. http://www.yctorah.org/content/view/739/10.

———. "Covenant and Conversion: The United Mission to Redeem the World." In *Covenant and Hope*, edited by Robert W. Jenson and Eugene Korn, 99–128. Grand Rapids, MI: Eerdmans, 2012.

———. "The Significance and Responsibility of Israel's Return to Zion." In *Returning to Zion: Jewish and Christian Perspectives*, edited by Robert W. Jenson and Eugene Korn, 99–128. Jerusalem: Center for Jewish-Christian Understanding and Cooperation, 2012.

Rosenak, Michael. "The Religious Person and Religious Pluralism." In *The Meaning and Limits of Pluralism Today*, edited by Alan Brockway and Jean Halperin. 13–20. New York: World Council of Churches, 1987.

Sagi, Avi. "The Punishment of Amalek in Jewish Tradition: Coping with the Moral Problem." *Harvard Theological Review* 87, no. 3 (1994).

Schwarzschild, Steven, "Do Noahides Have to Believe in Revelation?" *Jewish Quarterly Review* 53 (1962).

Seeman, Don. "Violence, Ethics and Divine Honor in Jewish Thought." *Journal of Jewish Thought and Philosophy* 16 (2008): 195–252.

———. "God's Honor, Violence, and the State." In *Plowshares into Swords? Reflections on Religion and Violence—Essays from the Institute for Theological Inquiry*, edited by Robert W. Jenson and Eugene Korn, 100–131. Jerusalem: Center for Jewish-Christian Understanding and Cooperation, 2014.

Shapiro, Marc. "Of Books and Bans." *The Edah Journal* 3, no. 2 (*Elul* 5763). www.edah.org.

Shapiro, David. "The Doctrine of the Image of God and *Imitatio Dei*." In *Contemporary Jewish Ethics*, edited by Menachem Kellner, 127–151. New York: Sanhedrin Press, 1978.

Singer, David, and Moshe Sokol. "Joseph Soloveitchik: Lonely Man of Faith." *Modern Judaism* 2, no. 3 (1982): 227–272.

Sklba, Richard. "New Beginnings: Catholic-Jewish Relations after 40 Years." *Origins* 35, no. 31 (January 19, 2006): 509–514.

Soloveichik, Meir Y. "God's First Love: The Theology of Michael Wyschogrod." *First Things*, November 2009.

Soloveitchik, Joseph B. "Confrontation." *Tradition* 6, no. 2 (1964): 5–28.

———. "The Lonely Man of Faith." *Tradition* 7, no. 2 (Summer 1965).

———. "Addendum to the Original Edition of 'Confrontation.'" 1967. In *A Treasury of Tradition*. Accessed April 28, 2022. https://traditiononline.org/confrontation-addendum.

———. "Redemption, Prayer and Talmud Torah." *Tradition* 17, no. 2 (Spring 1978): 55–72.

———. "*Kol Dodi Dofek*—It is the Voice of My Beloved that Knocketh." In *Theological and Halakhic Responses to the Holocaust*, edited by Bernhard H. Rosenberg, 51–118. New York: RCA, 1992.

Soloveitchik, Haym. "Religious Law and Change: The Medieval Ashkenazic Example." *AJS Review* 12 (1987): 205–221.

Twersky, Yitzchak. "The Rav." *Tradition* 30, no. 4 (Summer 1996).

Wurzburger, Walter. "Rav Joseph B. Soloveitchik as *Posek* of Post-Modern Orthodoxy." *Tradition* 29, no. 1 (Fall 1994).

Statements

Declaration of Repentance by the Roman Catholic Bishops of France. September 30, 1997. Accessed July 22, 2021. https://www.jcrelations.net/article/declaration-of-repentance-seeking-forgiveness-for-the-failings-of-the-church-during-the-holocaust-period.html?tx_extension_pi1%5Baction%5D=detail&tx_extension_pi1%5Bcontroller%5D=News&cHash=f0d431225705ae589d2697cfe7f0d25e.

To Do the Will of our Father in Heaven. December 2015. Accessed July 22, 2012. http://www.jcrelations.net.https://www.cjcuc.org/2015/12/03/orthodox-rabbinic-statement-on-christianity.

The Gifts and the Calling of God Are Irrevocable: A Reflection on Theological Questions Pertaining to Catholic-Jewish Relations on the Occasion of the 50th Anniversary of "Nostra Aetate" (No. 4). 2015. Accessed July 22, 2021. https://ccjr.us/dialogika-resources/documents-and-statements/roman-catholic/vatican-curia/crrj-2015dec10.

Guidelines and Suggestions for Implementing the Conciliar Declaration "Nostra Aetate," No. 4. 1974. Vatican City: Commission for Religious Relations with the Jews, 1975. Accessed July 22, 2021. https://ccjr.us/dialogika-resources/documents-and-statements/roman-catholic/vatican-curia/guidelines.

The Jewish People and Their Sacred Scriptures in the Christian Bible. 2001. Accessed July 22, 2021. https://www.vatican.va/roman_curia/congregations/cfaith/pcb_documents/rc_con_cfaith_doc_20020212_popolo-ebraico_en.html.

"Letter on USCCB 'Note on Ambiguities.'" National Jewish Interfaith Leadership. http://www.ccjr.us/index.php/dialogika-resources/themes-in-todays-dialogue/conversion/574-njil09aug18.html.

"A Note on Ambiguities Contained in *Reflections on Covenant and Mission*." Committee on Doctrine and Committee on Ecumenical and Interreligious Affairs. United States Conference of Catholic Bishops. (June 18, 2009). http://www.ccjr.us/index.php/dialogika-resources/themes-in-todays-dialogue/conversion/559-usccb-09june18.html;

Notes on the Correct Way to Present the Jews and Judaism in Preaching and Catechesis in the Roman Catholic Church. 1985. Vatican City: Commission for Religious Relations with the Jews, 1985. Accessed July 22, 2021. https://ccjr.us/dialogika-resources/documents-and-statements/roman-catholic/vatican-curia/notes.

Nostra Aetate. Accessed July 21, 2021. https://www.vatican.va/archive/hist_councils/ii_vatican_council/documents/vat-ii_decl_19651028_nostra-aetate_en.html.

Reflections on Covenant and Mission. Consultation of the National Council of Synagogues and the Bishops Committee for Ecumenical and Interreligious Affairs. United States Conference of Catholic Bishops. August 12, 2002. http://www.jcrelations.net/en/?id=966.

Statement of the German Catholic Bishops on the 50th Anniversary of the Liberation of the Extermination Camp at Auschwitz. January 27, 1995. Accessed July 22, 2021. https://www.jcrelations.net/fr/declarations/declaration/on-the-50th-anniversary-of-the-liberation-of-the-extermination-camp-at-auschwitz.html.

Statement on Interfaith Dialogue. Rabbinical Council of America. February 3–5, 1964. *Tradition* 6, no. 2 (Spring 1964): 28–29.

We Remember: A Reflection on the Shoah. Vatican, March 1998. https://www.jcrelations.net/fr/article/we-remember-a-reflection-on-the-shoah.pdf.

Journals

American Jewish Yearbook.
Jewish Law Annual.
Meorot.
Teḥumim.
The Edah Journal.
Tradition.

Biblical Commentaries

Abraham ben ha-Rambam.
Abraham Ibn Ezra.
Amar, Rabbi Shlomo. *Parashat Va'yishlaḥ.* http://haravamar.org.il/.
Chizkiya bar Manoach (*Ḥizkuni*).
David Kimchi (Radaq).
Meir Leib Ben Michael (Malbim).
Moses ben Naḥman (Naḥmanides).
Naftali Tsvi Yehudah Berliner (Netsiv).
Samson Raphael Hirsch.
Samuel ben Meir (Rashbam).
Seforno, Ovadiah ben Jacob.
Tsadiq ha-Kohen.

Talmudic Commentary

Meiri, Menaḥem. *Beit ha-Beḥirah.*

Midrash Collections

Kahana, Menachem. *Sifri on Numbers: An Annotated Edition* [Hebrew]. Vols. 1 and 4. (Jerusalem: Magnes, 2011–2015., 2011–2015), vol. 1, 167, and vol. 4, 474.
Mekhilta De-Rabbi Ishmael.
Mishnat R. Eliezer (*Midrash Aqur*). Edited by H. G. E. Enelow. New York: Block, 1933.
Sifre, Ha'azinu.
Sifrei.

Index

A

Abraham, 2–4, 9–12, 16–19, 21–24, 26, 28–32, 34–37, 39–42, 47–49, 55, 58–59, 126, 130, 135, 139, 154, 157, 161, 166–171, 174–178
anti-Judaism, 122, 133
antisemitism, 105, 119–122, 133–135, 149–151, 160
avodah zarah, 50, 52–54, 89–92, 94, 106–117, 125, 16, *see* idolatry
Augustine, 53, 170

B

Benedict XVI, Pope, 101, 123, 134, 136, 155, 173
Berger, David, 4, 111, 115, 123, 156
berit, 2, 10–11, 16, 22, 47, 123, *see* covenant
blessing, vi, 1–4, 9–10, 13–14, 16–20, 23–42, 58, 103, 105, 118, 120, 122, 131, 134, 139, 149, 151–152, 166–168, 172, 174–175, 178
Boys, Mary, 4, 105, 118, 120, 122, 134, 149, 151–152, 168, 172–174

C

covenant, vi, 1–5, 9–12, 14–22, 24–26, 28–30, 32–33, 35, 41–42, 47–52, 57–62, 64, 75, 93–97, 103–107, 109, 117, 121–130, 133–134, 136, 145, 147–148, 153–156, 160–162, 164, 166–178
Cunningham, Phillip, 4, 136, 151, 153

E

Emden, R. Jacob, 4, 71–73, 107, 112–113, 118, 125–126, 139, 168–169
Esau, vi, 3, 36, 132–133, 137–138, 160
Ezekiel, 26–27

F

Francis, Pope, 101, 134–136

G

Gellman, Yehuda, 4

Genesis, book of, v, 10–11, 17, 19, 21–22, 27, 32–34, 106, 127
ger toshav, 3, 54–55, 61, 64, 66–67, *see* resident alien
Greenberg, Irving, 4, 63, 90–97, 127–128, 164

H

Halevi, Yehudah, 61, 69
Hirsch, R. Samson Raphael, 4, 18, 112, 114, 125–126, 139, 168–169

I

idolatry, vi, 3, 17, 31, 50–55, 57, 59–60, 62–63, 77–78, 89–93, 96–97, 106, 108–109, 111, 126, 161, 167, 169
incarnation, 46, 90, 108, 167, 171, 174
Isaiah, 9–11, 19–20, 26, 28, 33, 59, 95, 161

J

Jacob, vi, 3, 11, 16, 22, 24, 31, 36, 45, 47, 59, 66, 71, 95, 97, 130, 132–133, 137–138, 160–161, 166, 168, *see* Esau
Jeremiah, 11, 26–28, 48, 59
John XXIII, Pope, 4, 141
John Paul II, Pope, 4, 101, 105, 119–120, 134–136, 150, 152, 154

K

Katz, Jacob, 4, 46, 73, 75, 91, 108–109, 111, 117–118

M

Maimonides, 4, 9, 12, 14–15, 17–20, 30–31, 33–34, 51, 53, 55–57, 60, 63, 66–92, 107–111, 114–115, 117, 119, 125–126, 130–131, 139, 142, 145, 157, 165, 169, 178
    Book of Commandments, 31, 59, 78, 126
    The Guide of the Perplexed (Guide)
        I, 53, 57, 70, 90, 108, 171
        II, 71, 78
        III, 9, 14–15, 17, 19, 20, 34, 84–85, 126, 166, 169

Mishneh Torah (MT), 12, 15, 17, 20–21, 31, 34, 50–51, 53, 55–57, 59–60, 66–67, 71, 75, 77–78, 82–83, 89–90, 92–94, 96–108, 125–126, 131, 139, 165, 169, 178
    Acts of Sacrifices, 17
    Book of Knowledge, 53
    Laws of Forbidden Intercourse, 83
    Laws of Idolatry, 17, 31, 59–60, 89, 92, 108, 126, 169
    Laws of Jubilee, 57, 83
    Laws of Kings and Their Wars (Laws of Kings), 12, 17, 20–21, 31, 34, 51, 55–56, 59–60, 66–67, 77, 82, 92, 94, 106–107, 131, 139, 165, 178
    Laws of Repentance, 56, 71, 83, 107
    Laws of Servants, 20
    Laws of Testimony, 56, 71
    Laws of the Foundation of the Torah, 78, 108
    Laws of Witnesses, 83
Commentary on Mishna Sanhedrin, 83
McDermott, Gerald, 4, 168, 171
Meiri, R. Menaḥem, 4, 54–55, 57, 90–92, 107–111, 115, 117, 142, 157, 165
Messianic era, 2, 9, 26–27, 34, 43, 48, 56–57, 59–60, 139, 147, 166
Micah, 9, 19, 22, 59–60, 97, 130–131

N
Noahide commandments, 21, 30–31, 50–52, 55, 57, 67, 69, 71, 77, 80–81, 86, 91, 106–109, 118, 126, 139, 167–168
Noahide covenant, 1, 50–51, 57, 59–60, 62, 64, 94, 109, 124, 168
Nostra Aetate, 95, 105, 114, 119–120, 122–123, 134–135, 147, 149–151, 153–154, 164, 172, 174

O
olam ha-ba, 65, 70

P
Pawlikowski, John, 4, 123, 170

R
Rambam, 18, 20, 31, 57, 65, 84, 91, 110, 139, 145, *see* Maimonides
resident alien, 54, 62, 66–69, 74–75, 77, 80, 82–83, 115
Riskin, Shlomo, 4, 13, 58–59, 128
Rivkis, R. Moshe, 112, 125, 139, 168–169

S
Sacks, Jonathan, 4, 48, 57, 97, 128
salvation, 9, 26–27, 48–50, 56–58, 71–72, 81–84, 104, 107, 113, 154, 168, 170, 172
Sinai, 3, 9–12, 14, 18–19, 21–22, 24, 32–33, 45, 47–48, 56, 59, 65, 69–72, 78, 83, 86, 91, 94, 111, 125–127, 139, 156–157, 166–169, 171, 173–174
Soloveitchik, R. Joseph, 3–4, 10, 14, 16, 18, 21, 86, 95, 102, 114, 122, 127, 140–149, 153, 156–165, 173
Soloveitchik, R. Velvel, 68, 86–87
supersessionism, 103, 122, 153–154, 156–157, 170, 175

T
tiqqun olam, 40, 178
trinity, 46, 90, 94, 108, 112, 167, 169, 171, 174

V
Vatican, 1, 49, 95, 101–102, 104, 107, 119–120, 122–123, 128, 134, 136, 141, 148–153, 155–156, 159, 172, 174

www.ingramcontent.com/pod-product-compliance
Lightning Source LLC
Chambersburg PA
CBHW051117230426
43667CB00014B/2627